THINGS I'LL NEVER FORGET

MEMORIES OF A MARINE IN VIETNAM

BY JAMES M. DIXON

THINGS I'LL NEVER FORGET

BY JAMES M. DIXON

COVER DESIGN BY JOHN DIXON

COPYRIGHT 2016
(REVISED AND UPDATED 2018)

PUBLISHED BY DO RIGHT PRESS

PRINTED IN THE UNITED STATES OF AMERICA

ISBN-13: 978-1533480095
ISBN-10: 1533480095

LCCN: 2016909668

W E ALL HAVE MEMORIES which make up our lives. This book contains memories of some of the most influential times in my life and some of the saddest moments in my life. These are the stories or memories of my time in the Marine Corps and in Viet Nam. In no way can this be an exact retelling of historical events. I kept a journal for one year so I know the dates and places are accurate. These are my memories. Other people who experienced the same things will have their own memories and recollections.

I wrote this for three reasons. The first was for my own therapy. For most of my life I tried to forget Viet Nam, but found myself constantly remembering bits and pieces in what many call flash backs. I never opened, much less read the journal I kept. By rereading the journal a million memories washed over me. I decided to write these stories in order to help me clarify and reflect on all that happened. The second reason for writing was for my family. After fifty years I hoped my wife, children, other relatives and even my friends would read this and perhaps understand what I and others went through. The third reason I will explain at the conclusion of the book.

James M. Dixon

Chapter 1

WHY JOIN THE MARINE CORPS?

ISN'T IT FUNNY how a song on the radio can bring back memories? You'll hear the music and instantly be taken back to a different time and place. Perhaps its summertime and you remember riding down the highway listening to that song. Or perhaps you'll remember that special person you had a crush on and how you danced to that song one winter night. I don't know about you, but the weather can also bring back memories for me just like a song on the radio.

Yesterday was the first day of summer, not by the calendar, but by the temperature. It was that first sunny hot day when only shorts and a t-shirt felt comfortable and only a cold glass of iced tea would do. Standing outside on my deck, I was taken back to the first hot day in 1965 when I announced to my family that I had joined the Marine Corps.

It was dinner time and we were all seated around the kitchen table. I'll never forget how my mother dropped her coffee cup and teared up. She left the table, went to the kitchen sink and began to sob. She knew I would be going to Viet Nam. My two younger brothers stared down at their plates and then peeked up at my father to gage his reaction. There was silence around the table and then he spoke, "It'll be a good experience for you."

In 1965 the war in Viet Nam was growing bigger every day. The United States had a military draft and our government was pulling more and more guys each day into the Army.

As I approached high school graduation my options were limited. I only knew three things. First, I didn't want to go to college because I didn't think I was smart enough and even if I had gone to college, there was not enough money to live on campus. Second, I was never going to get married. My mother and father had been fighting for years. I don't know which was growing faster, the war in Viet Nam or the arguments at my house. Many a night my brothers and I couldn't sleep for the shouting and screaming and there was no way I would live in that house a day longer than necessary. I wanted out. I loved both my mother and my father. And although the fights were loud, they were never violent. My parents were as opposite as any two human beings could be and they never should have gotten married in the first place. They realized the marriage was not working but decided to stay together for the kids' sake. That's something I would not recommend to any couple.

The third thing I knew was that I wanted a job and to be on my own. I could picture myself sharing an apartment with a buddy, working some manual labor job, and then waiting to figure out what life had in store for me. I really didn't have any idea what career I wanted. The problem was no one, and I mean no one, would hire me. You see with the draft and being eighteen, employers just laughed at me. Seriously, they laughed in my face. I had applied for work at every grocery store and every manual job I could think of. Whenever I even asked for a job application, employers would ask if I was a '4-F'. When I would answer no, they would laugh and not even give me an application. No sense wasting paper on someone who would be drafted into the Army in a matter of weeks.

After receiving that draft notice there were four options for getting out of the draft; the Army and being sent to Viet Nam. First, enrolling in college could mean a college deferment. And believe me lots of guys went to college just to get out of the draft. Second option was failing the physical. Between 1953 and 1963, when the country was not at war, the army would declare guys 4-F if they had flat feet, poor eyesight, asthma, were obese or suffered some other physical aliment. With the war in Viet Nam growing, the Army began taking virtually anyone who could walk and do a push-up. And they weren't too particular about the push-up! The third option was to become a 4-D "a dirty damn draft dodger" and run and hide in Canada. I never considered myself a hero, but 4-D seemed like a coward's way out. Of course, the fourth option was to join the Air Force, the Navy, or the Coast Guard, all of which had a waiting list to join. I had run out of options.

I realized I was destined to go to Viet Nam. My relatives, the Dixon's, had come to America in 1720 and had fought in every war this country ever had, from the French and Indian to Korea. Now it was my turn. All my relatives were Conservatives. Like them, I hated Communists and I firmly believed in stopping the spread of Communism in South East Asia. I believed that was what this war was all about, just like we stopped Communism in Korea. I also believed if we had stopped Hitler early enough perhaps we could have prevented World War II or at least saved millions of lives. Duty called. It was time to do my patriotic chore.

I should also mention that I was raised as a Quaker. Officially the religious sect is called the Society of Friends however the nickname is more recognizable. I still believe in many of their beliefs like, equality for everyone and not needing a preacher, priest, or minister to lead you in prayer. I believe I can pray to God in my own way. Where I differed in opinion and could not accept, was their belief in being a pacifist. Quakers would declare themselves 'conscientious objectors' or C.O. Several of my buddies who attended the Quaker meeting house with me were truly pacifists.

Many people believe that a conscientious objector, who refuses to carry a weapon or fight in a war, can get out of the military draft. They believe that pacifists or 'C.O.'s' are really just cowards. It simply is not true. Conscientious objectors were drafted like anyone else. They became Army medics or Navy corpsmen. The true believers still don't carry a side arm. They risk their lives to save the wounded and are often hit by enemy fire. Some guys have tried the conscientious objector route only to find out what they would be doing and quickly changed their minds. That gave the real C.O. a bad reputation. Sometimes conscientious objectors are given other jobs. One of my buddies, also a 'Friend', was drafted and instead of going into the Army, was trained to be a 'Smoke Jumper'. For two years he jumped out of airplanes into the edge of forest fires in Montana and Idaho. I would never call him a coward. I admire true believers. I never had the courage to turn the other cheek and not fight back. I only mention this because it is highly unusual for a Quaker to be in the Marine Corps.

At 18, I wasn't totally stupid, I didn't want to go to Viet Nam and get killed. I studied pamphlets from the Army with my best friend Dave. We were both faced with the same choices. The Army paratroopers seemed to have the best training, and therefore the best chance of survival. At the time, Army paratroopers required a three-year enlistment, while being drafted into the regular Army meant serving only two years.

A more rigorous physical had to be passed to become a paratrooper. I had been on the football team and had wrestled. Dave was on the track team. The physical didn't seem to present any problem. Except for one thing, I was 'color blind'. Not completely, but I can't tell the difference between certain greens and grays. A paratrooper had to have perfect vision. I believe the regulation is to prevent soldiers from jumping out of a plane and losing their glasses, which made sense. However, glasses don't correct color blindness. Why can't you jump out of an airplane if you're color blind? It was the first of many things in the military I would never understand.

Dave and I traveled to Philadelphia from Wilmington, Delaware to take the physical together. Dave passed. I flunked the color test and I felt like crap. When we returned to the recruiting office, the Army recruiter said it was okay because we could still join the Army. Dave could be a paratrooper and I could be a regular soldier. We wanted to join, together, and I wanted to be as good as Dave or anyone else. I was disappointed because I was good enough to be drafted, but not good enough to be a paratrooper. We walked down the hall past the other recruiting offices with their closed doors. The Marine recruiter not only had his door open but had been standing in the doorway listening to our conversation. He took our physical reports out of our hands and said, "Boys, come with me."

From then on everything he said turned out to be a lie! He told us we had to join the Marine Corps for four years. That was the first lie. We could have joined for two. Then he told us we could join on the **Buddy System**, which allowed us to go through Boot Camp together and through infantry training together. That was lie number two. We would then be stationed together for the first two years. The truth is once we got off the bus in Parris Island, S.C. I didn't see Dave Patterson until a year and a half later when he rode past me in a truck as I stood at the main gate to the air field at Da Nang, in Viet Nam. So much for the buddy system! Lie number three, we were told that the Marine Corps had the best training in the world. Everyone in the Marine Corps was trained to protect their own. That turned out to be only a partial lie, as I would later find out.

So, we believed the recruiter's lies and joined the Marine Corps. To this day I don't know if Dave blamed me for talking him into joining. I believed it was a joint decision. I'm pretty sure his Mom blamed me.

We spent the rest of the summer working for a tree trimming company. After work we rode our Honda motorcycles and I would ask Dave, "Where are we going?"

He would always reply the same way, "I don't know, but we're going to be the first ones there!" And off we would ride. Every weekend we tried to find a party or some 'easy' girls. The summer flew by. All I know is that to this day, on the very first hot day in May, I'm carried back to that kitchen table and I can still hear the clatter of my mother's coffee cup drop and remember my Mother's tears.

James M. Dixon

6

Chapter 2

WELCOME TO PARRIS ISLAND

S OMETIMES ON HOT SUMMER NIGHTS, when a cool light breeze starts to fan the heat away, I'll close my eyes and see the shadowy figure of a Marine Corps drill instructor with that 'Smokey the Bear' hat, back in 1965, standing in front of the entrance to a wooden building. He wasn't there to greet and welcome us to our new home. He was there to scare the shit out of us. He did a good job.

On Friday morning of Labor Day weekend in 1965, along with five other guys, Dave and I boarded a bus in Wilmington, Delaware at 8:00 am on our way to the Naval Yard in Philadelphia. We were sworn in there at exactly 11:00 am. I don't know about the other guys, but I'll bet they also didn't get much sleep the night before our swearing in.

Processing into the service took forever. I would soon learn that was typical of the military. After being sworn in, we went by bus to the Philadelphia airport and waited. We went by plane to South Carolina and waited six more hours for another bus to pick us up. This was followed by another long ride to Parris Island, SC. By the time the guard waved us through the Boot Camp gate on that Friday night, it was well after midnight. The whole place was dark and deserted like a ghost town. The only thing that proved we were at Parris Island was the well-lit statue of the Iwo Jima monument. As the bus slowly passed by it everyone stared in absolute awe.

I suppose the Drill Instructor was already pissed because of our late arrival and the fact that he had to work on Labor Day weekend. The bus pulled to a stop in front of a wooden two-story building that I would soon learn was called a barracks. The guy with the Smokey the Bear hat was a drill instructor. As soon as the bus door opened he stepped onto the bus and softly spoke to the driver. I couldn't hear what he said but he probably warned the driver to cover his ears. Then the cursing and yelling began.

"Get your asses off this bus! Move, Move, Move! Line up, asshole to belly button!" I had not noticed the other D.I.'s until I jumped off the bus. They were all yelling, **"Asshole to belly button!"** I didn't know what that meant, but I soon learned. We were to stand in a line with our belly button pressed up against the other guy's rear end, as close as possible. Once the guy behind you did the same, it was impossible to turn around.

A door opened, and we were herded inside the barracks. Two rows of bunk beds stretched the length of the building, perhaps forty bunks in all. In a formal letter received weeks before our induction, we had been warned not to bring anything with us. All would be provided for us by the Marine Corps. Some guys had brought suitcases or gym bags. The yelling continued.

"Every one of you scumbags, stand next to a bunk!" "Empty out your pockets and put everything on the top bunk." Everything was repeated, over and over again by each D.I., all yelled until it sounded like fifty D.I.'s shouting from every direction. We were told to stand facing a bunk and look straight ahead and "keep your fucking mouths closed." The only thing I had in my pocket was a hand full of dimes to call home with and a small pocket pad of paper with addresses written on it.

Others had not followed the "Don't bring anything" advice. Some guys had brought pictures of their mother or girlfriend. As two Drill Instructors, walked down each row of bunks, we could overhear the following conversations. "Why did you bring this picture of a whore into my barracks"?

"That's my mother sir."

"What are you going to do with this picture? Are you going to masturbate with it? Are you a motherfucker?

"No Sir."

"You don't want to keep this picture, do you?"

"No sir."

"Then get rid of it. Put it in that shit can over there!" That same conversation or ones similar were played out again and again as the D.I.'s worked their way down the two rows of bunks. Sometimes the yelling was about playing cards or paperback books or even toiletries. All were "voluntarily" disposed of. Surprisingly, I was allowed to keep my dimes and the address book, and some guys were allowed to keep a pocket Bible. The trash can, or shit can was nearly full.

Next, they shouted at us to move to an adjacent room that was set up like a huge classroom. We each hurried to a chair connected to a desk as we heard instructions yelled to keep our fucking mouths closed and look straight ahead. It was still pitch black outside probably one or two in the morning. In this classroom our weight and height were recorded on a government form. Paper and pen was provided, and we were told to copy sentences from a bulletin board. It was a letter to our parents or guardian and read as follows: I have arrived at Parris Island and all is fine. I am sending home things I no longer need. The Marine Corps will give me everything I need from now on. I will write again soon. The letter was signed, folded and we placed it in our pocket.

We spent an hour filling out paperwork: home address, jobs held, schools we attended and so forth. I think they wanted to find out if we could read and write English. Then it got weird. On the last page we were told to draw a naked man and woman. I don't know about the other guys, but I was sure confused.

"Now you fucking assholes draw a naked man and woman. And I don't want you to take all day and draw any fancy porn. I want to see the sex parts. If you can't draw just make stick figures." I guess they wanted to make sure we understood about the birds and bees. I thought how stupid did they think we were? We were all 17 and 18-year-old guys. Sex was all we ever thought about! Later I would find out how naive I was and how stupid some guys could be.

By now I guessed it was about five in the morning and still dark outside. Some of the D.I.'s huddled at the door and I could tell they didn't know what else to have us do but wait. So, we sat silently in our chairs and waited for the rest of Parris Island to awaken. Finally, we were told to go from room to room, for each step of our induction. Induction ran like a German train schedule. Our hair was cut off in one room. In the next room we undressed until we were completely naked. Our clothes, shoes, watches and jewelry, along with that letter we copied for home, were placed into a box, addressed and sealed.

Then we each followed the next guy into a shower room. As I washed I could see some sailors standing at the exit. What were sailors doing here? Had I joined the wrong branch by mistake? The sailors, I later learned were corpsmen and each held a flash light. As we exited the shower we were ordered to, "Turn around and grab your ankles." Was this some kind of perverted initiation? The light was shined up each butt. Some guys were told, "Go back and scrub that asshole, you scumbag and get it clean." Hearing this I scrubbed my butthole until it was red.

After showering and drying off, but still naked, we moved to the next stage in a long room where we were given a large green canvas bag, later called a seabag. We then proceeded down a long line of counters with large bins behind them. Each bin contained items of clothing arranged by sizes. Some uniformed men stood behind the counter, guessed your size and tossed the needed items at you. First came the underwear. One set was put on and four other sets stuffed into the bag. This process was repeated for each item of clothing, except for boots. Our feet were measured, and two sets of boots issued. Then we were given two hats: one we put on and the other went in the green bag. Once we were fully dressed, in our new green clothing we received what looked like a silver army helmet. I was surprised at how lightweight it felt. I thought no way would this stop a bullet. Lastly, we picked up a heavy galvanized steel bucket.

It was now dawn as we ran outside into the light of day and hurriedly ran across what looked like the world's largest empty paved parking lot. Many guys had trouble carrying the green bag filled with clothing, the helmet and the bucket. I put the silver helmet on my head on top of the green hat and hurried to keep up. On the other side of that giant parking lot we stopped in front of a wooden two-story building that we would now call home.

Welcome to Parris Island.

James M. Dixon

Chapter 3

A NEW WAY OF TALKING

WHENEVER I HEAR profanity on a public street or in the movies I recall boot camp and my introduction to a whole new language. I have never heard so much cursing in my life, not even on the football or wrestling teams or working alongside laborers. The drill instructors used language for intimidation and to berate us.

After we arrived in front of the barracks, the yelling continued. We were herded into the second floor of the barracks. I hadn't counted how many recruits there were but now there were more than the thirty-some that were on our bus. Instructions were shouted to place our gear on an empty bunk which held a folded pile of sheets, a pillow case and a green blanket. Before we had a chance to place everything on the bunk, the insane men in the smoky bear hats began yelling for us to **"Fall out into the street."** I wondered what that meant. Did they want us to run out into the street and fall down? As the orders were shouted we moved like a herd of spooked wildebeests out the second-floor door and down the steps. As I reached the bottom another D.I. was shouting for us to line up in four lines facing him.

Other DI's shouted, **"Where is your cover? Where is your cover?"** As some guys began running back up the steps and into the building, I figured they wanted us to get our blankets. As I started back up the stairs to get my blanket a DI stopped me and yelled, **"Where the fuck are you going?"**

"Ah, to get my cover sir," I sheepishly replied. With that he took my hat off my head and slapped me in the face with it.

"You got your fucking cover on your head, asshole!"

As we lined up and tried to form four straight lines more orders followed. Finally, the DI ordered us to "Right Face". We turned to the right. He ordered, "Forward March." We began walking down the street as the DI slowly yelled, "Right, left, right, left," as we tried to get in step. Several blocks away we reached another wooden building only this one was a single story with a grassy area beside it.

A different DI yelled at us to, **"Get over here and get down on one knee!"** We formed a semicircle around him, so we could all see. I would remember his speech for the rest of my life. He held up a metal spoon and shouted.

"THIS IS A FUCKING SPOON. YOU USE THIS FUCKING SPOON TO STIR YOUR FUCKING COFFEE, TO EAT YOUR FUCKING SOUP AND TO EAT YOUR FUCKING CEREAL. YOU PUT THIS FUCKING SPOON IN YOUR FUCKING MOUTH!" Oh my God, I thought, does this guy know any other adverbs besides fucking? Just how stupid does he think we are? Later I would realize just how dumb some of the guys kneeling next to me, actually were.

It continued. He held up a common fork and continued,

"THIS IS YOUR FUCKING FORK, YOU USE THIS TO SHOVEL FOOD INTO YOUR FUCKING MOUTH!" He held up a knife. "THIS IS

A FUCKING KNIFE! YOU USE THIS TO BUTTER YOUR FUCKING BREAD AND TO CUT YOUR FUCKING MEAT! YOU DO NOT PUT THIS FUCKING KNIFE INTO YOUR FUCKING MOUTH! DO YOU UNDERSTAND?" This was followed by a clatter of "yes sirs", and the D.I. yelling, "I CAN'T HEAR YOU!" This was repeated, over and over again, until we all replied, "YES SIR" in one loud voice.

Our next instructions had to do with a large metal tray with six divided sections.

"THIS IS YOUR FUCKING FOOD TRAY. YOU WILL SIDE STEP THROUGH THE CHOW LINE LIKE THIS." Then he demonstrated how to step sideways.

"WHEN YOU WANT SOME FUCKING FOOD, YOU HOLD OUT YOUR FUCKING TRAY LIKE THIS. IF YOU DON'T WANT THAT FUCKING FOOD YOU DON'T STICK OUT YOUR FUCKING TRAY." DO YOU FUCKING UNDERSTAND?" Again, we yelled, "YES SIR" followed by "I CAN'T HEAR YOU", from the DI. Again, and again this would be repeated ad nauseam. We were finally, allowed to enter the cafeteria.

We were told we had eight minutes to eat. I didn't realize the eight minutes included the three minutes it took to go through the food line. We sat in groups of eight at a table with four on each side. We stood until the order was given, "READY, SIT." Of course, this command was immediately followed by, "GET UP. WHEN I GIVE A COMMAND, I WANT TO HEAR EVERY ASSHOLE HITTING THAT SEAT AT ONE TIME!" The order "ready sit", was repeated several times until there was indeed one sound. This procedure really gave us only about four minutes to shovel food in. Then it was back out to the street and marching back to the barracks.

It was Saturday, of Labor Day weekend. Evidently the Marine Corps doesn't celebrate holidays. I guess they thought it meant we were supposed to labor, at least in boot camp. We spent the rest of the morning learning how to make a bunk and instructed how to fold 'hospital sheet' corners with a blanket pulled tight enough to bounce a coin off it. This lesson was taught through repetition. We worked as a team with our "bunky", the guy who shared either the top or bottom bunk. We were never given enough time to complete making our beds to the D.I.'s perfection, so we continued making and remaking them the rest of the morning.

Between tasks we were instructed to, "Stand in front of your bunk." Every now and then, a recruit would approach the screaming guys, and ask to go the bathroom, which was followed by laughter and an order to, "Get back in front of your bunk." Eventually we were called together in the center of the room and given further instructions.

We learned a whole new language. The Marine Corps is part of the Department of Navy and uses Naval terms. There are no bathrooms, and you don't go to the bathroom. The bathroom is called a *Head*, and you *make a head call*. Doors are called *hatches*. Stairs are called *ladder wells*. There is no floor, it's called a *deck*. Walls are *bulkheads*. These terms applied even when we weren't aboard ship.

We were also taught how to speak and address those crazy, screaming guys with the stripes on their shirt sleeves. Sometimes the lesson was explained in detail, while other times, an individual was humiliated as an example to all of us. For example,

"WHAT DID YOU CALL ME? DID YOU CALL ME A D.I.? DO YOU KNOW WHAT D.I. STANDS FOR? IT STANDS FOR DUMB IDIOT! IF YOU EVER CALL ME A DUMB IDIOT I WILL KICK YOUR ASS!" The same example was used on the poor slob who addressed him with the pronoun "You". A "ewe" is a female sheep and an ass-kicking would follow. They were called Drill Instructors and nothing else.

We, on the other hand, were never referred to as Marines. You don't become a Marine until you graduate from Boot Camp. We were called every kind of humiliating name imaginable: Puke, Maggot, Turd, Scumbag, and my personal favorite, Ladybug. Only ladybug was pronounced, "Laa-di-buggg!"

To speak to the Drill Instructor, you had to ask permission. Therefore, a request to go to the bathroom went as follows,

"Sir, Private Dixon asks permission to speak to the Drill Instructor sir."

"Speak Maggot."

"Sir, Private Dixon asks permission to make an emergency head call."

"No, tie a fucking string around your kidney!"

That first day several guys pissed their pants. I held my urine until I thought I would die. Eventually we were instructed that head calls would be given after each meal and other "appropriate times." Calling time out in the middle of a battle and asking to pee doesn't work.

Other terms were quickly learned. Pants were called *trousers* (children wore pants, men wore trousers), while underpants were *skivvies* or *skivvy drawers*. The long-sleeved shirt we had on was a *utility jacket*. The green trousers were *utility trousers* and were part of our *utility uniform*, or just *utilities*. The silver helmet was only the liner to a regular helmet and was called a *chrome dome*. Surprisingly, a tee shirt was called a tee shirt, which seemed to be the only thing that was the same as in civilian language. That giant parking lot we had run across to get to our barracks was a *Parade Ground* and was used for parades but mostly to practice marching. We didn't eat in a cafeteria but rather a *Mess Hall*, and after you witnessed the food being served you understood why. Food wasn't eaten but chow was, after going through a chow line. There was no breakfast, lunch or dinner. It was morning, noon and evening chow. These and many other terms had to be learned, seasoned with a good dose of profanity, as part of our new way of talking.

James M. Dixon

Chapter 4

A NEW WAY OF WALKING

APART OF MY TEACHING CAREER, I spent 12 years as an assistant high school football coach. My job during games was to videotape all the football plays. I usually stood high atop the stands in the press box or even on top of it, to have the best spot from which to view and record. Football coaches aren't concerned with the school band or halftime shows but I however, got to see a lot of them. Nowadays the band puts on more of a Broadway show rather than being just a bunch of marching musicians.

I'll never forget an 'away' game on a Friday night at Wilson High School just outside of Reading, PA. Wilson had a huge marching band with full color guard, baton twirlers, flag twirlers and four girls twirling white wooden ceremonial rifles. It was an impressive sight to see. At one point in the show the four girls twirling rifles stood at the fifty-yard line and tossed those spinning guns high into the air. Three of the girls caught theirs perfectly. The fourth girl caught hers, but not in her hands. She bounced the butt of that rifle off the top of her head. And down she went like she had been picked off by a sniper. She laid spread eagle on the fifty-yard line, out cold! A hush fell over the crowd as we all tried to process what we had just witnessed.

What was truly amazing was the rest of the band never missed a beat and like true professionals they just kept marching on. Trombone players and base drummers just stepped right over her and kept marching in perfect step and never missed a beat. Even when the athletic trainer finally ran out onto the field to see if she was even alive, they kept right on marching. My Drill Instructor would have been so proud.

When the half time show finally ended and the band marched off toward the end zone an ambulance pulled onto the field and took the poor girl away. As the ambulance passed by, the band members, all gave a salute just like any fallen comrade in combat. Just like Staff Sergeant Bozarth would have expected.

They say you never forget your Drill Instructors. I know I never did. The senior Drill Instructor was Staff Sergeant Bozarth. I believe his first name was Bill, but we were soon taught to only use last names. Making friends was discouraged, by only using rank and last names. I'm not sure where Sergeant Bozarth was from, although I thought I detected a slight New England accent. I know he was a baseball fan because he often used baseball analogies when explaining things.

Other Drill Instructors were Sergeant Henderson, who after about two weeks, was replaced by Sergeant Land. No explanation was ever given. Land was Bozarth's *hit man* or enforcer. He would sneak around while Bozarth gave commands or instructions and slap you on the back of the head if you were not complying perfectly. When we stood at attention he tried to distract us by pulling our chest hairs out one at a time. I thought he was a sadistic bastard.

Last was Corporal Knights, yes it was plural. SSgt. Bozarth introduced

James M. Dixon

Knights as an Indian. Knights, was quieter than Sgt. Land and would carefully pull our rifle in closer to our body, straighten our cover and whatever else needed adjusting. He didn't say much. At first, I feared all the Drill Instructors. Then I hated them, and in the end, I kind of respected them. It wasn't so much a change in them as it was a change in me and probably everyone else.

None of these Drill Instructors respected us because we were civilians and they had so much work to do to turn us into Marines. One of the things they did that first Saturday afternoon, while we stood at attention, was to ask each of us why we had joined their Marine Corps. Various answers were given until finally we figured out how to correctly respond: "Because I want to be part of the greatest branch of the service, The United States Marine Corps".

As they walked down each row asking the same question, I wanted to answer, "I don't know why Sir, I think I made a terrible mistake, because I think all you guys are a bunch a screaming nut jobs". Later I realized they were checking to see if any of us had been drafted into the Marines. The Marines had begun drafting guys. Being drafted would have meant even less respect, if that was possible.

The second reason for lack of respect was our scheduled time in Boot Camp. When Dave and I signed up in May of 1965, we were told Boot Camp would last twelve weeks. By July, we received a letter saying Boot Camp had been shortened to ten weeks. Good news for us. The Drill Instructor announced that Boot Camp had been shortened to eight weeks because the war in Viet Nam was escalating faster and we were being rushed through in just eight weeks.

Bozarth made the announcement, "You can do eight weeks standing on your head!" It was more good news for us, but not for the Drill Instructor. They had to cram twelve weeks of training into eight weeks. We were going to be busy and even then, the Drill Instructors didn't really think of us as true Marines. For them, even after completing Boot Camp we would be only two-thirds of a Marine.

No time was wasted. We finally went to bed that first Saturday after being up for 48 hours. My guess was a lot of guys, like me, had not slept much the night before leaving for boot camp so we were truly exhausted. When the lights finally went off I passed out. After what seemed like thirty minutes, we were shaken out of our bunks by the sound of metal garbage cans being tossed down the row of bunks and those same screaming Drill Instructors yelling, "REVEILLE, REVEILLE, REVEILLE, GET UP, GET UP, GET UP!" My first thought was, "What the hell just happened?" It was the beginning of the second day of Boot Camp.

It was Sunday and after breakfast, I mean "morning chow", we marched to the church for services. Formal classroom training was not scheduled so afterwards we practiced marching inside the barracks. I won't go into all the maneuvers you know: right face, left face, about face and so on. As we learned to march inside the barracks the Drill Instructor would call out *cadence*, "Left, right, left, right." At first, he went too slowly, to make sure we were all in step with his cadence. We had to listen to the exact pace or cadence. We spent the day marching around an oblong circle inside the barracks.

Whenever someone would turn left when they should have gone right, you could hear the Drill Instructor yell, "Your other left, asshole!" If the same mistake was repeated that person would have to do *Bends and Thrusts*. This punishment consisted of four parts and was done to the count of four. Beginning from standing at attention a recruit would: 1) squat down with the palms of his hands on the deck, 2) thrust his legs out behind him so he was in the push-up position, 3) thrust his legs back to squatting, and then 4) back to standing at attention. Try it once and it's easy. Do it twenty times or forty times and it gets old real fast!

I should mention that drilling or marching is still taught but not used in modern combat. The Greeks and Romans used marching formations in battle. The modern marching tactics were developed during the

Napoleonic Wars and were last used in the American Civil War. No one ever executed a left oblique maneuver in Viet Nam or any other modern battlefield. Drilling the troops was taught to develop teamwork and immediate obedience to commands.

Everywhere we went, we marched. The parade ground was supposed to be used to practice marching or *drilling*. Four weeks had been cut from our training, and one of those weeks was supposed to be spent drilling. Each Drill Instructor had his own style of calling cadence, so that when four or five platoons were marching at the same time you were able to keep in step and not get confused with others. SSgt. Bozarth was unique. After saying left, right, left, right, he would switch to one, two, three, four. Then he would say, "Reach for your left". With the command word, "Left" all eighty of our left feet had to make one thumping noise. However, his cadence was pronounced, "On, to, tree, four, reach or your left, reach or your left" and was sort of sung to his own marching song. We heard it in our sleep. It became our new way of walking.

James M. Dixon

Chapter 5

MAKING MARINES

I TAUGHT JUNIOR HIGH SCHOOL for 28 years. Usually students were divided into sections homogeneously with the top sections being college bound. The next sections were also capable of college work but might instead decide on a different path. The middle sections were the hardest to teach. They usually were smart enough, but because of laziness, difficulties at home, problems with the law or some other reason they were low achievers. The bottom sections probably weren't 'book smart' enough for college but they had other talents. Because we were an inner-city school, the very lowest sections probably should have been in 'special- education' classes. But that's a whole other story.

Each year my teaching schedule included mostly the lower, slower, sections. Once I complained to the principal and he gave me the following explanation. He said, "Jim, you are a good teacher and you can handle the problems of the troubled students better than some other teachers and the slow students seem to identify with you." It was a back handed compliment but was indeed true. I think part of the reason I related to the slow students was due to my experiences in the Marine Corps. For me the Marine Corps proved two things. The first one I already knew, I wasn't the smartest guy on the planet. Second, there were a lot of guys who were in worse shape than me. But by helping each other we all became Marines.

The wooden barracks where we lived were shaped like a large capital 'H'. The middle of the 'H' contained the offices, the head and showers, and the Drill Instructors' rooms. The two long lines that formed the sides of the H each contained the barracks of one, eighty-man platoon. Our platoon was on the second deck of one side. The H shaped barracks then held four platoons or three hundred and twenty men. Our platoon was number 275 and we were constantly competing with the other platoons. At least the Drill Instructors were competing to see who could pass the most recruits. Each platoon's barracks were laid out the same way. If you entered from the center, where Drill Instructors were, there were ten bunk beds to the right and ten to the left. These were along one *bulk head*, as it was called. On the opposite side were the same numbers of bunks which face the other row. The very middle of the barracks contained a large table opposite the entrance to the heads and offices.

Each of us had a bunk, a foot locker, and a bucket. The bucket was used for fire drills. During a fire drill each person was supposed to grab their chrome dome, rifle and bucket and fall out into the street. We only had two fire drills, one during the day as a demonstration and the other at night as a test. Most of us passed. The guys who forgot something, well, let's just say their punishment insured they never repeated that mistake. The primary purpose of the bucket was to sit on while we used the top of the foot locker as a work area to clean rifles, write letters, and polish boots, shoes and buckles.

Each night we were given *free time*. Free time did not mean what we thought it meant at first. During free time we were given tasks, which included: cleaning rifles, showering, polishing boots and shoes. Every night a different task was added such as writing a required letter home, polishing our belt buckle, washing our belts, and so forth. During this free time talking was permitted, but no grab-ass. That meant we could whisper but not fool around. It always seemed that we never had a chance to complete all these tasks. So, there was little time to talk with other guys.

We however had plenty of time for sleep. 'Lights out' was at 10:00 p.m. or 2200 hours. Reveille occurred at 5:45 a.m. or 0545 which meant we had almost eight hours sleep. After a couple days of being wakened by crashing garbage cans it was explained that reveille was at 0545, but there was no rule about getting up earlier. By waking up a half hour earlier we could dress, make a head call, make our bunks and avoid a lot of shouting. Eventually the drill instructor only needed to walk out into the middle of the barracks and say, "Reveille" and all eighty of us would already be standing in front of our bunks, dressed and our bunks made. We were learning.

The second Saturday in Boot Camp, we were still too new to realize that the Drill Instructors were human, and their only entertainment was 'fucking with the troops' by having us do something stupid. Sometimes it was necessary and at times it was to teach a lesson. That Saturday afternoon the Staff Sergeant announced, "All right, I want all the Jewish guys front and center." This meant the Jewish guys were to run to the center of the barracks and stand at attention in front of the Sergeant. No one moved. He repeated the order again with the same results. "You mean to tell me that none of you fucking morons are Jewish?" He then told Corporal Knights to, "Hand me the roster sheet." He looked down the list of names and finally said, "Goldblat, front and center!" Goldblat ran to the center of the barracks and stood at attention. Staff Sergeant Bozarth then continued. "Goldblat, are you Jewish? And I don't give a fuck if you are or not? You are not in trouble. Do you understand?"

Goldblat replied, "No sir, I'm not Jewish sir."

Bozarth took a deep sigh and continued. "Well, Goldblat sure sounds like a Jewish name and every Company needs at least one Jew, or the commanding officers will think something is wrong. So Goldblat you are now the Company Jew."

Goldblat started to speak, "But sir, I'm Catholic and..."

"Goldblat, you are the company Jew, and in ten minutes you will fall out in the street with the other Jews and March to the Synagogue. Do you understand?"

Goldblat sheepishly replied, "Yes sir."

Staff Sergeant Bozarth emphasized his point, **"I can't hear you Goldblat."**

"Yes sir, Drill Instructor!"

Satisfied, Bozarth dismissed him and said, "Now get back in front of your bunk and get your shit locked up and wait for the order to fall out." And that's how platoon 275 met the requirements for a Jewish Marine.

Later that same evening while we sat on our buckets working on our many tasks during free time, Sergeant Land announced, "All right you fucking Pukes. You have been here for one week. Is there anyone who wants to call home?" I thought, *Oh my God yes! I want to call my parents and tell them to get me the hell out of here. These people are crazy!* There were four of us who stepped forward and were ordered out into the street. We stood at attention in a straight line and for what seemed like an hour, we called home. We shouted, "Hello Mom!"

Sergeant Land standing at the top of the ladder well called down to us, "I can't hear you! How is your momma supposed to hear you?"

So, we yelled it repeatedly, **"Hello Mom!"** Now I know we didn't yell for an hour, it just seemed that long. It was probably only ten or fifteen minutes, just long enough for our voices to become hoarse and for the point to be hammered home that there would be no phone calls home. Finally, Sergeant Land came down to the street and dismissed each of us individually.

Asking, "Have you called home enough, turd?" I was last. When Land stood in front of me with the brim of his Smoky the Bear hat touching my forehead he paused as he thought of a new term. "I think I'm going to call you *Shit for Brains*. Now get back in the barracks Shit for Brains!" That became his new nick name for me.

I only mention this story of calling home to illustrate that I was not the smartest guy in Platoon 275. I was not the dumbest either. We all had to help each other. I helped one guy, from some cowboy state who, had only ever worn cowboy boots and didn't know how to lace up regular boots. I showed him how the laces wrapped around the hooks on the boots.

During free time when we showered we were supposed to wear shower shoes or flip flops. 'Cowboy' went walking into the shower barefoot and when the Drill Instructor stopped him he explained, "I have to let my 'dogs' air out." This statement was met with ridicule, and many bends and thrusts for his dumb excuse. The Drill Instructor never smiled, but all of us laughed.

Later I helped one guy write his required weekly letter home. He could only write in capital letters, much like a second grader, and I wondered how far he had gone in school. When it was time to put a stamp on the letter he could not believe that one stamp was enough to send a letter all the way to Louisiana. And I had to help him spell Louisiana. He also couldn't understand that no additional postage was needed for air mail.

The guy next to him explained, "All letters go by air mail! Do you think the post office has some guy drive your letter all the way to Louisiana?"

His reply, "But we live pretty far out in the river country."

His bunky agreed, "Oh I'll just bet you do."

Not everyone was a country bumpkin or an idiot. Some guys were very clever and we all seemed to have some unique talents or abilities. These lessons I learned about people would serve me well as a teacher.

James M. Dixon

Chapter 6

BUILDING BODY, MIND AND SPIRIT

I HAVE A FRIEND retired from the Marine Corps. He was called back to duty after his retirement and as of the date this book was published, is officially still in the Corps. He signs all his E-mails, *Semper Fi*, which is short for *Semper Fidelis* which is Latin for "Always Faithful". The United States Marine Corps flag is often seen flying just below the American Stars and Stripes. Rarely is a flag from one of the other branches of the services seen displayed. Seeing that red and gold Marine Corps flag reminds me just how proud Marines are.

All through boot camp, and even in their brochures, the Marine Corps preaches about how they would build Marines in body, mind and spirit. I initially thought spirit referred to God and religion. Later I realized spirit referred to the confidence, duty and honor of being a Marine. By the time

I left boot camp the Marine Corps had achieved that goal of spirit in me.

In boot camp, as in many classrooms, we lined up in alphabetical order. My bunk was at the end of the barracks in a row with Devlin, Dishaw, Dixon, Dochterman, and Donald. Yes, his last name was Donald. Dochterman and Donald's bunk was directly across from mine. I thought they looked like two of the goofiest guys I had ever seen. Dochterman was barrel-chested with long muscular arms. He had the build of a wrestler and with his shaved head he looked like a moron. Donald had buck teeth and with his shaved head he looked like a cartoon character. Then I looked in the mirror one morning at my skinny body and shaved head and quickly realized I looked as stupid as they did. I didn't know it at the time but the three of us would be together for the next two years and would become like the Three Musketeers, or perhaps more like the Three Stooges.

Training the body meant building muscles, and the physical part for me was not that difficult. I can honestly say nothing I did in boot camp was any harder than two-a-day football practices in the August heat or any harder than wrestling practice.

Every day before morning chow we went for about a half mile run around the parade ground. The pace was double time, which meant twice as fast as marching. No one ever won a marathon running double time. We also had PT and anyone who ever took gym class in school knows what that stands for. However, in boot camp they always called it P.T. training. I always thought that was redundant and puzzling, like a lot of other things in the Marine Corps. Sometimes, PT training involved exercise like jumping jacks and push-ups. Oftentimes it involved holding our rifles for an hour in various positions and different rifle maneuvers. This was frequently done in combination with bayonet training. We also ran through an obstacle course which consisted of climbing a rope, swinging across a ditch and several stations of climbing over and under things. We also were required to do six pull ups and carry another Marine 25 yards who was of similar weight to ourselves. Records were kept for those who could not complete all stations, but I never had any problem with any of them.

One day we marched double time to the Confidence Course. I remember seeing the tall two-story obstacles made from long telephone poles. From ground level, looking up, they appeared as giant imposing death traps. We stood in formation as an instructor ran through the entire course demonstrating how to complete each station. As I watched I realized that there was no way I could do half of those things. I have never been afraid of heights but not only were we up high, but we also had to climb up and over other barriers while we were two stories in the air. We had to swing from one station to another and finally use a rope to climb down. The rope was attached to a two-story high tower. It hung at a 45-degree angle which we had to climb down head-first using our arms and legs. Three fourths of the way down we had to let go with our legs and hang from the rope by our arms. Then we had to swing our legs back up on the rope in the other direction, so you now were coming down feet first. Below this contraption was a large dirt pool filled with muddy water about four feet deep.

I knew this was where I would *wash-out* of boot camp. Washing-out meant several bad things could happen: One, a general discharge, which meant you were not good enough to be a Marine. Or two you could be sent back two weeks to another recruit platoon and repeat what physical training was needed. This meant two more additional weeks in boot camp. The third option was being sent to a motivational platoon. We had all seen those guys crawling through mud to get to the mess hall and then doing bends and thrusts as Drill Instructors washed them down with fire hoses. We were told the punishment continued for days until they begged for a dishonorable discharge.

It's amazing what a human being can do when those kinds of options are hanging over your head and a screaming Drill Instructor threatening bodily harm. To my amazement I was able to complete the Confidence Course. Even more amazing was the fact that just about everyone in our platoon also completed the course. However, many guys fell into the muddy water to the delight of the Drill Instructors. We were told that our platoon would have to come back and do it again each week until everyone passed. It didn't happen, because they were pushing us through. Viet Nam was calling. I do remember a feeling of pride and accomplishment as we double-timed back to the barracks. I guess that's why they called it the Confidence Course.

The only other physical test that I worried about was the Physical Readiness Test. The test had to be accomplished with a full knapsack, containing a blanket, poncho, mess kit, and a brick. We also wore a cartridge belt with two full canteens and carried our M-14 rifle. We went to the obstacle course and completed several additional stations. We had to climb a rope, run and jump across a ditch, crawl on our belly, carry a fellow Marine 25 yards and do eighty step ups to simulate climbing a hill. All of this had to be accomplished wearing all our gear. After completing these tasks, we were nearly exhausted. The final stage was a three-mile run in platoon formation while carrying our rifle out in front of us.

To practice for the test, the Marine Corps believed in over-training. We left the barracks in formation and ran to the obstacle course. Then after the three-mile run we ran back to the barracks. If anyone dropped out of the run, and someone always did, we continued running around the parade ground until several guys passed out. Then it was back to the barracks for public humiliation for those who dropped out and punishment for all of us for letting them dropout. I'm proud to say I never dropped out. Dochterman with his barrel chest was not built for running. After his first drop out, public humiliation and our punishment, we were instructed to help guys who were about to drop out by carrying their rifle, knapsack or even carrying them. Several times I helped 'Doc' as he was soon nicknamed.

Just to show you how dumb I could be, one day we were told to get ready for the brutal running test. As we prepared, the Drill Instructor demanded to know if there was any of us who knew how to type. I had

taken typing in high school and figured typing had to be easier than running three, four or five miles. I volunteered. Doc gave me a funny look. I
figured he was going to miss my help! The entire platoon lined up in formation and began running to the obstacle course. The Drill Instructor
handed me a shovel. "Here Shit for Brains. You see this drainage ditch
that goes around the barracks? Well, I want you to shovel all the shit out
of that ditch. Do you understand?"

With a very loud voice I replied, "Yes Sir." I was still digging out that
ditch long after they returned from that run. When I finally finished digging completely around the H shaped barracks and came back inside,
Doc looked at me as if I was an idiot. I remembered my father's advice,
"Never volunteer for anything." Now I knew what he meant. Volunteering
for anything would mean being tricked into some extra work. Or even
worse, it could get you killed.

When the day came for the official running test the Drill Instructors
wanted the whole platoon to pass so they would look good. We were told
to wear our knapsacks, minus the brick and the mess gear. Guys who
had a history of not being able to finish were told to replace their gear
with a pillow. The two canteens which we trained with were always full.
Today they were empty except for a swallow we took just before the final
run. And our rifle could be carried over our shoulder. When our platoon
crossed the finish line we stopped running and just marched. This time
no one dropped out of the test. We all passed. The Marine Corps' *over-
training* had worked. We were given time to celebrate by having nine
minutes to eat evening chow!

Like I said the physical stuff never bothered me. It was the mental
part that gave me difficulty. There was so much to memorize. We had to
learn our serial number. Mine was 2145242. Months before, my father
passed over, he suffered from severe dementia and couldn't tell you what
day it was or even who you were. But he still remembered his service
serial number from World War II. We had to memorize and identify

every Marine Corps rank from private to the freaking Commandant, plus every rank in the Navy. The Eleven General Orders, which if I wrote them here would take up a full page; they had to be memorized exactly. If you ever see a Marine in uniform, ask him his 5th General Order, I'll bet he can repeat it flawlessly. We also memorized the combination to our foot locker, our M-14 rifle serial number, along with all the nomenclature of the rifle including: the caliber, all the parts, how fast the bullet traveled, how many rounds per minute it would fire, and Lord knows what else had to be memorized!

The day we were issued our rifle we were taken to a classroom and for two hours Drill Instructors told us everything we would have to memorize. We were instructed step by step how to take the M-14 apart and how to put it together again. I got stuck several times and needed help. I was never mechanically inclined. We were told that by the end of boot camp we would have to disassemble our rifle and reassemble our rifle in two minutes, blind folded. I thought to myself; *"That's not going to happen!"*

Each night during free time we disassembled the rifle, cleaned it, and put it back together. I, along with many others got stuck and frustrated. Staff Sergeant Bozarth announced that we had to work together and learn that weapon. Old goofy-looking Donald sat next to me and showed me a trick with the parts. By taking each part out and positioning it exactly as it had come out and placing the next part right in front of it, the parts would be lined up in the exact order they went back in and exactly in the direction they were taken out. I still found it difficult but after several nights I could do it without any help. To my amazement after weeks of practice it became second nature. When we took the blind fold test I completed the disassembly and assembly of that rifle in one and half minutes. I surprised even myself! I was becoming a Marine, thanks to Donald, who would become a lifelong friend, right up to the day he died.

Chapter 7

LEAVING PARRIS ISLAND

PETE SEEGER helped to write a song called; *"Where Have all the Flowers Gone?"* I'm sure everyone has heard the 1960's group, Peter, Paul and Mary or some other artists sing the lyrics. Whenever I hear that song I am reminded of leaving Parris Island.

Toward the end of boot camp, we all began to feel like Marines, but we sure didn't look like Marines. Every two weeks we marched to the barber shop and had our hair cut so short our heads looked like they were shaved. With our covers off, we all looked like morons. Back in 1965 that was not the normal civilian look. We washed all our own clothing on Sunday afternoons. Our utility uniform was never ironed or pressed. It made us all look like Beetle Bailey from the comics. During boot camp we would march past real Marines in their starched and pressed utilities. Even their covers were starched and stood up, unlike our covers, which looked like baseball caps pulled down over our ears. Seeing those guys made us feel like Beetle Bailey.

About once a week we got naked in front of some navy corpsmen for a physical exam. It was called a 'short arms' inspection. I'll let you figure out how they came up with that name. During these exams we were often given vaccines, in the form of a shot, usually in the arm. The needles were given with some sort of pneumatic hand-held gun that literally shot the vaccine into our arm. With about two weeks left in boot camp we each received an injection in the ass. Of course, no one ever told us what the shot was for and no one ever dared to ask. However, this one shot we got in our right ass cheek was particularly painful especially the next day. It hurt to even get out of our bunks. That was the same day we got measured for our dress uniforms.

Unlike the first day, when they guessed our size and then threw clothing at you, these uniforms would be seen in public and represented the Corps; they had to fit perfectly. Professional tailors measured each one of us. We stepped up on a tall box, so the tailor could drop a tape measure from our crotch down to where our trouser cuff would be. Then he marked the leg with a piece of chalk, slapped you on your right ass cheek and yelled, "Next". I guess it was their way of having fun after measuring hundreds of legs per day. The pain stung clear through to your hip. That night during showers we each checked out the damaged cheek. They were all black and blue and we wondered, "What the hell was in that shot?"

The next week we got our dress uniforms and prepared for our final inspection. Each night the Drill Instructors would call us to the center of the barracks. We would sit like Indians with our legs crossed as they showed us how to perform certain tasks with our uniforms. They demonstrated how to starch our utility cover, so it stood up, so the Marine Corps emblem could be seen. They showed us how to put a spit shine on our shoes. A good spit shine was good for looking up women's skirts or, so we were told. Some guys really believed it and were more motivated to shine on. They gave us advice on how to answer questions that would be asked by the inspecting officer. Then each night the Drill Instructors would practice or rehearse the inspection. Every time something was wrong, punishment was handed out.

The night before the final inspection we were all sitting in front of the Drill Instructors. Staff Sergeant Bozarth was listing all the final details of what had to be accomplished that night. Suddenly one of the guys stood up and interrupted Bozarth.

The boot quickly shouted, "Sir, the private requests to make an emergency head call, Sir." Bozarth looked at him in stunned disbelief. No one had requested an emergency head call since the first day of Boot Camp. The other 79 of us sat staring at the Sergeant wondering what would happen next.

Bozarth asked, "Just how bad do you have to go?"

Immediately the reply came back, "Sir, the private is going now, Sir". Bozarth gave a quick wave of his hand toward the head, as the guy ran off. None of us could believe what had just happened, but we all knew it was the funniest thing we had seen or heard in a long time. The real humor was that none of us had ever seen any of the Drill Instructors ever crack so much as a hint of a smile. Now we watched as each Drill Instructor bit their lips and made grimacing facial movements in order not to laugh. The harder they tried the funnier it became. Finally, they each looked at one another and burst out laughing. All the guys who were sitting next to the poor unfortunate guy scooted over as if they might be sitting in his accident.

Sergeant Land in a stage whisper, spoke to Corporal Knights, "I guess somebody's going to be washing out his skivvy drawers tonight." That was the first I ever saw a human emotion from any of them.

Staff Sergeant Bozarth quickly regained his composure and shouted, "All right you fucking shit birds get back in front of your bunks and get hopping for that inspection". As we worked, I looked up at the three Drill Instructors and I could tell they were still making wise cracks about the incident and still trying not to laugh.

We all passed the final inspection and were ready to ship out. The whole process went quicker than I expected. Everything was moving faster, and nobody really cared how shiny our shoes were because we weren't going to be wearing shoes in Viet Nam anyway. That Saturday, after the inspection, we had a parade and graduation ceremony. My father traveled to Parris Island to attend the occasion. That afternoon I got to spend a few hours with him. It was a proud moment for him.

Sunday, we packed everything we owned into that same sea bag, issued to us on our first day. On Monday we boarded Greyhound buses. Staff Sergeant Bozarth and Corporal Knights waved to us from the steps of the barrack. Sergeant Land refused to attend. For him we had missed too much training in Boot Camp to be called real Marines. We had missed four full weeks, spending only two weeks on the rifle range instead of three. We had only one night at Elliott's Beach, where we practiced setting up tents and slept on the ground. Other Marines spent at least four or five nights on that bivouac. Everyone has seen pictures of Marines doing drills lifting those heavy telephone logs. We never touched them. Some people may not have called us real Marines, but many of these guys from boot camp would end up real dead, very soon.

As we drove out of Parris Island, I realized something I had sorely missed. The bus driver turned on the radio. It was the first music we had heard in two months, except for the marching songs played at graduation. We had no radios in boot camp. I'll never forget the song on the radio as we exited the island: "Where Have all the Flowers Gone?" Marines don't like to be called soldiers. But the lyrics were not lost on me. The last stanza of the song is particularly poignant. Without permission to print any of the lyrics, you may want to look it up for yourself.

Chapter 8

INFANTRY TRAINING AT CAMP LEJEUNE

I HAVE EIGHT good buddies that I taught school with and have known for 35-plus years. We play poker together and go out to breakfast once a month now that we are retired. The other morning at breakfast we were all telling stories and jokes. I told them a story about training at Camp Lejeune and the use of hand grenades. As I finished they all looked at me as if I was the biggest liar in the room. I couldn't understand their reaction. Later, on my way home, it dawned on me that I was the only one of my friends who had ever thrown a hand grenade. Their only knowledge of grenades came from Hollywood. I never talked about my experiences in the Marine Corps because I learned a long time ago that most people don't have a clue what it was like. That's one of the reasons I'm writing those stories now.

Riding in the Greyhound bus from Parris Island, South Carolina to Camp Lejeune, North Carolina took several hours. Doc and I sat next to each other talking. I learned he was from New Jersey, but we both followed the Philadelphia teams. It was Halloween and I remember the Spanish moss hanging from the trees and thought those eerie looking vines made it look like Halloween all the time. As the bus pulled into the gate at Camp Lejeune, we were filled with trepidation. The landscape didn't help. I have no idea what Camp Lejeune looks like today, but in the Fall of '65 it was mighty creepy looking. All the base utility pipes, like water and sewage, ran above ground. When I say above ground I mean twelve to fifteen feet above ground. The pipes hung by tall metal poles. I figured they had to be tall so vehicles like our bus could drive underneath. I wondered why everything was above ground and I still wonder today. Perhaps it was because the base was built in 1942 during World War II and we needed training bases finished quickly. Why would building utility pipes above ground be faster than putting them underground? Maybe they were there because the whole base was built on top of a swamp and the pipes couldn't be buried in a swamp. I don't know. No one ever explained, and no one ever asked.

Above ground hot water pipes with steam vapors rising above them looked like a creepy Sci-Fi movie scene. But the strangest thing of all was seeing the men running on top of the pipes. Yeah, they were running in groups of four, twelve to fifteen feet up in the air. One slip and a man could easily break a leg, or worse, his neck. And why were they running up there? Later I would learn these were the 'force recon' guys, which was the Marine Corps answer to the Green Berets.

Before the bus came to a stop, someone said, "Wouldn't it be funny if some Sergeant gets on the bus and starts screaming, 'Get the fuck off my bus and line up asshole to bully button." I thought, *"Yeah, wouldn't that be funny!"*

As it turned out the sergeant stepped onto the bus and said, "Welcome to Camp Lejeune. My name is Sergeant Bunning. When you get off the bus line up, in formation, for roll call. Any questions?" I guess the other guys were as startled by his politeness as I was.

Several guys replied, "No Sir."

The sergeant quickly responded, "Don't sir me. I work for a living."

And work we did. Infantry training is nothing but hard work. The United States Marine Corps takes great pride in saying that all Marines: cooks, truck drivers, mechanics, clerks and wing wipers (guys who work on the planes used by the Marine Corps Air Wing) all are trained for six weeks to be infantry riflemen. In 1965 everyone except Women Marines went through infantry training.

We were placed in ITR (Infantry Training Regiment) in alphabetical order. Dochterman, Donald, Dixon and Dishaw were still together. I should also mention that while we were in boot camp we all had taken a series of aptitude tests lasting several hours over the course of three days. These tests were supposed determine what job or occupation we would be assigned. By sheer coincidence everyone whose last name was between Anderson and McNutt were surprisingly perfectly suited for the Military Police. And by another strange coincidence everyone else was suited to be a mechanic. Go figure, or as Gomer Pyle often said, "Surprise, Surprise!"

Your occupation in the Corps is known as your M.O.S. or Military Occupation Specialty. I remember when I got my assigned MOS in boot camp and was told I was going to be an M.P. (military policeman) I felt a sense of relief. Perhaps I won't have to go to Viet Nam after all. That point was completely shot down during ITR when each instructor told us, "Don't fool yourselves. You're an 0300 (infantryman) you're going to Viet Nam."

On our second day in camp the new instructors announced that the training time for ITR was also being cut from six weeks to four weeks. Again, our training would be crammed into a shorter time period. During ITR we learned how to fire machine guns, mortar, and rocket launchers. The Army and most Hollywood movies call rocket launchers, bazookas. Therefore, most civilians do too. Live ammo was fired at targets and we fired blanks at each other when training how to fire and maneuver.

Instructions were demonstrated on how to walk on a patrol, keeping eight feet apart, so a grenade would kill only one Marine. Other instructions included such as how to set up an ambush and what to do if you were ambushed. Marines are trained to shoot accurately at long distance targets. However, in a combat situation you often find yourself shooting at someone who is only five or seven feet away. There is no time to take careful aim. 'Point shooting' or shooting from the hip was taught and practiced continually. Point low at the ground and as the rifle fires, the muzzle blast will kick and raise the tip of the rifle up. It is human nature to fire high when shooting from the hip. By shooting low we could see where our bullets hit the ground and then easily move the rifle accordingly. We practiced this, repeatedly. I don't know if it was because I had grown up with guns and had done some bird hunting and shooting at clay pigeons, but I was good at point shooting and hip shooting, something that I would use often in Viet Nam. What they didn't teach us was, the first time you kill someone you will be so scared, you would want to empty your twenty-round magazine into the victim. That fact we would learn on our own.

A typical day in ITR went from before sun rise to well after dark. Reveille came much earlier than in boot camp. Each day we would wait in the dark, in formation outside the barracks for tractor trailers, called cattle cars, to pick us up and take us to the field. We carried our knapsack, cartridge belt, canteens, rifle, and now our full helmet not the chrome dome we wore in Boot Camp. I don't know anyone who ever picked up a helmet and wasn't surprised to realize how heavy it is. After arriving in the field (anyplace outside for training) there would be an outside classroom set up with wooden bleachers with a chalkboard. We would climb out of the cattle cars and force march to morning chow usually a couple miles away. Why didn't the cattle car drop us off at the chow hall which would have made sense, but then we would have missed all the fun of a forced march to and from chow.

Once back at the outdoor classroom instructions were given about some weaponry or technique used in maneuvering. These were usually tedious and boring. Learning about the muzzle velocity of a machine gun, how many rounds it fires per minute, the bullet speed, who invented it, how much it weighs loaded and unloaded, and on and on, was boring. After the lesson we would force march again to noon chow and back. Then we would fire the weapon or practice the technique. Afterward, it was back on the cattle cars to camp. After evening chow, we returned on the cattle cars to the field, to fire the weapons at night or practice that technique in the dark. Then another ride on the cattle cars back to base. We often returned at 2200 or 10:00 p.m., just enough time to clean our rifle and shower so we would get to bed by midnight. Reveille came at 0430 and we would do it all again. That kind of schedule gets old fast.

We also learned how to throw a hand grenade. I should begin by saying that no one ever pulled the pin on a hand grenade with their teeth. That pin is in there for safety and your teeth would be pulled out before it came out. The pin holds the handle of the grenade down. Everyone was taught to grasp the grenade with the handle in the palm of the hand so that it is firmly in place. The pin can be pulled out and if the handle remains in place the grenade can stay safe forever. Then the pin can be pushed back in and the grenade would never go off. However, once the handle pops off there are only two choices. Either you get rid of the grenade or the grenade will get rid of you. The Viet Cong would pull the pin and carefully place the grenade, with the handle still intact, under dead bodies. When the body was lifted the handle came off and a few seconds later it exploded, killing whoever tried to move the body.

Needless to say, after several weeks of getting four or less hours of sleep per night we became exhausted. Sitting in a boring class and listening for hours about the nomenclature of a weapon, it became hard to pay attention. No matter how boring, the lessons were still extremely important. Our lives, and our buddy's lives, depended on how well we learned these lessons. This message was hammered into us repeatedly. This was not a game like, 'I bet you five dollars'. This was, 'I bet my life'! More than once someone would fall asleep. They would be awakened with a slap on the back of the head by one of the many instructors. The second time that person fell asleep the instructors would make him stand in the back of the outdoor classroom and hold a live hand grenade with the pin pulled. No one ever fell asleep holding a grenade! This was the story I relayed to my poker buddies who didn't believe me. They just didn't know how a grenade works and they didn't know the life and death importance of what we were learning.

We learned how to read a map and work a compass. Then the cattle cars would drop us off in groups of four, about 100 yards apart. We had a card with a compass direction and a specific number of paces to walk. We had to find a marker with a letter or number or combination of each nailed to a tree. After writing the information down, the next guy followed the instructions to the next marker. Once the four-man group found all the markers, it led us back to the road to be picked up by the cattle cars. It's a simple exercise that every Boy Scout has used. I was amazed at how many guys had trouble learning it, especially when we came back and did it at night. We were very late getting back to the barracks that night.

Even though ITR only lasted for four weeks it was all done in the field. The weather in North Carolina in November is not bad. But it does rain, and it gets colder each day. We spent way too much time standing around waiting our turn to fire a weapon or walking down a trail to be ambushed. We waited in the rain and cold for many a cattle car to pick us up. They never waited for us, we waited for them.

The other hard thing about ITR was following the typical Marine Corps schedule. Every Thursday night was *field day night*, which meant the barracks and head had to be cleaned and by clean, I mean spotless. So, no matter how late we returned from the field we had to clean the barracks and head, which took several hours. Then on Friday mornings after we left on the cattle cars the officers would go through and inspect the barracks.

Not passing meant another field day night.

Saturday was a rifle and uniform inspection in the morning instead of going to classrooms. Passing inspection meant the rest of the day and night off. We never passed! So, a second inspection was held again on Saturday afternoon.

Finally, we had Saturday night and Sunday off. We weren't allowed off the base, so I never found out what the nearby town was like. We were able to go to the 'Post Exchange' or P.X. where we could buy soap, shoe polish, tooth paste and so on. On Saturday night they would show a movie outdoors like a drive-in theater, except there were no cars, just wooden benches. By late November it was too cold and uncomfortable to sit outside so we seldom watched a movie. Sunday was for washing clothes. There were no washing machines only scrub brushes and wooden tables. We hung our clothes on a line to dry. If it rained that Sunday, the clothes were hung in the barracks. Can you picture 100 guys' underwear hanging from their racks?

After four weeks all the guys who were not actual riflemen went home on leave. Then they would attend another school for additional training in their MOS. Doc, Donald, Dixon and Dishaw stayed for Advanced ITR which was more of the same thing only the activities and training were longer. I'll never forget what one of the instructors told us. "There are lots of men in the military. But it takes a special kind of man to run up to an enemy, stick a bayonet in their stomach, fire a bullet into them and scream in their face all at the same time. Not everyone can do it. But an infantry rifleman has to."

Advanced ITR took another four weeks or most of December and it got colder each day. Our final test was an overnight bivouac for three days in the field using everything we had learned. We dug foxholes and slept in them just like we would do in Nam. I remember waking up one cold morning after a very heavy frost had formed, coating everything in white. We shaved using our metal helmets (minus the liner) to hold the icy water.

I pictured how it must have been at Valley Forge or at the Frozen Chosin in Korea. I suspect we had it easier than they did.

I would never pretend to know what those guys went through. I realize that anyone that was not in Viet Nam will never be able to know what it was truly like. Unless you did those things, you would never fully appreciate them. I hesitated all these years to tell these stories partially because I know that most people will never understand, just like my poker buddies didn't understand how a hand grenade works or what it's like to throw one or kill someone.

Chapter 9

HURRY UP AND WAIT

THE OTHER DAY I had a colonoscopy. Anyone who has ever had one knows it's no big deal, except for the preparation the day before. That's a shitty experience. I was scheduled to arrive at 9:30 am for a 10:30 am appointment. Always punctual, I arrived a little early and then of course wasn't called until 11:00. Sitting in the waiting room of the hospital I remembered all the times in the Marine Corps that I had to wait and wait and wait some more.

After Camp Lejeune, we were all given 20 days of leave. I was home for Christmas to see all my relatives and show off my new uniform. I especially wanted to impress my high school friends. However, many of my buddies were either also in the military or in college. No one seemed too impressed.

While in high school I knew three girls whom I considered friends. Becky and Annette were in vocational agriculture class with me for three years. We were all friends but not boy / girl friends. Annette went steady with a guy in the class ahead of us and eventually married him. Becky was cute, prim and proper. I'm not sure she was even allowed to date until her senior year. I took her out to some events that she wanted to see but they were not real dates, just good friends doing things together. I considered both Annette and Becky to be more like sisters than even friends. There was a third girl named Grace. She was different. I liked her, and she liked me. We went out on real dates such as the senior prom and movies. I believe she liked me, but I also knew we did not share enough in common to ever be lovers or get married. She was shy and introverted. She also had a dislike (which was almost a fear) of any animals. I grew up raising animals and loved them. It would never have worked out for us. I was going to Viet Nam, so I never tried to pursue a relationship with her other than dating. When on leave, I met up with all three girls while wearing my uniform. Annette was engaged. Becky had a steady boy friend. Grace and I went out for dinner. None of the girls seemed too impressed. They all promised they would write to me and me to them, which we did.

When leave ended I returned to Camp Lejeune to await further orders. Always fearful of being late or AWOL (absent without leave) I arrived the night before I had to return. The Marine Corps and Navy now calls it U.A. (unauthorized absence). UA meant punishment and the infraction went on your permanent record. Also, after six months in the Corps everyone automatically became a private first class, if they had not gotten into any trouble. Since I arrived at camp the night before, no one on base was prepared for my early return so they had no place for me to sleep. I was given a bunk and mattress but no sheets or blankets. It was two days before New Years. It was cold, and the barracks had only minimum heat to keep the pipes from freezing. It was a long night for Private Dixon.

The next day I was assigned to a holding company. This company was just a place to await further orders and for the other guys to return from leave. We waited for orders to find out where we would be stationed next. We would fall out each morning into formation and march to chow. Then hang around until noon so we could march to chow again then wait again until evening chow.

On New Year's Day the base was practically empty. The Marine Corps only served a late breakfast and an early evening chow. I don't know what I had for breakfast but whatever it was would ruin my day. Some guys said there was a USO building across the base that had a television where we could watch some college football games. So, I hiked to the building and figured I'd enjoy watching some football. By 10 am I began to feel funny in my stomach. By 11am I knew I was going to be sick. After leaving the USO building I threw up along the side of the road. I knew I was not finished, so I headed to sick bay. In sick bay were three other guys who were also throwing up and one poor Navy Corpsman to treat us. I started to puke again, and he quickly asked me to go outside. Once outside I continued until I had the dry heaves. I asked the corpsman if he could do anything for me. I'll never forget what he said. "All I can tell you is, if you taste something hairy in your mouth, you better swallow hard, cause, it might be your asshole." At the time it wasn't the least bit funny, but now... He gave me some Pepto Bismol. By the time I left sick bay the place was full of sick marines all having eaten the same chow and now throwing up. Later that afternoon they were going to serve a nice New Year's Day dinner. I debated whether to eat or not. I finally decided it would be better to put something in my stomach than to not eat at all. I was not the only guy to ask for a bowl of cereal and some milk. That was my first case of ptomaine poisoning. I hoped it would be my last.

The next day was a typical work day. The Marine Corps does not like to see guys standing around with nothing to do, so we were assigned to a work detail. Forty of us boarded a cattle car after morning chow and drove out into the field. There, we discovered three old buildings. They were probably old, World War I barracks, all single story and in horrible shape. Our job was to demolish the buildings. The Corps supplied us with one hammer and one crowbar for forty of us. Thirty-eight of us, with nothing to do, were told to stand in the other two barracks and "stay out of sight". It was 40 degrees outside and raining. The buildings had no doors, no windows and no heat. When tearing down a building, if the only tools you have are a crowbar and hammer, the only thing you can take apart are doors and windows. We stood around in those cold damp buildings for four hours, while two guys worked with the hammer and the crowbar. At noon we got back on the cattle cars, rode to chow, then after four more hours of standing in the cold and we returned to the barracks. Like I said, the Marine Corps does not like to see men standing around with nothing to do.

Lucky for me the next day we were given our written orders. All the guys who were going to the MP's were put in a separate barracks where we were instructed what to do and what we needed before going to Camp Pendleton, California. Of course, Doc, Donald and I were reunited. Dishaw was not there. Evidently, he was still only 17 years old. He was too young to go to Viet Nam and would have to stay at Camp Lejeune and continue with the work platoon. I never saw Dishaw again.

The next day we flew to California and drove by bus to Camp Pendleton, near San Diego. Spending a winter in Southern California is not a bad place to be. However, it wasn't always sunny and warm. Daylight was still short. The nights were kind of cold, temperatures in the 40's. We were the first guys to arrive to form the new 1st M. P. Battalion. We were so new we didn't even have a commanding officer yet, so they put all of us on v or as the Army calls it K.P. (Kitchen Police).

Most old movies about World War II portray KP as punishment. We were on mess duty not for punishment but simply because we arrived in camp early. We had to wait for the other 600 guys to arrive, that would make up the battalion, and what better way to wait than on mess duty.

Most people have seen the famous Norman Rockwell picture of a soldier in uniform at home helping his Mom peel potatoes. It's a touching, iconic picture. However, we never peeled potatoes. In 1965 the Marine

Corps had automatic machines to do that. We ate a lot of mashed potatoes from a powdered mix. Instead of peeling potatoes all day, we cleaned the mess hall, chow line, tables, decks, and scrubbed pots all day.

I should mention that the food in the Corps' mess halls was not bad. My mother was one of the worse cooks in America perhaps because my father insisted that all food be cooked well done. I never knew that a pork chop could taste good until I ate one in a mess hall. My mother's pork chops tasted like shoe leather. Some guys complained about the food, but I thought it was better than home.

What made mess duty seem like punishment was the work hours. The mess hall began serving morning chow at 0600 and ended when the last guy went through the line about 0800. However, the mess hall opened before 0600 so the cooks could begin work. Therefore, we had to arrive at 0500, which meant we had to wake up way before that to brush our teeth, get dressed, and make our bunks. The mess hall served evening chow from 1700 (5pm) to 1900 (7pm). About an hour later at 2000 (8pm) after the mess hall was completely cleaned we could leave. In effect we worked from 5 in the morning until 8 at night. Yes, that's a 15-hour day, six days a week. On Sunday only two meals were served beginning at 0800 for morning chow and ending at 1800 for evening chow. Therefore, on Sunday we only had to work a 12-hour day. Each evening we had to shave, shower, wash our clothes, and of course on Thursday night, we held field day to clean the barrack and head. In our free time we could write letters home. But mess duty wasn't punishment!

The other thing that made it seem like punishment was the way it was run. The person in charge of the mess hall was a 1st Lieutenant who oversaw ordering the proper amount of supplies, taking care of the paper work and inspecting the final food serving. If he was at the mess hall he must have had a separate office because I only saw him twice, both times when higher ranking officers were inspecting.

The real guy in charge was a sergeant E-5. He was a 'lifer' who probably had been in the Corps for 15 years. Anyone who had been in the Marine Corps for 15 years and only made E-5 meant one of two things. Either he was an asshole, or he had been in trouble a lot. In this case I guessed it was both. I don't remember his real name, but we just called him Sergeant Grumpy. The guys who did the real work of cooking were Lance Corporals and Corporals or E-3's and E-4's. They too worked 15-hour days, but they only worked every other day and every other weekend. For the most part they were guys like us who joined for four years and happened to have an M.O.S. as a cook. Sergeant Grumpy was always on our case. He was a little skinny guy who had a habit of standing around doing an imitation of James Cagney. It wasn't intentional it just looked that way. He would stand around and lift his shoulders up with his hands down at his sides as if to say, "You dirty rats." I studied him each day and tried to figure out what he was trying to do. He was so skinny that his trousers would slip down, but instead of putting his fingers inside his belt and lifting them up he would pull them up with his wrists on the outside of the trousers. Each time he did this he reminded me of Cagney.

After the first week we were informed that mess duty was going to last four weeks instead of one. That bit of news was not well received. Mess duty was hard work cleaning up after each meal, wiping down the tables, the chow line, sweeping the floor, and swabbing the deck. It was boring work, but we usually finished an hour or so before the next wave of troops poured in to eat. For that hour we stood around and tried to look busy.

You must remember we were all still teenagers. Boredom and fatigue became the ingredients for trouble. One time between meals someone threw a wet sponge at another guy. Within seconds the entire mess hall was in full battle mode. Dozens of sponges, even some from the corporals, were hurled around. Tables were arranged into battle formation. The wet sponge war, as it was later referred to, lasted for several minutes until Sergeant Grumpy came out of his office. I don't know if it was an accident or not but Grumpy caught a heavy wet sponge in the face and chest. I thought he was going to have an aneurysm. Of course, all of us pretended we were busy working and weren't even aware of any sponges, even though the deck and bulkheads were covered with water. Sergeant Grumpy, not knowing what to do, simply told all of us to, "Give me 20! And get this place cleaned up." For us, 20 push-ups were nothing. One of the guys even joked, "I was going to ask him which arm he wanted us to use!"

I learned a lot while on mess duty. Some guys would get an 8-hour pass on Saturday night and take a bus to Tijuana and get back at three in the morning to start work at 0500, just so they could be with a Tijuana whore. I thought they were crazy. Doc, Donald and I often were too tired to even go to the base movie. I also began to realize that the lifers and most of the officers didn't really care about the enlisted men at all. There was a separate section of the mess hall for Staff Sergeants and above, including Lieutenants. They never went through the chow line with the troops but were served restaurant style by the cooks who acted as waiters. The higher-ranking officers ate in a separate mess hall with table clothes and silverware like a real restaurant. The only officer who went through the chow line was the Duty Officer of the Day who was required to visit the mess hall. Some of the Duty Officers would inspect the chow line before the meal but most didn't even do that. I never saw or heard of an officer asking how the chow was, or if we were getting enough to eat or any questions at all. They didn't seem to care.

We continued waiting and working on mess duty for the rest of the month of January. Finally, we were assigned to 'D' company, the last company to be formed. We were the first to arrive in the M.P.'s and the last to form a company. At last I thought the waiting was over. Boy was I wrong!

James M. Dixon

Chapter 10

THE 1ST M.P. BATTALION

THE OTHER MORNING I witnessed our city police arrest a man for purse snatching. I didn't see the crime, only the police officer cuffing the guy, reading him his rights and shoving him into the patrol car. We have all seen it a thousand times in movies and television, this time it was live and only six feet away. I recalled that's just how they taught us to do it in the 1st MP Battalion. I also remember how during the training I thought I might someday want to be a police officer. As M.P.'s we received some of our training and instructions from the California Highway Patrol and I imagined it would give me a head start on applying for any local police force.

The problem, however, was none of the training we got in the 1st M.P. Battalion would ever be used in Viet Nam. All the officers in charge really had no idea what we would be doing in Viet Nam. Some thought we might be guarding a prisoner of war camp or patrolling the streets of Saigon or DaNang looking for drunken Sailors, Soldiers, and Marines. One thing for sure, we all agreed, we would not be going around and arresting the

Viet Cong!

Every one of us was a 0311 (infantry rifleman) so they organized the battalion like a typical infantry battalion. An infantry battalion has four companies each with four platoons. A platoon has four squads all with the smallest unit a four-man fire-team. Therefore, a battalion should have well over 800 men. I don't know what the Marine Corps is like now but at that time we were never at full strength. Instead of over 800 men in the 1st M.P. Battalion we had just over 600 or about 150 men in each Company.

Dochterman, Donald and I were still together in the same platoon, only now we were each in a different squad. We still hung around together on weekends and evenings. But, we still hardly had any free time. Each day we had classes on police work, such as: how to use hand cuffs, how to wrestle someone to the ground, how to search a suspect, and how to warn them of their rights. Each morning we began with a run through the hills and in the afternoon, we did P.T. exercises. I was amazed at how out of shape I was after 20 days of leave, five days of waiting and 30 days of mess duty. We had classes each morning and then practiced what was taught in the afternoon.

After every chow we stood in company formation with all four platoons. The platoon Sergeant could take roll by asking each squad leader and team leader if anyone was missing. If someone was missing or late the Sergeant would still report, "All present or accounted for," so they wouldn't look bad. Then when you showed up the Sergeant dealt with your punishment and the Lieutenant would not have to make a formal report. I was only late one time. I tried to make a phone call home and waited in line, which took longer than I had planned. For my punishment, I was not allowed off the base that weekend, which was not as bad as it sounds since we only had Saturday nights off.

I have talked to guys who were in the other branches of the service. They all had weekends off after basic training, we never did. By a weekend off, I mean they had off Friday night until Monday morning. For us a weekend off went from Saturday afternoon until Sunday night. We had to be back in the barracks by 2200 (10:00 pm) Sunday night.

Of course, every Thursday night was field day; clean the barracks and the head for an inspection Friday morning. In many places in the service, after passing the inspection on Friday morning, you were dismissed and didn't have to return until Monday morning. Lots of guys who lived within driving distance could go home and visit friends and relatives. I don't know if it was because of the war, but I think our superiors were afraid guys would not come back or perhaps with too much time off we would get in trouble. I guess that's why we only had Saturday night off.

Our platoon sergeant was Sergeant Deluca. He was a *lifer* and had 19 years in the Corps which made him about 37 years old. He had risen to the rank of Staff Sergeant (E-6). He wasn't a bad guy, and always treated us fair. He was always amazed at how little we knew.

We were told each week we would have a *general inspection*. They wanted to make sure we had all our equipment, clothing and our gear was ready to go to Viet Nam. In our case, because we would be leaving, our inspection was even more important. I thought a general inspection meant that a real life General would come and inspect us. No, a Commanding General's or CG's inspection is usually held once a year throughout the Marine Corps usually in the Spring. A general inspection is when they check or inspect everything: our uniform, our rifle, our equipment, the barracks and the head, everything. When I say they check our uniform I mean the uniform we were wearing and all our other clothing. They checked uniforms that would be hanging in a wall locker and all our other clothing laid out on our bunk. All our equipment was displayed on our bunk: our knapsack, cartridge belt, canteens, first aid kit, poncho, mess kit and anything we would carry into combat. These inspections were called a *junk on the bunk inspection*. We had the normal Friday morning inspection of the barracks while we were at class. Then on Saturday morning we had the 'junk on the bunk' inspection.

The first time Sergeant Deluca told us not to worry about the inspection, "It's no big deal." He didn't realize that the junk on the bunk inspection was one of the things they skipped in Boot Camp. The results of the first inspection were appalling. Sergeant Deluca complained, "Didn't they teach you anything in Boot Camp?" They didn't teach us that!

When I say they checked all our clothing, that's exactly what I mean, all of our clothing. You had to lay out five pairs of skivvy drawers, five tee shirts, five socks, five utility jackets, five utility trousers and so on. Everything had to be folded a certain way. Our name had to be stamped in ink or sewed on every item. We washed our clothes on Sunday, therefore by Friday morning most of our clothing and underwear was dirty. Many of us set dirty underwear on our bunk; after all it was called junk on the bunk. The Marine Corps didn't appreciate dirty clothes on their bunks.

Our platoon consisted of mostly guys like me who were just out of Boot Camp and ITR. There were however, several Lance Corporals who had served in the Dominican Republic conflict, when the Marines were sent in to evacuate and rescue Americans trapped in a rebellion. They had already been in the Corps for two years. They took us under their wings and explained some of the tricks and secrets to passing inspections. What we needed to do was buy five sets of everything. Then pay a tailor to have our name sewed neatly on everything. They explained we needed to carefully fold each item to the specific regulation and place each piece of clothing in the bottom of our foot locker. We never touched or wore those clothes. They were for inspections only.

That sounds easy. Problem was where did we get the money for a complete set of five uniforms? In 1965 a Private made $105.00 a month. After taxes that didn't leave much. We also had to purchase our own soap, toiletries and shoe polish and to pay for stationary and stamps if we wanted to write home. After the first inspection the Lieutenant noticed that the bottoms of our boots needed new soles. Guess who had to pay for new soles on our boots. Lucky for us we were all promoted to Private First

Class and given a $5.00 a month raise. We also had to pay to have our single stripe sewed onto all our uniforms. We set about trying to purchase all the needed new items but even after I received $100 from my father, I still needed another month's pay to buy everything.

That's why I was phoning home to ask my father to send me some money, so I could pass those inspections. It's also why I was late for formation and grounded to the base for a entire Saturday night.

Each Friday night we would clean the barracks and head, a second time, to prepare for the general inspection on Saturday morning. We gave extra care to cleaning our rifle and polishing everything. We set everything out on our bunk the night before and checked each other's uniforms and gear so that we could all pass the inspection and have Saturday afternoon off. Friday night we slept on the floor, so we would not disturb our junk. We still never passed. They always found something wrong, so we always had another inspection that afternoon. In reality, we were never dismissed until at least 1500 (3 pm) on Saturday.

With so much time preparing for inspections and training we had little time to really get to know each other. I only got to know the guys in my squad. One thing I noticed were the things we had in common. We had all played high school sports like football, basketball or wrestling. Most of us had graduated from high school and all had some girl back home to whom we wrote. Other than learning what state they came from there was little time to know much else. I still hung around with Doc and Donald who were in other squads. Doc had a girl back home who he had promised to marry. He wanted me to be his best man, which I thought odd and figured the chances of both of us making it back from Viet Nam were slim. One Saturday night the three of us went into Oceanside, California, the nearest town. Doc got a tattoo of the Marine Corps emblem on his shoulder. He wanted me to get one also. I thought about it but after I saw the ugly swollen scabs that took a week to heal, I decided never to get a 'tat'.

Donald was an odd sort. In the Marine Corps, a guy who was squared away was someone who always had his gear, equipment, and uniform exactly the way the Corps wanted. A shit bird was just the opposite. Most of us had our shit bird days when we got our asses chewed out for something. I don't remember Donald ever getting his ass chewed. He was the most squared-away guy I knew.

There were two Mexican guys in my squad. I say Mexican because they spoke fluent Spanish and had an accent when they spoke English. They were second generation Mexican. They graduated from high school and their accent was a combination Mexican and Texan. Garcia was a short, small guy with handsome features. Gonzales was short and heavy set. They used to do an imitation of the Cisco Kid and his sidekick Poncho saying, "Oh Cisco." and "Oh Poncho". They made us all laugh.

Donaldson was a big farm boy from the Midwest. He was smart and usually more squared away than me. We were all horny young men, but I remember Donaldson always seemed to have women on his mind.

Our squad leader was Corporal Fussner (not his real name). He was a hillbilly. He was skinny, missing a front tooth, and kind of slumped shouldered. I could tell in high school he would have been one of the 'greasers'. He was impressed with himself even if we weren't. He liked to smoke in the barracks which was against the rules. He would often hide between the wall lockers so as not to be seen and spent more time trying to see what he could get away with than doing anything productive. He was always trying to impress us with his worldliness and foul language. He would say things like, "This rifle is dirtier than a Mickey Spillane fuck book", which really made no sense at all. He warned us about going to Tijuana. "You be careful down there. Take along lots of rubbers. Some of them ladies have diseases that doctors don't have a cure for. Hell, the scientists don't even have a name for them yet." Fussner fit the description of a true 'wind bag'.

All the guys who were Lance Corporals and had served in the Dominican Republic were promoted to Corporal even though they had only been in the Corps for less than three years. Corporal Fussner had been a Marine for four years and reenlisted so he could get promoted to Corporal. Even the Marine Corps knew Fussner was an idiot. He was our leader.

After being in the M.P.'s during February and March, a bunch of us finally had saved enough money to go to Tijuana. We would have preferred to go to Disneyland, but it was much farther away and cost way more. So, Donald, Donaldson, Dixon, Dochterman, Garcia and Gonzales boarded a bus and took the short trip to the Mexican border. The bus let us off and we walked across a bridge into the infamous town. What a pig-sty! The whole town stank. It smelled like a combination of B.O., beer, and burnt barbeque. Even our two Mexican buddies were shocked. The place was one bar after another with prostitutes everywhere. And I don't mean good looking prostitutes. I remember Donaldson summing them up, "I wouldn't fuck these whores with my worst enemy's dick!" They weren't just ugly they looked like you could catch some disease if you walk too close to them! We went into several bars looking for a place clean enough to sit. We all had to try some Mexican beer and of course some tequila.

It was a good thing we had Garcia and Gonzales with us. They spoke Spanish and kept us from getting ripped off. Doc had too much to drink and decided to get another tattoo, but I was able to talk him out of it. I didn't want anyone having their blood drawn in that filthy place. I told him that he could get a cheaper tattoo back in Oceanside California. We all had too much to drink especially for guys who were not used to drinking.

We decided to spend the night in Tijuana. Garcia and Gonzales found a fairly clean hotel. Donald and Donaldson shared one room, Doc and I were in another and Garcia and Gonzales in a third. Doc passed out on his bed. I showered and managed to crawl into mine. Sometime before dawn I awoke to a strange sound like a toilet flushing or a pump sucking water. I sat up and looked around the room but all I saw were Doc's stomach muscles moving up and down. Suddenly his stomach erupted like a volcano. Vomit shot out of his mouth with such force that it went straight up and bounced off the ceiling and splattered off the walls. Thank goodness, I was awake in time to pull the covers over my body and avoid getting hit with liquid shrapnel. I have seen projectile vomiting since then, but nothing compared to what Doc had just done. Being stupid, I didn't think to roll Doc onto his side so that he wouldn't choke on his own vomit. Fortunately, he survived. As a matter of fact, the explosion from his mouth had hit the ceiling with such force that hardly any dripped down on Doc. In the morning I woke Doc, so he could go into the head and finish throwing up. I was dressing when the other four guys came to our room. I remember the look on Donaldson's face as he studied the art work on the ceiling. He cocked his head to one side like a puppy watching you pee into a toilet for the first time. He looked at it for the longest time. Garcia's only comment, "I knew we should have told him not to drink the worm."

After we got cleaned up and left the room we put Doc on a bus back to Camp Pendleton. The rest of us spent the remainder of the day shopping. I had my picture taken, super-imposed with two very attractive women. I had seen similar pictures and was foolish enough to think all the woman in Tijuana looked like that. Now I could have fun telling other guys they needed to go there and check it out. Donaldson bought a deck of playing cards with a different naked woman pictured on each card. My favorite was the ten of spades.

We returned to the barracks later that day, broke, hung over and a little bit wiser. Doc was already in his bunk. On Monday we would continue our other MP training.

Chapter 11

A ROAD TRIP TO JAPAN

MY GRANDFATHER used to say, "The way you can tell the difference between a fairy tale and a bullshit story is a fairy tale starts out, once upon a time... and a bullshit story starts out, now listen, this is no shit now..." Everybody has heard both types of stories. I have a story that is so incredible that whenever I tell it, people think it's a bullshit story. Some true stories are so incredible they are hard to believe. You can't make this stuff up!

Since we might be patrolling the streets of some town or city in Viet Nam, the Marine Corps decided some of us should be trained to drive jeeps as patrol cars. Two men from each platoon were picked to learn how to drive a jeep and use a radio. The Lieutenant picked me, and a guy named McDonald. I don't know about Mac, but I was honored to be picked. Mac was from Massachusetts and was a huge Boston sports fan. He had played high school football, as a quarterback and safety. His dream was to follow his brother and get a football scholarship to college. He told me he was shorter than his brother and since no one offered him a scholarship he decided to join the Marine Corps in the hopes that he would grow a little taller. Then he would go home and work on that scholarship. Eventually Mac and I would become good friends.

We and two guys from each of the other platoons, a total of eight, were sent to a school on base. We spent one week learning how to drive a jeep and one week learning how to work a radio. We all had one day of radio operation in infantry training. We learned the phonetic alphabet: Alpha, Bravo, Charlie, Delta, Echo... We also were taught how to change frequency, certain code terms, and the rules of radio operation. One major rule was to never use the word 'repeat' on the radio. Repeat was only used when calling in artillery fire. Whenever the 'cannon corkers', as the infantry called them, heard the word 'repeat', it meant to continue the artillery barrage. So, when a message had to be said again, the operator replied, "Say again your last." It was a cardinal sin to use the word repeat.

Once we mastered the radio it was time to learn to drive and take care of a jeep. I was amazed at how many guys didn't know how to drive a stick shift and use a clutch. I had been driving a stick shift since I was 12 years old. My father gave my brothers and me an old Austin Healey to drive around the farm fields near our house. In the Marine Corps we learned how to drive a jeep in four-wheel drive over hills and ruts. The final test was driving out in the middle of nowhere, at night, one car length away from the next jeep, without any lights. That was kind of hairy. Using lights in a combat zone makes for an easy target. On Saturday, instead of a rifle inspection, we had a jeep inspection. Luckily the jeep's canvas tops were off, along with the two doors, so we had less to clean. But the engine also had to be cleaned, which was the real hard part.

I was better at driving the jeep than McDonald, but he was better at using the radio. I never seemed to get the part about ending a radio message. When talking and wanting the other person to respond we were taught to say, "Over." When finished we said, "Out." but never "over and out." For some reason I could not keep that straight.

The last test with the jeep was to ford a river. Fording is crossing a river when there is no bridge. A jeep can be adapted to drive through deep water, so deep that the entire engine can be under water. They showed us a movie on how to waterproof the jeep. Basically, a pipe is attached to the intake valve, and another pipe to the exhaust pipe. The pipes stick up in the air about six feet and higher than the roof, somewhat like a snorkel. Pasty caulk is wrapped around all the engine parts so that no water can get in. I have absolutely no motor skills when it comes to engines. I was amazed the Marine Corps didn't make me a mechanic, since everybody seemed to be assigned the opposite M.O.S. as to their abilities. The only thing I knew about an engine was if it runs out of gas it will stop. Running out of oil means the engine will stop forever. Staff Sergeant Deluca kept emphasizing that if water got into the engine it would be ruined.

The last day of our jeep training we had to waterproof the jeep and test it by fording a river. Apparently, there weren't any fordable rivers near Camp Pendleton, so it was decided to take one of the jeeps to the ocean and run it into the water. Eight of us rode in a 6 x 6 truck down to the ocean. A 6 x 6 is like a 4 x 4 or all wheel drive vehicle only it has six axles, hence the name. They found a small inlet where the waves were small. The Sergeant tied an empty white plastic bleach bottle to a six-foot piece of clothesline. The other end was tied around a concrete block. A volunteer was selected to carry the block and bottle out into the water about waist deep and drop it off. When I say volunteer was selected I mean, "I need a volunteer." And then the sergeant handed the bottle to the nearest guy who had an expression of 'oh shit' on his face. It was late March and even though we were in Southern California it was not very warm. We were still wearing our utility coats, or field jackets as we called them. That water had to be cold as Mac and I would soon find out!

Two guys would test the waterproofing by driving one jeep into the inlet. With only one jeep we took turns putting the pipes on and off and wrapping the caulk around everything. Some guy from the motor pool watched and checked to make sure we didn't miss any part of the engine. Again, they stressed that if any water got into the engine it would be ruined. The term 'vapor lock' was used, whatever that meant. By the time all four teams of drivers and radiomen were finished it was well after 1100 and time for afternoon chow. Sergeant Deluca announced that, "When we come back from chow two of you guys will test this jeep by driving it into the water and around that buoy", as he pointed to the bleach bottle. That's when I committed the unspeakable sin of asking a question.

The Marine Corps has an expression, which comes from a famous poem by Alfred Lord Tennyson or John Keats or Robert Kipling. They all seem to have been given credit at one time or another for the line. The actual quote is. "Yours is not to reason why, yours is but to do and die." The Marine Corps always says, "Yours is not to reason why, yours is to do or die." Simple meaning, do it without questions, or we'll kill you. So, when I asked, "Hey, Sarge, why do we have to have two guys in the jeep?" I could tell I had blundered by the expressions on everyone's face that said, *did he just ask a question?*

The immediate response from Sergeant Deluca was, "Because Dixon when you get to Nam you will always have two guys in every jeep! One to drive and one to work the radio! And guess what? You're going to be the guy riding shotgun when we get back! Now who's the guy you're teamed up with?" Mac sheepishly raised his hand, so I wouldn't have to point him out.

We then piled into the truck to go to chow as Mac looked at me and said, "Nice going Dixon."

We returned from chow and stood around on the beach while Sergeant Deluca and the guys from the motor pool finished their smokes. I remember looking out at the white bottle that was being used as a buoy and thought to myself, "Man, that buoy sure looks far away." I had spent many a summer on the Chesapeake Bay and the Sassafras River and I knew about high and low tides. I also knew it had been six hours since the buoy was placed at waist deep water. It had to be high tide by now. I wanted to say something but: A) I had already opened my mouth once today and B) perhaps the sand beneath the water stayed at nearly the same level far out into the inlet. So, I kept my mouth shut.

When we got the order to begin, Mac and I took our field jackets off, so we would have something dry to wear after our mission. As ordered Mac sat in the driver's seat and I got in the passenger side.

I commented only to Mac, "That buoy sure looks a long way off!"

I remember his reply, "It probably just looks farther because we're sitting down." The waves rolling in were not like the Atlantic Ocean waves where they come crashing onto the shore. These waves were only about a foot high and gently rolling across the inlet.

The jeep was pointed toward the water. Mac put the jeep in first gear, slowly let off the clutch and away we went. The first wave hit the tires and we hardly noticed it, so we kept on going. The second wave hit the bumper and slightly jolted the jeep. We kept going. The third wave hit the grill and water started pouring into the jeep, but we kept going. Looking at the buoy it still seemed a long way off. The next wave rolled up to the hood and splashed inside the jeep up to and over our seats. As it washed over our testicals we both inhaled deeply. Man, that water was cold! We kept on going. The next wave lifted us out of our seats and we began to float out of the jeep.

We could hear Sergeant Deluca yelling, "You don't have to drive around the buoy, just up to it." It was way too late for advice. Mac and I were hanging onto the jeep, but we had floated out. I had my right hand on the dash and my left hand on the top of the seat. Similarly, Mac had one hand on the steering wheel and the other on the seat. The jeep, still in gear, kept on going. With the next wave we were forced to swim or drown. Fully clothed and with our boots on, swimming was not easy.

The jeep kept going without us. Sergeant Deluca, now standing knee deep in water, was screaming orders at us, "Put the brake on! Take it out of gear! Put it in reverse!" These instructions were way too late now. Mac began to try to swim toward the drowning jeep, but swimming in cold water when you are fully dressed was nearly impossible. We all watched the jeep as it proceeded on its journey. Just like a submarine periscope, the intake pipe went slowly underwater, quickly followed by the exhaust pipe. The last we saw of the jeep, it was headed for Japan.

We swam the short distance to shore and walked out of the water. Sergeant Deluca had his cover off, sweating, and rubbing his head. We had just drowned a United States government jeep. To be honest, the jeep was old, having been manufactured in 1946, which was indicated by the serial number. Who knows how many times the speedometer had rolled over? I began calculating how many pay checks it would take to pay it off.

The guy from the motor pool radioed for some help. Eventually the motor pool sent two guys in wet suits to rescue our jeep. They swam out and found the jeep, hooked a tow rope to the back end of it, and with the 6x6 yanked the jeep out of the ocean. We towed the jeep back to the motor pool as we returned to our barracks and I was amazed at how much water kept pouring out of the jeep on the ride back. The other surprising thing was that the incident was never mentioned. To his credit Sergeant Deluca took full responsibility. He told the Lieutenant he had not calculated on the change in the tides. Being a lifer, he was forgiven. I thought for sure Mac and I would be court martialed, but we never heard another word. That is except for the ribbing we got from the other guys. That went on for weeks!

As far as the Marine Corps was concerned the incident was finished and forgotten. As for me, it would never be forgotten. However, when I relate this story it's so unbelievable that it may as well have never happened, because it is so ridiculous, everyone I tell it to think I'm bullshitting them. But as I said before, you can't make this stuff up.

Chapter 12

WHAT'S FUNNY AND WHAT'S NOT

THROUGHOUT MY LIFE, as with everyone else, I have had my share of mishaps, blunders, heart ache, disappointments, death, and sorrow. I have suffered through horrible jobs and terrible bosses. And every married couple has experienced troubles and worries especially if you have children. That's why life causes baldness and gray hair. Throughout most of my life I have been blessed with a certain irreverent sense of humor. I try to find the 'funny' in everything. Joking has been my way of coping with all the difficulties in life for as long as I can remember. However, some things that happen in life are just too sad where even I can't find any humor. Laughter won't help you cope with some of life's tragedies.

Our last week at Camp Pendleton was a busy one. We prepared for the final General Inspection, had dessert at the Platoon leader's house and packed all our gear to go to Nam. We signed important papers and generally made ready for the trip. My squad and the fourth squad had to clean the barrack's deck, bulkheads and everything in the barracks including the two, galvanized shit cans (trash cans). Each week two guys were picked to take the cans outside, empty them, scrub them out and make them shine. Of course, all week guys tossed all sorts of foul, disgusting litter into the shit cans. Everything from letters from home to soda cans and human spit were discarded in those cans. I don't know which was worse, cleaning out the head or cleaning out the shit cans. However, for the final inspection, brand new cans were brought out and unwrapped. The old nasty cans were hidden out of sight. No one wanted to take any chance of not passing.

We passed with flying colors. Only some minor picky things were written up, so the higher ups would know that a thorough inspection was diligently carried out. We didn't have time to celebrate but it was a relief when the final inspection was over, and we had gotten a good grade. As a reward we were given the afternoon off. That was the first and only Friday afternoon we ever had off. However, we were confined to the base because we were to leave the next day for Viet Nam.

While we were sitting around feeling good about passing inspection, suddenly someone shouted, "Officer on deck, attention!" It was the Battalion Colonel who had entered our barracks. We stood at attention in stunned silence. It was the first time we had ever seen the Colonel in our barracks. Hell, the final General Inspection was conducted by his X.O. *Had the Colonel come by to give us a pep talk or was the final inspection not over.* The Colonel began cursing at us and complained about dirt everywhere. Then we heard some guys laughing from the other side of the wall lockers. The Colonel continued his tirade but as he continued to chew us out, more and more guys began to laugh. It turned out it was not the real Colonel. A guy named Coultern (I'm not sure of the spelling or pronunciation) had dressed up like the Colonel, painted a mustache over his lip and was strutting around doing a remarkably funny and accurate impersonation. He continued his charade even as guys began to throw things at him. He caused so much laughter and commotion that Sergeant Deluca came in. Even he was at first fooled by the look-a-like. After a stern warning about the consequences of impersonating an officer, Deluca got the sergeants from the other platoons to come and take-a-look. We all had one well-earned laugh. I remember that day with fond memories, thanks to Private Coultern. Thirteen months later when I had to identify the remains of Coultern's body, well, that was not so funny. Today I like to remember Coultern and his hilarious impersonation rather than his body lying in a zippered bag.

Several weeks before the final inspection, Lieutenant Evans began inviting everyone in our platoon to come to his house for a visit. We got to meet his wife and have dessert in an informal setting. Lieutenant Evans was the only officer I knew that treated his men as if we were all equal, if not of equal rank. I had a lot respect for him. I'm sure it went against all Marine Corps protocol.

Also, in that last week before shipping out to Viet Nam, we had to sign all kinds of papers. There were papers concerning our life insurance policy for $10,000, including the beneficiary, which was to go to my mother. We also had to sign a legal paper about going into combat in Viet Nam. We all lined up and signed with little or no comments. However, when it came to me, I was asked additional questions. "You know Dixon, there is no turning back now?"

"Yes Sir," I replied.

"Once you sign this, if you don't show up on Saturday you will be court-martialled and imprisoned."

"Yes Sir, I know."

"There is still time to change your mind."

"Yes Sir, I understand." I signed the papers just like every other guy. Afterwards several guys asked me,

"Why did they ask you all of the questions?"

I only shrugged my shoulders and said, "I don't know."

"Do they think you are going to desert or something?" I gave the same answer, but I think the questions were more about the word Quaker stamped on my dog tags than my desire to desert.

On Wednesday the jeep drivers from all four platoons drove the jeeps down to the harbor in San Diego to be loaded onto the ship. Of course, neither Mac nor I had to go. We had no jeep! I found that amusing then and still funny today.

After the final inspection on Friday we were given an extra sea bag. A work detail had placed special stencils on the bags and had painted the words, '1st **M.P. D Company**'. We filled out a tag with our initials and last name and attached the tag to the bag with a piece of wire. We carefully took all our folded skivvy drawers, socks and tee shirts and placed them in the sea bags instead of in our foot locker. Our dress uniforms, winter and summer, dress shoes, dress socks along with our winter coat was stuffed into this extra sea bag. Where we were headed we wouldn't need any clothes other than our utilities. We hooked the strap over the clip and placed a combination lock on the whole bag, so it would be secure. Then we carefully wrote the combination down on a piece of paper, so we would be able to remember it after our 13-month tour was over. Finally, we carried this extra sea bag down to the parade ground where several 6x6 trucks were waiting. I remember tossing my bag into one of the trucks. There were more than 150 bags from 'D' Company. The idea was that these bags would be flown to the Marine base in Okinawa, Japan. Thirteen months later when we flew out of Viet Nam we would be reunited with those very same bags. And that is exactly what happened.

When my tour of duty was finished, I and several other guys walked into a giant cargo hanger in Okinawa which could have held several airplanes. In front of us lay dozens of long rows of green sea bags where over 600 had originally been placed. In one row lay bags marked D Company. I walked down the line until I found the one marked J.M. Dixon. I was one of the last guys from D Company to leave Viet Nam. Looking for my bag, I passed by many a bag with the names of guys who I knew were dead. I remember carrying my bag over my shoulder through the exit door and turning to look back at all the unclaimed bags. A lot of guys, who threw their sea bag onto the trucks at Camp Pendleton, that Friday, would never be reunited with their bags. I couldn't think of anything funny that day. Humor could help me cope with lots of things, but not the sight of dozens and dozens of bags from D Company, that would never be reunited with their owners.

Chapter 13

A BOAT RIDE TO VIET NAM

EVERY YEAR on the first Saturday in May, the famous horse racing spectacle known as the Kentucky Derby is held. For well over one hundred years thousands of people flock to Churchill Downs to watch it. The race is televised all over the world and is watched by millions of horse racing fans. Each year when I hear about the race I am immediately taken back to the day we left for Viet Nam.

I remember the day, May 7, 1966, because Corporal O'Leary was a huge horse racing fan. When he found out I was from Delaware, he asked me if I had ever been to the Delaware Race Track. I had grown up within walking distance but had never been there. Quakers are not real big on gambling. I told him I had not. He began telling me how beautiful it was and that he had been to all the race tracks from Saratoga in New York to the Preakness in Baltimore. O'Leary was putting together a derby pool. A dollar got you a chance to draw a horse's name out of a hat. If your horse won, you got all the money in the hat. I kind of figured O'Leary had already drawn the name of the favorite horse, so I passed.

Summer had arrived in Southern California and that Saturday was hot. Temperatures reached the 90's by afternoon. In the morning after chow we finished packing our gear. We each carried a knapsack and a gunny sack. Our poncho and blanket were rolled up and tied around the top edge of the knapsack. We wore our cartridge belt which contained two canteens, our first aid kit and the canvas pouches for our M-14 ammo magazines. We each had eight mags (ammo magazines for the rifle) but no cartridges. We wore our helmet and had our other sea bag with all our extra uniforms and some civilian clothes, and of course our M-14 rifle which we would lug everywhere. That morning we had one final inspection. It was more of a check to make sure we were all present and had all our gear.

After noon chow, we formed ranks in our respective platoons. When given the order we picked up everything we owned and boarded cattle cars that took us through San Diego to the loading docks by the bay. Looking out of the cattle car windows was impossible because they were higher than where we sat elbow to elbow. I never even got a glimpse of the city and only saw the ship after we arrived at the dock.

The ship was named the U.S.S. Upshur and was an old cargo vessel that was converted into a troop carrier. After the first day aboard the vessel, we all nicknamed it the U.S.S. Up-chuck. Almost everyone has seen pictures from World War I or II, of Sailors, Soldiers, and Marines in long lines walking up a gang plank alongside a troop transport ship. What you can't tell by the pictures or even movies are how slow the line moves. We stood in line for over an hour. We'd walk three or four steps and stop, two more steps and stop again. It was 90 + degrees outside and the sun was beating down on us. I don't know the total weight of all the gear and equipment we carried, but it was probably close to 100 pounds. We all struggled with that sea bag. Each time we tried to shift the bag from one shoulder to the other and move our rifle at the same time, we either dropped something or knocked something off some other guy. Helmets were constantly falling off. Finally, someone came up with the idea of fastening the chin strap and letting the helmet hang off our rifle barrel. It allowed our heads to breathe. It also kept the helmet from rolling down the gang plank.

I couldn't wait to finally set foot inside the ship where I would be out of the sun. But once inside it wasn't any better. We found ourselves still in a long line headed up ladder wells, down passage ways and then down, down, down, into the belly of the ship. There was no air conditioning and no air, period! The only thing you breathed was other guys' carbon dioxide, body odor and sweat. It was hotter inside the ship than outside. A and B companies were placed in one of the converted cargo bays and C and D companies in another. Imagine 300 Marines with all their equipment crammed in space about the size of a basketball court. Our sea bags were tossed up into an area where the bleachers would have been. The bags remained there for the duration of the voyage. We had to sleep in racks (bunks) stacked four high. Each rack was only two feet wide, much smaller than a normal bunk. The distance above each rack was also two feet. There was never any sitting on your bunk. We couldn't even sit up in the bunk. The racks were laid out and fastened end to end in long rows, so close that tall guys' heads could get kicked by another tall guys' feet. Long rows of these metal racks were laid out with two bunks connected side by side to each other. Rolling over in bed meant falling on the deck or rolling onto the guy in the next bunk. Between the rows was about three feet of passageway.

We were all ordered to make our bunks at once. Here's a math challenge for you. If guys sleep four high in a set of bunks and the next row is three feet away, and all eight Marines must stand in the three-foot space between racks, how in the hell can eight men make eight bunks at the same time? It was elbowing to elbow of mass confusion. Tempers flared, and I don't know why fights didn't break out. It took several hours to make up all the bunks. The term 'cluster fuck' was heard repeatedly. I had hoped to watch the ship pull up anchor and slip through the harbor but by the time we finished making the bunks and stowing away our gear, the ship was out of sight of land.

The ship was equipped with a P.A. system which allowed announcements to be heard from the holes to the heads and even on the top deck. When an announcement was made for evening chow call, 600 men headed for the only mess hall which sat fewer than 50 men at a time. Some guys stood in line for two hours. We joked that after each meal we should just go get in line for the next meal.

After chow we returned to the hole. Sergeant Deluca came into our compartment and made several announcements. First, there would be no showers that night because the ship had to make water. That meant salt water would be de-salinated for drinking and showering. Second, certain areas of the ship were off limits to enlisted men. We could go to the main deck, but no higher. Above that deck, civilians, officers and the ships headquarters were located. Enlisted people like us were not permitted to associate with the higher-ups. Even the staff sergeants would not be sleeping down in the holes with us. Third, guards would be posted starting the next day. There were four companies and four platoons and only our platoon would be doing the guarding. There were four squads, and do I need to say which squad would begin the guard duty? We were all exhausted that night when we hit the racks. It would be the last good night sleep I would get for a long time.

The next morning, I noticed when I rolled out of my bunk onto the deck the ship was rocking and rolling. I had spent many a summer on small boats on the Chesapeake Bay and had even ridden on a large ferry boat on a two-hour trip from Lewes, Delaware to Cape May, New Jersey. But I had never been on a ship this big. I thought the larger the ship, the less you would feel the movement of the ocean. That turns out to be true, however this day the ocean was really moving. They called it high seas.

When I woke up in the morning the first thing I wanted to do was take a leak. So, I made my way to the head where I found a huge line to the entrance. I decided to hold my urine and wait. As I tried to walk back to the bunk area the ship was moving so much I had to hold onto the sides of each bunk to keep from losing my balance. The ship would go up and down to the right, then up and down to the right again. The next time it would go up and down to the left. You never knew which way the ship would roll. Which is just like most women, you never know what to expect. I guess that's why they refer to a ship as 'she'.

With each unexpected movement I starting to feel queasy, so I decided if I put some food in my stomach it might help. I headed to the chow line. If I live to be a hundred I'll never forget that mess hall. Of all the meals I ever ate in the Marine Corps, they never served 'eggs over easy'. They often served scrambled eggs and even some kind of weird omelet, but never just fried eggs from a greasy grill. The movement of the ship caused the eggs to slide from one side of the giant grill to the other side and then back again. A dozen or more fried eggs rolling back and forth across a greasy grill ruined my appetite. I took one look at those eggs and decided to pass on breakfast.

Feeling I might be sick, I walked to the head. This time the line was shorter and moving faster. I soon realized why, when I reached the hatch to the head. Guys must step over the six-inch strip of thick metal that encircles the hatch to enter the head. I will never forget the sight before me. The entire head was filled with human vomit, some urine and shit tossed in. It was at least four inches deep and moved as a wave with the motion of the ship. As it moved from side to side it would splash up on to the bulk head and then return like a wave to splash up against the other side. Incredible as that sounds, it was even worse to see and smell. In the middle of the head stood a single Marine private in his shower shoes and with his trousers rolled up over his knees as waves of human waste rolled past him and over him. In his hand he held a mop with the end resting in a bucket to keep it from floating away. His job was to clean the head. It was an impossible task. On his face was the look of a lost wet puppy sitting on a door stoop begging to come in or looking for help. After gazing at that unforgettable sight, I could only help him by not throwing up and adding another layer to his misery. Like the guys in front of me, I made an about face and headed to the nearest ladder well that would take me to the bow (front) of the ship.

Once on the main deck another unforgettable sight awaited me. Dozens of guys were hanging over the railing of the gunwale (side edge of ship). They were heaving up whatever was in their stomach. However, as the ship would proceed on its downward motion, gravity and wind would blow the vomit high into the air and back onto anybody standing in the line of fire. Announcements came over the P.A. warning men to move to the stern of the ship if they had to be sick. I worried that because of the ship's movement and guys hanging over the gunwale, it would end in someone accidentally falling overboard. The seas were so high I knew if anyone fell over there would be no way to save them. They would be gone forever.

I made my way back to the stern but stopped half way and leaned up against the outside bulk head. I was protected from the wind but still had some fresh air to breath. There really wasn't anything in my stomach anyway. I stayed there until the nauseous feeling passed. I'm proud to say I never did throw up, but I sure felt like I wanted to. I wrote in my journal that Sunday, half of the men were sick two-thirds of the time and two-thirds of the men were sick half of the time. At any rate the sight of 600 seasick Marines was burned into my brain forever.

Announcements were made to report to sick bay to receive some saltine crackers that would help with sea sickness. I got in line for crackers but by the time I got there, the crackers were all gone. I did manage to eat some noon chow and began to feel better. If I kept something in my stomach I was okay. Most of the guys were not so lucky. Some guys stayed sick all day. That Sunday we saw no sign of Sergeant Deluca or Lieutenant Evans. I wondered if they too were sick. The next day the weather changed, and the sea calmed down, however there were still a handful of Marines who remained sick. The nickname U.S.S. Up-chuck would remain forever.

Sunday night our squad began guard duty. Some guys were stationed at the foot of the stairwells leading to the upper decks. I and three others were picked to walk around the main deck from midnight until 0400. Being on that deck at night was beautiful. The stars were a hundred times brighter and more numerous than I had ever seen. The sky was clear, and it seemed we could see forever.

There were two of us patrolling the deck and we were told to walk in opposite directions, so we could cover more ground. The other guy with me was Donaldson. Each time we passed we would stop and shoot the shit. He gave me a master's degree in sex education. Like I said before, he always had women on his mind.

At 0400 the other two guys relieved us and they walked until 0800. They got to watch the sun come up. There were always two men stationed on that deck 24 hours a day. The main problem with standing watch was the lack of sleep. Lights out in the hole was 2200 (10:00 pm). That's when most guys bunked down, but some guys continued to talk or fool around. If I fell asleep at 2230 and was awakened at 2330 to get ready for guard duty, that gave me one hour of sleep. I returned from guard duty at 0430, went to bed and reveille was at 0530 which gave me another hour of sleep. The next morning Donaldson and I expected to be allowed to sleep in. No such luck. Sergeant Deluca rousted us out of our bunks.

When Donaldson asked, "When do we get to sleep?"

The answer was, "You can sleep when you're dead!" We spent one week on guard duty then another squad took over. It was a very long week.

Eventually, we fell into a routine aboard ship. Most of our time was spent in line waiting for chow. Eventually they synchronized the chow calls so that each company was called separately and therefore we didn't have to wait as long.

Each morning we had some type of class. We had instructions on how to take a ship shower which went as follows: Thirty seconds of fresh water on our body. Then, with the water off, we could wash with soap for as long as we wanted. Then we finished with one minute of water to rinse. You might ask how someone can wash their hair in that short of time. The answer, we didn't have any hair, except pubic. Other classes were on how to keep your rifle dry, how to clean and lube the rifle when in Viet Nam.

Many of the classes were useful while others were not. We were instructed on how to brush our teeth and how important it was to change our socks each day. A doctor talked to us and showed a film about venereal disease. The movie was sickening. Donald said, "I don't think I ever want to have sex again!" I agreed. Donaldson however said, "I'll have to give that some thought."

After noon chow we had P.T. on the deck on top of the huge hatches that covered the cargo bay hole. We did jumping jacks, bends and thrusts, running in place and push-ups. P.T. lasted for about an hour. At the end of our trip we had a contest to see who in our platoon could do the most push-ups. I found that if you could pump out five or six push-ups as the ship was going down with a wave and then one or two as the ship came back up you could do more. They made us stop at 100. I'm proud to say I was one of the few who did 100 push-ups. In those days I weighed only 155 pounds and was a tall, skinny kid, but I was in the best shape I would ever be in. When I came home from Viet Nam I would only weigh 135.

Two companies, A and B, were selected for a research test. While we did our P.T. on the top deck, where we could breathe, companies, A and B put on their ponchos and went down into a storage area below deck where the temperature was much hotter and did the same exercises until someone passed out. After we arrived in Viet Nam they would test both groups to see which group was better able to adapt to the climate. More about that test later.

In the evenings we had free time. There was a ship's store where we could buy shaving cream, soap, boot polish, letter writing stuff, and buy candy and other junk food. Books and magazines were also sold. Amazingly a lot of guys bought comic books, I guess because they were easier to read. Free time was supposed to be for letter writing and relaxing.

I was shocked at how many ways there were to make or lose money aboard ship. Hair longer than a quarter of an inch had to be cut. Some guys invested in hand trimmers and would cut your hair for 25 cents. 25 times 200 haircuts added up to 50 dollars, which was more than two weeks pay. There was always a card game or a dice game going on somewhere.

My grandfather had warned me about such games. He had fought in WWI. He didn't tell me not to gamble, but he showed me something. He shuffled a deck of cards, then he had me cut the deck, and then he dealt out five cards face down in a semicircle. He then pointed to each card and told me what the card was. He got five out of five right. He explained that he really wasn't very good at that trick, but I would meet guys in the military who were much better. He explained that dice could be rolled in a way, so they always came up seven. The dice had to bounce off a wall to keep the game legit. I steered away from those so-called games of chance.

Another way guys made, or lost money was lending it. A day or two before pay day many guys were running short of money. To borrow five dollars meant paying back six after pay day. I borrowed money, so I could go on a bus trip once we got to Hawaii.

We also had some entertainment while on board ship. On Saturday night they showed a free movie, which was nice. On Sunday evening many of us would sit around the edge of the room and sing church hymnals. One of the guys who always sang the loudest and enjoyed it the most was Donaldson. I guess you can't think about women all the time.

The U.S.S. Up-chuck was not all bad. We stopped in Hawaii for three days. Evidently during the first day of high seas something had broken, and it took three days to repair it. While in Hawaii, several of us went on a bus sightseeing trip. We saw the World War II Memorial, some famous gardens, statues and some guys went aboard a launch to see the sunken ship the U.S.S. Arizona at the bottom of Pearl Harbor. I went for a stroll on the beach and had my picture taken in front of Diamond Head. I thought, *"Man wouldn't it be great to be stationed in Hawaii?"* I changed my mind when I went to buy a Coke which cost two dollars. In 1966 a Coke anywhere else cost only a quarter. Be careful what you wish for.

A week later the ship stopped in Japan. We got to spend one day on shore. Doc, Donald, Mac and I went to a bar in Yokohama. It was completely different from Tijuana. The bars were clean and so were the ladies. They spoke perfect English. It was nice to talk to a woman after only hearing guys voices for the past few months. After only one afternoon in Japan I knew I wanted to return someday.

We left Japan and headed south towards Viet Nam. The temperature in Japan in late May was 80 degrees. It took us a week to sail to Vietnam. The temperature went up five degrees each day. Do the math. We had spent about a month on the U.S.S. Upshur before arriving in Viet Nam.

Chapter 14

A MARCH IN THE SUN

I SUPPOSE WE HAVE all experienced hot days. Even people who live in North Dakota, Minnesota, and the Upper Peninsula of Michigan have hot days. We have all heard of people who have visited Arizona in July or Disney World in Florida during the summer and complain about how hot it was. I often feel sorry for our fighting men and women over in the Middle East, where they deal with extremely hot temperatures. People say, "But it's a dry heat!" I say, "Bull shit!" 120 degrees is 120 degrees, and it's hot. However, it's not as hot as Viet Nam where it was over 120 degrees and not a dry heat. We were in the tropics!

I remember an old Tom Hanks movie. Hanks' character had just stepped down off an airplane in some tropical country and he looked up at the sky and complained, "What are we, about a mile from the sun?"

That's what I thought when our ship docked at DaNang. I think it was Donald or Doc who said, "Man is this fucking hot?"

Mac replied, "No, this is too hot to fuck! How do these people even manage to make babies?"

The U.S.S. Upshur pulled into port at night while we slept. After morning chow, we gathered our gear and prepared to carry everything we had carried onto the ship, off again. First to depart however were the jeeps, trucks and other vehicles. It would have been neat to watch giant cranes lift them out of the cargo bays. But we were down in the disembarkation area waiting. This time the Marine Corps decided to stagger the disembarking, allowing more time between each group leaving. Of course, they never told us about the staggered time, so we waited ready to go. I suppose they began with A company and then B and C and finally D. Still waiting at noon, we put all our gear down and went to chow. We never even left the ship until 1600 (4:00 pm). Another hurry up and wait. It was much easier disembarking because we didn't have to wait with all our gear on our shoulders. This time we walked uninterrupted off the ship. The heat hit us in the face like when an oven door is opened to check on a Thanksgiving turkey. We had sweated like pigs on a rotisserie while waiting on the ship but now, *"Oh My God!"* I'll never forget the way the heat sucked the energy and oxygen out of our bodies as we walked off the ship.

We lined up in platoon formation and waited as cattle cars arrived to pick us up. One cattle car pulled up near our platoon and out stepped a guy who looked like no one I had ever seen in the Corps. He was wearing no cover. This was a cardinal sin, one we learned the first day of boot camp, and he desperately needed a haircut. He wore the same olive drab utilities we wore except his were so faded they were a lighter color and unstarched. His utility jacket (work shirt) was not tucked into his trousers. The sleeves had been cut off making it a short sleeve shirt. Our utility trousers were neatly tucked up inside our boots, which was called blousing.

His trousers hung down like a civilian. He wore corporal chevrons on his two collars proving he was indeed in the Marine Corps.

This driver walked right up to Lieutenant Evans, didn't salute, and spoke to him like he would any enlisted man. We stood in formation and watched in stunned silence. The driver spoke, "I'm here to pick up some MP's. Whenever you want you can start loading up." Lieutenant Evans stood at attention and saluted, even though the enlisted man was supposed to salute first. The corporal gave a half ass salute in return and walked away. The Lieutenant looked at Sergeant Deluca and said something and Deluca whispered something. I couldn't hear the exact words, but I figured the conversation went something like this;

"I guess people don't salute around here."

"I told you Sir, things would be different over here."

The driver paused on his way back to his vehicle, and then walked over to our formation. He stood in front of the first guy and spoke, "I'm going home in eight days. How much longer do you have to go in country?" A collective sigh went through the ranks and I got a sick pain in my stomach. The driver then turned and walked away. We all had 365 plus days to go. I tried to imagine what kind of hell that guy had been through and what I would look like a year from now. Then I wondered if I would even be alive in a year. I thought there is no way I'm going to survive a year in this heat. We boarded the cattle cars in silence.

As usual we could not see out of the windows of the vehicle unless we stood up and risked falling. The drive lasted a long time. How far were we going? When we left the ship, we could see and hear planes landing at the air base but now as we continued our ride the sounds became fainter. We continued driving. We all began to wonder and worry where were we going? Perhaps all this M.P stuff was just a ruse, and we were really going to be an infantry company. After all, we were all 0311's (infantry riflemen).

After driving an hour, the cattle car stopped, and we disembarked. We weren't completely out in the middle of nowhere because there were lots of tents.

Garcia asked out loud, "Where the hell are we?"

Mac replied, "I don't think we're in the middle of nowhere, but I think we're right next door to it!"

The so-called tents were ratty old, World War II platoon or squad tents. A squad of twelve to fifteen men could fit nicely into one. Of course, our entire second platoon of 45 men was told to unload all our gear into one tent. We then marched in formation to evening chow.

The mess hall was about a half mile away. We took along our mess gear which consisted of one small size metal container that unfolded into two halves. Inside were a steel fork, spoon and knife. We had often used these mess kits whenever we trained in the field. Little did I know that for the next year this would be the best way we would eat chow. Most meals would be C-rations which were eaten right out of the cans.

Before entering the chow line, we had to rinse our mess kit in boiling water. The hot water was kept in a large galvanized trash can, just like the shit cans in all barracks. The water was kept hot with a gas stove attached to the side of the can. Imagine what the water looked like after 600 to 1000 men dipped their mess kits into it.

The food wasn't what you would call gourmet, but it was hot and plentiful. It never looked appealing when it was piled into a mess kit the size of two dessert plates. In the mess hall huge galvanized pots about half the size of a trash can held Kool Aid. It was kept cold with a giant hunk of ice. Evidently there was electricity for making ice somewhere not far away. Because of the extreme heat I wanted to drink lots of Kool Aid. In the 1960's we were taught not to drink too much liquid. It was thought to be bad for you. We were told to take salt tablets instead. The sergeants instructed us not to drink too much because we needed food to keep up our strength. Of course, today all that is considered wrong.

We marched the half mile back to the tent. It was hot and very dry and a platoon of men marching in step kicks up lots of dust on a dirt road. We of course were sweating like football players in August. Dust and sweat is the exact recipe for mud, a layer of which formed on any exposed skin. When we finally got back to our tent we all looked like coal miners except our faces were covered in brown dirt instead of black coal dust. That's when they announced there would be no showers that night!

Most of our gear was left sitting outside the tent since the entire platoon would sleep in one tent. We lay elbow to elbow on the floor. The tent had a wooden floor which was made from old wooden pallets laid next to each other and then someone had nailed plywood over the whole thing. Surprisingly, the whole floor was stable if not perfectly flat. Our helmets became our pillows with our rifles kept at the ready by our sides. We fell asleep listening to distant rifle and machine gun fire, along with the whirl of helicopters and noise from airplanes flying nearby. Off in the distance we could hear the sound of artillery, which reminded me of thunder during a summer storm. These were the sounds of war that we would hear nightly for the next year.

To this day I have no idea where exactly this camp was in Viet Nam. No one asked, and no information was forthcoming about our whereabouts. We had to be an hour's drive from DaNang. Since DaNang was a sea port we could have been an hour north, south or west of DaNang. East would have put us in the middle of the South China Sea. But exactly where would forever be a mystery.

The next morning, we began our first full day 'in country' a term used to describe Viet Nam. The opposite of 'in county' was 'back in the world'. Viet Nam was so different it was a world unto itself. It was decided that our location was not secure. We were assigned to work details to dig trenches, fill sand bags, and string barbed wire around our immediate area. The other platoons and companies did the same thing in their sections. The task would take many days to complete. Working in this oppressive heat took its toll on us.

The old tents had holes in the seams and for some reason the sides of the tent, which could be rolled up to allow air to circulate and keep the inside somewhat cooler, were kept rolled down. If the sides of the tent were at least rolled up, we would be in the shade and the heat would not build up to unbearable temperatures. Looking back, it's unbelievable that someone didn't die of heat stroke. On the second day in camp someone found an outdoor thermometer. I kept checking each hour to see how hot it became. At nine in the morning it was 90 degrees and at ten it was 100 degrees. When we marched to noon chow it was 120. I stopped looking.

That afternoon one of the test companies either A or B, fell out into the road in front of the rows of tents. They carried their full battle equipment and were preparing for a 20-mile forced march. A forced march is where the company forms two columns, which straddle both sides of a road and walk with a stride like speed or power walking. Each Marine will try to stay about five paces behind the guy in front of him. Guys with short legs or guys at the end of the column end up jogging to keep up. We performed forced marches during infantry training and while we were at Camp Pendleton. It was never any fun and, in that heat, it was down right dangerous.

This forced march was all part of the so-called test study done aboard ship to prepare us for the tropical climate. Two companies, ours being one did P.T. exercises on the deck of the ship while two other companies performed exercises below deck wearing ponchos to simulate the heat. This day would begin the next stage of the test. Company A and another the next day would go on a forced march. The third day one of the companies like ours would also do the forced march. The results of the two groups would be compared.

I stood in the opening to our tent with my arms held out grabbing onto the sides of the tent entrance. I distinctly remember the sweat dripping off each arm as I watched the men standing out in the road waiting for the march to begin. Finally, two pick-up size trucks with canvas covers pulled up behind the company. Painted on the sides of the trucks were large red crosses. These were military ambulances and were to follow the marching company and pick up anyone who became ill. The problem was that two men had all ready collapsed in the road before they even started marching. The corpsmen in the first ambulance picked the two up and drove them to a hospital or sick bay. The company captain gave the order and the entire company began moving. They had not totally passed in front of our tent when the second ambulance picked up three more guys. Luckily the first ambulance returned in time to pick up the third group of victims as the company disappeared out of sight.

I thought to myself, first, this was unsafe and insane. And second, if those guys were in better shape than our company, how many of us would be able to finish that same march when it was our turn? The answers came shortly. Within an hour the company began to straggle back to their tents. The whole march had to be cancelled because of a lack of available ambulances to pick up all the guys who passed out. Luckily, saner heads prevailed and the whole test was cancelled because of the unsafe conditions.

To this day whenever it's hot outside someone asks, "Hot enough for you?" -and some asshole always asks that question- I think back to that march in the sun and I thank God, it's not **that** hot.

James M. Dixon

Chapter 15

THINGS CAN ALWAYS GET WORSE

I'M NOT A COMPLETE pessimist but I have been around long enough to know that things don't always get better. I was a public-school teacher for 28 years in an inner-city school district. Every time we got a new principal or a new superintendent I hoped things would get better. They never did. It either stayed the same or got worse. Each year of teaching I was reminded of my time in Viet Nam.

We spent our first week in Viet Nam in that makeshift camp. I hated it. Every day the temperature reached at least 110 degrees. The second day they issued each of us wooden cots with a canvas bed to sleep on. Because we were in squad tents, but each tent held four squads, we were more crowded than on board ship. Each cot butted up against the side of the next cot, so we had to crawl in and out of our cot from the end. There was no exit from the side because some other poor guy slept there. The sides of the tent remained rolled down, so no air could circulate. The officers in charge thought the Viet Cong would be able to see inside the tent and make us accessible to sniper fire. The closed tent made the temperature inside at least ten degrees hotter. Once we were outside on work details no one seemed to worry about snipers. I was confused. It made no sense, but then again...

We continued each day on work details including filling sand bags, digging trenches and stringing barbed wire and other jobs. We had two kinds of heads located nearby; one for pissing and another for shitting. The pissers were nothing more than a hole with a large metal pipe 12 inches around sticking out of the ground. Every few days a new hole had to be dug and the pisser pipe moved and then the old hole was covered up. Not a fun job when it's 110 degrees outside. The shitter was similar only it looked more like an old outhouse. We sat on a wooden board with a crude hole cut out of it and did our thing into a 55-gallon metal barrel that had been cut evenly in half. Once a week some poor PFC dragged the half barrel far away from the camp and dumped the contents into a hole. Then he poured kerosene over the contents and set the whole thing on fire. He stood there as the fire burned and occasionally pouring on more fuel. How much more fun can you have in 110-degree heat than standing next to an open fire of burning shit?

After the first night in camp we were given permission to take showers. But the showers were a half mile away. By the time we walked back after the shower along the hot and dusty road with jeeps and trucks passing by, you were ready for another shower. The water was at air temperature, but at 110 degrees, the shower was plenty hot. On Saturday June 4th we had a thunder storm and all 150 of us in D company grabbed our soap and took a shower in the rain. It was the best shower we had the whole time in that camp. While we stood naked in the rain, I wondered what any Viet Cong sniper, who happened to be watching, would have been thinking.

The afternoons were so hot, we were told to clean our rifles which really needed cleaning. I firmly believe the officers and sergeants were too hot to stand outside and supervise us on work details. Our sweat which dripped on to the rifle whenever we touched them, caused rust to form and we carried the rifles everywhere: chow, work details, showers, they were always with us. The heat caused lots of dust to form on everything. We breathed it, we drank it and we ate it in our chow. And of course, we cleaned it off our rifles. We used to joke that we could sit and watch the rust and dust form on our rifle. If you went two days without cleaning your rifle the rust and dust would be dangerous because the rifle wouldn't fire well.

Each night we had to stand guard duty. It was kind of like the fire watch we had in boot camp and everywhere else. Fire watch lasted for one hour and then we were relieved by the next guy. We might have fire watch every eight or ten days. In this camp, guard duty was for two hours and we took turns in groups of four. So, we stood guard for two hours and got to sleep for six hours, but it was every night. Another difference here we could see mortar and artillery fire up on the nearby hills. It was not unusual to hear sniper fire. No one was ever hit because the shooter was much too far away. During guard duty we walked a certain part of the parameter between the two other guys in our squad who were also on duty. It was pitch black outside with even the light from a cigarette forbidden. We couldn't see the guys next to us until the two of us approached within a few feet of each other. Those first few nights we were all a little shaky and scared. I remember seeing Garcia with his bayonet fixed to the end of his rifle. He was a little guy about the size of most of the Vietnamese and he was taking no chances.

Most evenings between chow and guard duty, we would sit around the outside of the tent. It was noisy with guy's bullshitting and teasing each other. After being in country for two weeks, (on Sunday June 12th) we received our first mail from home. I remember the guys all sitting around the outside of the tent silently reading letters. It was the quiet I remember.

Sergeant Deluca announced on June 8, 1966 that we would be leaving this area and moving to the DaNang airbase. We would be more like an infantry battalion guarding the base. Our company was issued extra weapons: shotguns, grenade launchers, and machine guns. Since we wouldn't be doing much MP work we would also be reorganized but were not told how. I couldn't wait to go to the airbase where we would be farther away from the Viet Cong and closer to civilization. We were even promised that at the base we would get a 'two can' beer ration per day. The news was received as a reprieve from danger. We would be in the rear with the gear and the beer.

Little did I know that soon I would be looking back at this first week fondly. Things were about to get much worse.

Chapter 16

GUARDING THE DA NANG AIR BASE

MY WIFE AND I love going to the beaches in Delaware and Maryland. From our home in Pennsylvania we drive past the Dover Air Force base going to and from the beach. On each trip I see those cargo and jet planes, and I am reminded of the air base at DaNang and the months spent guarding and working to secure the base. I don't know what my sons thought each time they saw those giant cargo planes at Dover AFB, but I know they weren't reminded of the sights I had seen.

We boarded 6 X 6 trucks one squad at a time and rode to the Da Nang Air Base. The Air Base, like all airports or military bases was huge, almost beyond comprehension. The four Marine Companies were each assigned a fourth of the area surrounding the base to guard and keep secure. Our D Company took the area from the south gate to the west gate. I never knew which companies guarded the other three parts. The west gate was the major entrance and exit to the whole base.

On June 14, 1966 we arrived at what would become our new base camp and home inside the Air Base. Company D's camp was the size of a football field. From an aerial view of the whole Air Base our camp would appear as a speck. The camp was laid out with two rows of squad tents lined up perfectly the way good little Marine tents should be. Nine tents were on each edge of the field with a large common area down the middle like the commons in many small New England town, which are often called the 'Greens'. Except these commons were supposed to be a parade ground and was anything but green. It was all dirt.

The camp was divided by the four platoons with their separate tents running the length the camp. At the far end of the camp were two tents, one for the officers and a separate one for the NCO's. At the front of the camp was the company headquarters on one side and two tents on the other side for a barber shop, laundry and a tailor. Near the officer's tent was a supply tent and a tent that would eventually be converted into a bar.

There were some good changes for us at this camp which would make our lives easier. We could use the Vietnamese tailor to shorten the sleeves on our utility jackets (work shirt). Yes, we would be able to wear short sleeve jackets in the 100-degree plus temperatures. The tailor could also make us a civilian suit at an incredibly cheap price. After several guys had suits made and I saw the quality I too had one made. We could also use the Vietnamese to do our laundry. The cost was cheap and faster than washing our clothes by hand. However, when we got the clothing back it had a strange smell, like it had been washed in oil. The explanation was simple. It was the hot and dry season and the Military oiled all the roads to keep the dust down. The oily smell clung to the clothes as they dried. It would have happened even if we washed our own clothes. The last good thing about the new camp was, we were given a beer ration of two beers a night, if we didn't have guard duty. The trouble was we would have guard or patrol duty three out of four nights. The one supply tent next to the N.C.O. tent was converted to a bar.

Before I joined the Marine Corps, I was not much of a drinker. Alcohol is kind of frowned upon by Quakers and I never liked the taste of beer anyway. They say beer is an acquired taste. In the evening when we didn't have duty we had three drink choices. They included cold beer, or warm sodas which on its journey to Viet Nam had been chilled, heated in the sun, chilled again and once more brought to room temperature (100 plus degrees) before finally being served to anyone who wanted to drink a hot soda that had lost all its carbonation. Yum! The third choice was water. The only available water came from giant canvas bags that hung from poles located between some of the tents. The tents provided some shade to hopefully keep the water cool. Water that sits in the sun becomes stagnant and therefore poison. We would fill our canteens with this water and then add a tablet of iodine to prevent getting sick. The iodine tablets made the water taste like, well, iodine! With those three choices of drinks I soon developed a taste for cold beer.

Other than the laundry, the tailor and the beer, everything else was worse than the first camp we had just left. Here we had no showers at all. They would have to be built. We were immediately put on our new schedule. Sleep deprivation and exhaustion would become the norm.

The entire company was reorganized. Every rifle company has four platoons, one of which is called a weapons platoon. Guys in the weapons platoon are experts with machine guns, or mortars, or flame throwers. During our M.P. training the weapons platoon had the same training as everyone else. Now that we were acting like an infantry company the weapons platoon was divided up and placed among the other three platoons. We still had four platoons so nearly everybody was moved like reshuffling a deck of cards. I moved to the third platoon but still had Sergeant Deluca and Lieutenant Evans as my leaders. I also still had Corporal Fussner as my squad leader. Dochterman went to the first platoon and Donald went to the second. I would see less and less of them. In return our squad got guys I knew of but was not yet friends with.

Our new schedule consisted of four separate days of duty. On day one we would be sent to the 'line' of bunkers and foxholes that encircled 'D' company's part of the Air Base. We spent the entire day and night, all 24 hours on guard duty. One guy would sleep while the other watched for a Viet Cong (V.C.) invasion, which of course never came. During these 24 hours we were issued two boxes of 'C' rations, or enough food for two meals. Day two we returned to camp for 'work parties' and then went back on the line to stand guard duty at night. The work parties consisted of various details but mostly filling sand bags and digging trenches in the hot sun. On day three we left the camp and went to an outpost closer to the front line. This outpost was called the 'reactionary force' and we stayed there for 24 hours. The outpost was used for running patrols outside of the base into the civilian population. During the day we ran four-man patrols and at night six-man patrols. Two patrols over lapped at all times. One squad also had to stay awake at all times, in case of an emergency or problem. Therefore, day three allowed for little sleep. I remember someone asking the question, "When are we supposed to sleep?" The response from Sergeant Deluca was always the same, "You can sleep when you're dead!" Outpost day also meant 'C' rations.

Finally, day four was our day off. In the morning they always held an inspection of our tents and our rifles. Then in the afternoon we had other work parties. At night, one of the four squads had fire watch. So, each guy in that squad had to stand fire watch for one hour, which allowed time to finally get some sleep. This was also the only night we were allowed our two can beer ration, if we didn't have fire watch. Some guys would ask non-drinkers like me to trade and stand fire watch for them. Sometimes I would if the trade was worthwhile. Others would offer cans of fruit from the their 'C' rations or some junk food purchased at the P.X. This so called '4th day off' was the only time we could take showers, once we built the showers. There were three sets of showers, one for the officers, one for the N.C.O.'s and one for the enlisted men. The enlisted men's showers were the last to be built, of course.

If that fourth day, our day off, fell on a Saturday or Sunday, and if we passed inspection, we could travel to the P.X. or sometimes go to 'China Beach'. The P.X. was outside of the airbase on a hill called 327, so called because it is 327 feet above sea level and on a topographic map has 327 labeled on it. Strange enough, the P.X. was much closer to the enemy than where our camp was located. In this war without battle lines it really didn't matter. China Beach was a hospital and recreation center located near the city of Da Nang and sat right next the ocean. During my six months in the MP's we could go to China Beach twice. I got to swim in the ocean and bought a hamburger and milkshake. It was like heaven! Those so-called days off that fell on Saturday and Sunday were few and far between. The drudgery of this four-day schedule went on and on and seemed endless. Letters and packages from home were the only break we had from the boredom and drudgery.

All wars have their share of boring times. The war in Viet Nam has been described as endless hours and days of boredom followed by short bursts of adrenaline-filled terror. In the MP's we spent countless boring hours guarding the line. The so called 'line' was mislabeled because as almost everyone knows there were no real lines facing the enemy. Our part of the line encircled our own position where most of the people were friendly. However, the Vietnamese civilians were on both sides of the lines. Some of the civilians were the Viet Cong, some weren't.

When we manned the line of bunkers and fox holes surrounding the air base we were safer than probably most places in Viet Nam. The French had built the Air Base (air port) at DaNang and the surrounding defensive positions. The French knew what they were doing. They built a string of concrete bunkers, re-enforced with steel, about every quarter of a mile surrounding the entire air base. The bunkers weren't bomb proof, but they were bullet proof and had slits in the sides for shooting rifles and machine guns. The roof of the bunker was made of cement a foot thick and then we added several layers of sand bags. The best part of the bunkers' construction was that they were totally above ground with slanted roofs that allowed rain to run off, so no water would flood the inside floor. They provided cool shade in the summer heat and a dry living space during the monsoons. Each French bunker could hold six to eight men.

About 25 yards in front of the bunkers ran a long strand of circular barbed wire, (concertina wire) about four feet high, held in place with long stakes cemented into the ground. Next, in front of the barbed wire, was 25 yards of anti-personnel land mines. They were nasty little buggers. On the other side of the mine field was another row of concertina wire. The wire wasn't there to keep the Viet Cong out. It was to prevent one of us or a local civilian, (or some animal) from accidentally walking into the mine field. There were very narrow, marked paths about two feet wide, that weaved their way to the other side which enabled us to cross the mine field. Several strands of straight barbed wire on each side of the path guided us through the field. We used these paths when we went on patrols into the many villages located outside of our parameter. On the other side of the mine field was several hundred yards of cleared space for unobstructed rifle fire. Sometimes all the trees were defoliated, or cleared, or sometimes the line of fire was simply a mile of rice paddies. For the Viet Cong to mount any kind of attack, they would have to go over or through two rings of barbed wire and 25 yards of mine fields. Even James Bond would have had a tough time.

We only had two things to worry about. First, could a single V.C. somehow sneak through our marked path in the mine field at night? Or could a sniper shoot us from nearly a thousand yards away? Occasionally the V.C. did shoot at us but we were too far out of range for a regular small caliber rifle. Only a highly trained sniper would ever be able to pick off anyone. The V.C. were not highly trained and they certainly weren't snipers. However, we all quickly learned the sound a bullet made when hissing through the air, something that would pay off later.

Stationed near us was a battalion of engineers. We shared the same mess hall. One of their many jobs was mine sweeping or mine removal. They didn't use a machine like a re-enforced tank with a roller for crushing and setting off mines. No, these guys used an old, World War I bayonet. Those bayonets were eighteen inches long. The engineers probed the field on their hands and knees, using the bayonet to carefully slice through the dirt to find mines with their hands. Yeah, it was way too dangerous for me to imagine.

One day while I was sitting on a French bunker I witnessed the effect an anti-personnel land mine had on a human being. On Monday, October 10, 1966 I was standing guard duty on top of one of the French bunkers. An engineer was working on his hands and knees trying to make one of our paths a little wider. I was writing a letter home and the guy on post with me was asleep down in the bunker. As I wrote that letter I dreamed about being back at home. Suddenly I felt the shock wave of an explosion that startled me back to reality. A corporal from the engineers' squad had accidentally slid his boot too far inside the mine field and set off a mine. I instinctively climbed off the bunker and ran to his aid. He was still conscious and on his knees. He yelled at me to stay back. He was afraid I would rush in to save him and accidentally set off another mine and get us both killed.

Today if I close my eyes I can still see the toe half of his boot hanging by a tiny sliver of his boot sole. The toe half of his foot was totally gone. Bones, tendons and hunks of flesh stuck out from the ankle half of his boot as blood flowed into the mine field. I knew he had to be in terrible pain, but he dared not move for fear of setting off a bigger explosion. My buddy in the bunker radioed for help and it seemed like forever before an ambulance and corpsmen arrived. I feared he would bleed to death and pleaded with him to let me try to pull him out. He ordered me to stay away and took his belt and tied a tourniquet around his ankle. Other engineers came and carefully slid him out to safety and to a hospital.

For the engineer it was his so-called 'million-dollar wound'. He would be sent home, honorably discharged, and would receive a small percentage of his corporal's salary every month for the rest of his life. Of course, he would never walk right again. The sight of the bloody stub of his foot sticking out of what was left of his boot was the most disgusting thing I had seen since arriving in Viet Nam. I'm sorry to say that I would see much worse before I left this country. I have never forgotten that day. I'm sure he would remember it every day for the rest of his life as well.

That engineer was lucky the exploded mine was only a small one designed to wound. If he had stepped on it with his heel, the concussion from the explosion would have shattered the bones in his leg all the way up to his knee or higher and the doctors would have had to amputate part of his leg up to where they could find intact bone. There were much bigger mines in that field designed to kill him and wound anyone standing nearby. There were also tiny mines or booby traps designed so that when you tripped the wire a small grenade, a little bit bigger than a golf ball, would pop up about two or three feet in the air and explode between your legs. These were called Bouncing Betties and were designed to blow off dicks and balls. Men feared those mines, most of all. We would all rather lose our life than the family jewels.

Day after day we worked in the sun digging ditches and filling sand bags then stood guard duty all night. The boredom and drudgery took its toll on all of us. Briefly it changed one day on our platoon's so-called day off, after we worked all day in the hot sun filling sand bags. A huge thunderstorm dropped a deluge of water on the camp that evening filling all the trenches with several feet of water. The entire parade ground was covered in four to six inches of water. Someone, I don't know who, found a football and a game between our four squads quickly ensued in the rain and mud. The officers and N.C.O. stood in their tents watching us. It was the most fun we had in these first months in Viet Nam. It was the first I had heard anyone laugh. For the first time, I thought I might survive living and working at the Da Nang Air Base.

Chapter 17

TRICKS FOR STAYING AWAKE

THERE HAVE BEEN TIMES in my life when I have been bone-tired. We have all been overly tired when we've driven on a long trip or been up all night with sick babies. When I was working my way through college I ran an old PBX telephone machine working as an operator, from two in the morning until seven thirty a.m., and then went to classes. By the end of the week I was more than exhausted. Of course, there were times when I pulled all-nighters studying for finals or trying to wrap up a term paper. We've all had times in our lives when we've had sleepless nights for one reason or another. But I have never experienced exhaustion like I felt standing guard duty in Viet Nam.

Our four-day schedule of working all day and standing guard duty, all night allowed for little sleep. After several weeks we began to crave sleep. Years later I would learn the military believed that sleep deprivation would make men more aggressive towards the enemy and therefore better fighters. They thought we would take our aggression out on the enemy. All it did was piss us off at the seemingly unsympathetic officers who put us through this ordeal.

It felt like the officers were out to get us. Work us all day in the hot sun until we were near exhaustion and then they would try to catch us sleeping on guard duty. They always put two men in a bunker or foxhole. One guy had to be awake at all times. Also, we both had to be awake one hour before sunrise and one hour after sunset. That time was called 'stand by'. The time in between could be used for some sleep. We The most we could get was four hours sleep per night but usually less. We slept outside with bugs and in the rain, with an occasional alert for some unusual sound or checked by one of the N.C.O. or officers. With the mine field and barbed wire in front of us we feared an officer or N.C.O. more than any Viet Cong. I often stood guard duty outside the foxhole or bunker with my back toward the mine field and facing the path from which a sergeant or lieutenant would approach.

Over the endless days, weeks and months of sleep deprivation we learned tricks for staying awake. Smoking on duty was prohibited for many reasons, the most important being it made a Marine an easy target. It is amazing how the red glow of a cigarette can be seen from such a long distance. However, the action of smoking a cigarette and keeping anyone from seeing it became a favorite trick for staying awake for many guys. It was one of the many reasons some guys learned to smoke. Another reason was for burning blood sucking leaches off your skin. Another method for staying awake was to sing out loud, if the guy with you didn't mind. Usually we were too exhausted to even care about anyone singing.

Radios were forbidden, but many of us listened to them anyway. I bought one at the P.X. with two ear plugs. I would put one plug in one ear and listen to music while I listened for approaching sergeants and officers with my other ear. The only station we could pick up was Armed Forces

Radio. That station was forbidden from playing rock and roll music. So, we listened to show tunes and old music from the 30's and 40's. At night they liked to play classical music which only made me sleepier. Sometimes I would try and make up my own lyrics to the music.

I know I wasn't the only guy listening to the radio because in the morning we could hear lots of guys yelling, "**Good Morning Viet Nam**" up and down the line. They were simply repeating what they had just heard on the radio. If you've seen the movie by the same name, you know what I'm talking about. The catch phrase was started by Adrian Cronauer, played in the movie by Robin Williams. Cronauer's replacement was Pat Sajak, the game show host, who continued saying it to begin each morning. Thousands of Americans, perhaps hundreds of thousands, awoke to those words each morning. When my wife and I saw the movie in the theater, the audience laughed each time he yelled the line. It only brought back memories for me, unpleasant memories of trying to stay awake.

My favorite way to stay awake was to eat or drink. I would buy a soda whenever possible from the company bar and take chips, cookies, or crackers out on the line. Just the process of opening the packages would help to keep me awake. Some guys would drink coffee. We got either coffee or hot chocolate inside each 'C' ration box. I don't drink coffee so I would trade my coffee for hot chocolate. The problem was heating it. We found if we dug a small hole, placed an old empty 'C' ration can in the hole with a heat tab in the can we could heat our drink. Hiding it, in the hole kept the glow from the burning heat tab out of sight. We could mix water with the chocolate and stir it over the flame and it wasn't bad to drink. The whole process could take almost an hour and was good for keeping you awake.

Everyone developed his own trick for staying awake. Some were more successful than others. Guys were caught sleeping and were 'busted' or reduced in rank. All received office hours which was one step away from a court martial. It went on their permanent record and kept them from getting the next promotion. In the M.P.'s, often their record would be wiped clean if they would volunteer to transfer to an infantry company. Some guys did.

My friend, McDonald, who everyone called 'Mac, you might remember he and I had driven a jeep into the Pacific Ocean, had a special trick he used to keep awake. Somehow, he had found, bought, or traded for a pilot's survival knife. It wasn't illegal to have one, but this knife was never issued to infantrymen. Each night Mac would sit and sharpen the knife with the wet stone that came with it. My God, it was unbelievable how sharp that blade became after hours and hours of sharpening. He literally could and did shave with that knife. Shaving and running a razor-sharp knife up and down his throat, was his way of staying awake!

All these tricks worked for awhile, but the hours of boredom took their toll. It's hard to imagine just how bored and tired we became. Whenever I felt myself starting to dose off I would stand outside the foxhole. Standing there for endless hours, suddenly the ground would jump up and slam you in the face. Yes, that's right. That's what it feels like when you fall asleep standing up. I know I wasn't the only one it happened to because other guys would confess to the same thing. We used to laugh about it.

Today as we all grow older we sometimes complain about sleepless nights. Like most fathers, I have lain awake many a night worrying about my two sons. The next day we kind of run out of gas about the middle of the afternoon. We all know the feeling. It's nothing compared to being so tired you 'fall asleep standing up'. But like Sergeant Deluca always said, "You can sleep when you're dead!" The monotony of guarding the Da Nang Air Base would seem much better than the nerve wracking time I would eventually spend in the grunts.

Chapter 18

LEADERS

B Y THE TIME someone reaches my age they have experienced many types of leaders and bosses. I place bad bosses into two categories. Some are bad because they are inept or simply out of the realm of competence. The old 'Peter Principle' theory where people rise to their level of incompetence is true, more often than not. The other type of bad boss is mean-spirited and out to make other people's lives miserable because they don't care about other peoples' feelings. They are just interested in results and their own self promotion. I have experienced all kinds of leaders and bosses as a school teacher. Luckily, I didn't deal too often with the mean -spirited bosses but sadly I knew too many inept leaders. The same was true in the Marine Corps.

Let's see if you can put 'D' Company's first Sergeant into one of these categories. I never saw the man without a cup of coffee in his hand or one on his desk. On days we had work parties, which was any day that we didn't spend the whole day on guard duty, one of our jobs was to polish the officer's and N.C.O.'s boots. They evidently were too busy making important decisions to polish their own boots. One afternoon I was assigned to work in the company bar. It was not a bad job and at least I was in out of the sun and heat while nearly everyone else was outside on work parties. The company first sergeant was the only other person in the bar. He made sure I kept busy sweeping the floor, wiping the bar down, oiling a squeaky door and filling the cooler with ice. He spent the entire day sipping beer, and I'm sure making important decisions.

Everyday the company first sergeant stood in front of his tent and supervised us in the seemingly useless task that I always thought of as a 'make work' job to keep us busy. In front of both rows of tents that ran the length of the common area, or parade ground, was a trench. The trench was two feet deep and three feet wide. The dirt from the trench was shoveled out and used to fill sand bags. The bags were carefully placed two deep and four rows high and laid just like a brick layer would build a wall of concrete blocks double thick. This construction enabled us to jump into the trench if we were under a mortar attack. The unique part of this trench was it was deliberately built so it was not in a straight line. Every ten yards the trench took a 45-degree turn. It zigzagged its way down the length of tents. The idea was if a hundred men jumped into the trench and a mortar landed inside, it would only kill a few men because the 45-degree angle prevented the shrapnel from killing a long line of troops. This type of trench was called a 'zipper trench'. Each day that we had work parties two guys were selected to flip over each, and every one of the top layers of sand bags. They were perfectly good bags and weren't bothering anybody, but several hundred of them, each weighing 40 pounds, had to be flipped over. To my way of thinking it was just 'make-work' to keep us busy and make us tired.

After cleaning and sweeping out our own tent, one of us would have to sweep out the NCO's tent. As I said they had to have time for thinking and making important decisions. One day, I was sweeping their tent. Of course, I was not doing it to the first sergeant's liking. He took some time to explain something to me. He pointed to the zipper trenches with the hand that didn't have a coffee cup in it, and said, "Do you see that zipper trench?"

I nodded, "Yes."

"You ever wonder why I make you men flip them bags over every day?" I didn't answer. So, he continued speaking. "You see in the Marine Corps everything is straight and green." He was correct. Just several weeks before we were all issued new skivvy drawers and tee shirts. The new ones were all green. Everything we wore was 'olive drab' the official color of the Marine Corps. So, I replied yes to his rhetorical question.

He continued, "You know if you leave them bags alone with all this sun and rain, grass will start to grow out of them bags? Green grass, and them zipper trenches ain't in a straight line like Marine Corps trenches should be." At first, I didn't know if he was joking or just crazy. He finished by concluding,

"That's why those zipper trenches shouldn't be green." I simply replied, "Okay" and continued sweeping. I realized that he wasn't a bad leader, he was just a windbag.

Corporal Fussner had been my squad leader since I joined 'D' Company. Even after the re-shuffling of the entire company, I was still stuck with him. It had not taken long for me to realize Fussner was not the sharpest bayonet in the Marine Corps. The more I was with him the more convinced I became that he was mentally challenged. I taught many special needs classes as a teacher and Fussner could have fit right in. He didn't try to mess up, no more than the 'Three stooges" did, but he just naturally did. Donaldson used to say, "Fussner could fuck up a wet dream." And I had to agree.

Most civilians don't realize that there are several different kinds of hand grenades. The most common 'fragmentation' grenades used for killing people are usually referred to as "frags'. They are the ones you see in World War II movies and they look like pineapples, which is another nickname for them. Another type of grenade is a smoke grenade and it is shaped like a soup can with a ring sticking out of the top. Both types of grenades are colored differently and have a unique shape, so anyone can tell them apart, even in the dark.

One-day Corporal Fussner took me and two other men from our squad on a patrol and got us lost. Getting lost on a patrol at night was not that uncommon. During the day, getting lost was hard to do. On his order I radioed back to the C.P. (command post) for help. They instructed him to throw out a smoke grenade, so they might locate us and give us directions back to our lines. Fussner accidentally threw out a fragmentation grenade. Lucky no one was killed or hurt. But it sure scared a lot of people. I had to change out of my brand-new olive drab skivvies when I got back to camp. Yes, he was an idiot.

Corporal Edwards was another kind of leader. I met him when he was a lance corporal. Once he became a corporal his personality changed. We would go on work parties filling sand bags and loading them onto trucks for the construction of bunkers.

He would say, "All right men, get busy". He would stand around and 'nit-pick' at us. Either we put too much dirt in the bag or not enough. The bags were never stacked straight enough. It felt like he was always trying to show that he was in charge. No one liked his attitude and even the other corporals and sergeants didn't get along with him. One time he got into a fist fight with one of the other corporals. I firmly believe being a leader went to his head or perhaps it brought out his true personality.

Corporal Waters was our best leader. Whenever we went on a work party he would pitch in and help.

He would say, "All right men, let's get this done." He didn't work as hard as us because he would occasionally check that the bags were all filled to the same level or that they were all stacked correctly. If the bags weren't right, he would help you correct them. We would follow him any-where. And we all worked to please him because we respected him.

On Monday, July 11, 1966, seven other guys and I were promoted to lance corporals. I was proud. I had been in the Corps for less than a year and became an E-3. Soon I would oversee daytime patrols and the respon-sibility that went with it. I hoped I would be like Corporal Waters and not like Corporal Edwards.

Just outside the main or west gate was a road that led up to hill 327 where the P.X. and movie theater were located. Along that road was a fairly large Vietnamese village called 'Dog Patch', nicknamed after the Little Abner comic strip village. All the buildings were thatched huts just like in the comics. Soon after we took over the Air Base, I chipped a filling out of a tooth and had to hitch a ride from the main gate to the dentist located up on hill 327. It was my first trip down the street in Dog Patch. Dozens of whores lined the street and waved to any G.I. who drove by.

They would yell, "Sucky sucky, fucky fucky, one dollar!" Only it came out sounding like, "dorwar". Also, licky licky one dollar came out, "ricky ricky, one dorwar". Many of the Vietnamese woman and men would put something called 'betel nut' on their teeth, which turned the teeth black and eventually would cause them to rot and fall out. These were not good-looking whores, and even at a dollar, were overpriced.

As an MP, we often had to run patrols through Dog Patch looking for the Viet Cong. During the day the whores would run and hide because we had orders to arrest them. At night no one could be outside at all. Breaking curfew meant arrest or accidentally getting shot. Men were constantly sneaking into Dog Patch at night to rent a dollar whore. One of the other M.P. companies still patrolled the streets in jeeps dressed as M.P.'s and would arrest any G.I. they found in Dog Patch. The punish-ment was a court martial.

On Monday night July 11th, the same day I was promoted, Fussner took me and four other guys on a night patrol through Dog Patch looking for

V.C. We were supposed to weave our way back and forth through the village but stay off the main street because that was still patrolled by the M.P.'s in jeeps. Fussner rushed us through the patrol almost at a trot. Then on the way back he stopped at one of the huts (or hooch) on the main street for what he called some "Boom Boom" time. (During his first enlistment he had been stationed in Japan and liked to impress us with his bilingual Asian skills. By adding the word 'San' to the end of any word he thought he could speak Vietnamese. So, Poppa-san meant father and Momma-san meant mother). While he was in the hooch having boom-boom we stood outside. Sure, enough an M.P. jeep came by and asked us what we were doing. I explained we were on a patrol and were heading back to 'D' Company which was part of the M.P. Battalion. The M.P. took my name down and I knew they were going to report me. We left Fussner in the hut and headed back to our company. He sneaked back on his own. I knew we were in trouble and none of us wanted to take the blame for asshole Fussner.

Two days later, on our day off I had to report to Lieutenant Evans and explain what had happened. I let it all out. I told about Fussner getting us lost and the mix up with the grenades and the night in the whore's hooch. I tried to explain that Fussner wasn't trying to screw up. He wasn't deliberately trying to hurt anyone, but... I believed at the time the lieutenant understood. Fussner faced 'Office Hours' which was one step below a court martial. Office hours went on your permanent record and could lead to being busted in rank. Fussner could be reduced to a lance corporal like me. Rather than being busted, it was decided to put him on six months probation. Eventually corporal Fussner was transferred to an infantry company.

Once he left we all worried that Corporal Edwards would be our new squad leader. I worried the other guys would then blame me, not for speaking up about Fussner, but for having to put up with Edwards which might be worse. Lucky for us Corporal Waters was promoted to sergeant and became our squad leader with a capital 'L' for real Leader.

Chapter 19

THE 'D' WINGERS OF COMPANY 'D'

I DON'T KNOW WHY but throughout my life I seem to be attracted to people who seem to have one or two 'screws loose'. I'm not sure if perhaps they saw the same thing in me which explained the mutual connection and friendship. But from the time I was in junior high school through senior high, I always hung around with guys who all shared a slightly demented or twisted sense of humor. Our high school was divided into four wings, A, B, C, and D. The 'D' wing housed the Special Ed. and the shop classes. Those students were nicknamed "D Wingers", an uncomplimentary term, given by the more superior college bound students to the special education or "Speds" because of their perceived stupidity. I studied both college 'prep' classes and some shop classes. But for some reason, I liked hanging around with the 'D' Wingers more than with the 'Preps'. The few friends I had who went to college also possessed my weird sense of humor. Even today, I still get together with my buddies from my teaching days for breakfast or cards. I still laugh at them and with them because of our shared sense of 'D' Winger humor.

In the Marine Corps I met lots of different and unusual guys. There were guys from the southern backwoods to the biggest cities in America. The guys I hung around with were usually the half goofy ones. And I'm sure they felt the same way about me. Getting to know and understand a lot about a guy was easy after spending eight hours together in a foxhole with nothing to do but talk. We all had several things in common. We all hated being in the Marine Corps and the way we were treated. We all had hopes and dreams of what we were going to do once we got out. It didn't matter where you came from or what color your skin was or what language you spoke, we all shared the same feelings. I learned a lot about human nature in general as I got to know these guys.

Each night the sergeant would pair us up with a different guy usually in a different foxhole or bunker to stand guard duty. Sometimes it was a new guy you knew nothing about. I learned that by asking certain questions I could quickly get to know them better. I would ask where they were from? Then, why did they join the Marine Corps? And finally, what were they going to do when they got home? All the guys I got to know had their own individual dreams and plans. But mostly I learned to like them because of their sense of humor.

I already told you about Dochterman and Donald. Doc's dream was to marry his sweetheart. I was to be his best man at their wedding. Donald was very 'squared away' and probably liked the Marine Corps more than most of us.

Garcia was from Texas and had played in his high school marching band. He joined the Marine Corps because the recruiting sergeant promised they would put him in the Marine Band, so he could practice playing his trumpet. Of course, he never even saw a trumpet in the Corps. His dream was to go back to Texas and play in a professional band. His buddy from Texas was Flores and they were like the old Cisco Kid and Poncho. Flores joined because the recruiting sergeant told him the Marines would make him a cook. His dream was to have his own restaurant someday. Garcia also hung around with a guy from Michigan named Kreh. Garcia and Kreh went on R & R (rest and relaxation) together. Kreh was a crazy guy. I never knew when he was bull shitting or when he was telling the truth. He was going to buy a fancy car like a Camaro and ride around Flint, Michigan and pick up women.

Hernandez was a Puerto Rican from New York City. He was very quiet. At first, I thought it was because of his Spanish accent, but he spoke perfect English. He was very good at poker, too good if you know what I mean. Some of us would not play if he was in the game.

Then there was Jonas. Yes, that was his last name. His first name was Jim like mine. He was from one of the Carolinas. He used to tell bullshit stories about the mountains where he grew up, stories about "hoop snakes and such". Northern and city guys used to make fun of his southern drawl. He once got in trouble and he could have easily blamed it on me, but he took full responsibility. I always admired him.

Carden was also from one of the Carolinas but didn't have quite the southern drawl that Jonas had. Carden joined the Marine Corps to follow a family tradition. His brother also was in the Corps. Carden wanted to go to college or some other type of school when he got out. He was one of the guys who first gave me the idea that college could be in my future.

McDonald, 'Mac' was probably my best friend. We had driven a jeep into the Pacific Ocean. I already related his method of staying awake. He joined the Marine Corps because he wasn't big enough to get a football scholarship. His goal was to go home, marry his sweetheart and go to college on the G.I. bill.

Payne was from somewhere out west. He was 'gung ho'. He claimed he joined the Corps to learn how to fight and planned to become a mercenary when he got out. He kept saying how he wanted to be in the action and away from this 'chicken shit outfit' where all we do is stand guard duty. For the most part I thought his story was total B.S. However, the first month they asked for volunteers to go to the infantry he jumped at the opportunity. I lost contact with him and heard he died soon after leaving the M.P.'s. He was one of the few who admitted to joining because he wanted to.

A common reason I often heard for why guys joined the Marine Corps was because they claimed they had wrecked their Dad's car and didn't want to face the consequences. Or they got in trouble with the law and the judge gave them a choice of jail or the Marine Corps. I don't doubt it happened to some guys, but I also think a lot of guys didn't want to admit they made a horrible mistake by joining the Corps.

Kreh told the best story of why he joined the Marine Corps. We were all sitting around one day eating 'C' rations in the rain on what was supposed to be our day off. I asked him,

"So Kreh, why did you join the Corps?"

His answer had everyone waiting for an explanation. "I joined for the sex." Nearly everyone asked, "What?" He continued,

"Yeah, the recruiting sergeant told me if I joined the Marine Corps I'd have all the sex I could handle." Now, we all knew how the recruiting sergeants lied. Even Dave and I were supposed to be on the so called 'buddy system', but we had not heard any promises of sex. Then Kreh continued,

"And you know he was absolutely right. Cause everyday that I have been in the Corps, I've gotten fucked!" Yep, that was the best reason I ever heard.

One of my buddies, for this story I'll just call him Private Bill Hilly. I believe he made it out of 'Nam alive and I wouldn't want to embarrass him with this story by stating his real name. Private Hilly wasn't real bright and having grown up in rural America, was very trusting of others. Some guys took advantage of him, while other guys took him under their wing to protect and befriend him.

On one of the endless nights we spent sharing a fox hole or a bunker on guard duty, Private Hilly admitted that there was something he didn't understand. As I mentioned before we took turns staying awake and sleeping. Most guys owned a watch but many of us didn't wear one. We needed one, so we could tell what time to wake the other guy up when it was his turn to be on duty. I had never liked wearing a wrist watch. Usually we would sleep for two hours and then switch and try to stay awake for two hours. One morning after our squad awoke and we were sitting around waiting to be picked up by a truck to go back to our base camp for work parties, Hilly began to complain.

"I don't know what's goin' on around here but some'n sure is wrong."

Someone asked Hilly, "Why, what's the matter?" Hilly replied,

"Here it is 11 o'clock in the morning and the sun is just now com'n up!" We all laughed because we knew what had happened. The guy in the fox hole with Hilly had the wrist watch and each time Hilly went to sleep the other guy had moved the watch ahead by an hour and a half. That gave Hilly only half an hour of sleep and the other guy got three and a half hours of sleep. Who knows how long that had been going on before Hilly wised up?

When Sergeant Deluca arrived with the truck to pick us up, Hilly told him, "I have to go to the P.X. and buy me a watch." When Sergeant Deluca heard what had happened he gave Hilly the day off to buy a watch. We all chastised the other guy. Deluca told him,

"You ought to be ashamed of yourself for taking advantage of a poor soul like that. Imagine if that poor bastard fell asleep and some gook snuck up and killed both of you?"

The first chance I got I went into Dog Patch and bought a pocket watch from a gook for five dollars. It lasted one week. Little old Garcia went with me and he talked the gook into giving me my money back. Garcia had a way of talking to anyone. I don't know if it was his smile or his size, but he got along fine with the Vietnamese. I later bought a real pocket watch at the P.X.

One of the things we did to entertain ourselves was to tell stories.

They were mostly tall tales or bullshit stories. I already mentioned how my Grandfather explained how you could tell the difference. There were a lot of stories that began with, "Now listen..." A typical conversation in the mess hall or in one of the endless lines we stood in would sound something like this:

City slicker, "You's guys better not talk like that if you are ever in _____, (whatever city he was from)

Southern boy, "Why's that?"

City slicker, "Because somebody will cut you up! Hell, there are some parts of the city you don't dare go into. If you ain't part of that gang they'll slice you up like you were salami in the deli."

Southern boy, "Well we don't have no gangs where I'm from. But we do have some mean critters."

City slicker, "Yeah, like what?"

Southern boy, "Well down in the South we got some crock-a-gators, and they are about the meanest critter on planet earth!"

City slicker, "What the fuck is a crock-a-gator?"

Southern boy, "Well, its half crocodile and half alligator. You see one end of it has the head of a gator and where its tail should be, it has another head of a crocodile. It has two heads and no ass end."

City slicker, "Well if it has no ass end how does it take a shit?"

Southern boy, "It don't. You see that's what makes it so mean. And that's no shit." Most bullshit stories ended with, "And that's no shit."

City slicker, "I swear you southerners are all full of shit."

Southern boy, "Now don't you go say'n that. You know the South shall rise again!"

Any Northern guy, "Yeah, cause shit floats."

Then a northern farm boy would jump in.

"We got some strange animals back on the farm where I come from. We had a cow, and a pig and a chicken that we lived off. One day my sister accidentally fed some sawdust to that chicken. And wouldn't you know it, the next time that chicken laid eggs, when they hatched, six of them baby chicks had wooden legs. And the seventh was a wood pecker."

One day we were on a patrol. It was hotter than hell and we were running ahead of schedule, so we took a break. We had been walking in a dry rice paddy, so we sat down on the dike. As we sat there the guy next to me looked over the other side of the dike and yelled, "Holy shit!" I looked and right behind me were several eggs in a nest with some tiny snakes crawling out of the shells. I happened to be carrying the shotgun that day. So, with the first blast I destroyed over half of them. By the time I emptied the gun they were more than all gone.

Sergeant Waters said, "Easy Dixon. What's the matter with you? Are you afraid of snakes or something?"

Fisher, who had been to college before he dropped out, and was drafted said, "Those looked like the 'Johnny two-steppers'." They were so named because if you got bit from one, you were supposed to be dead before you could take two steps. It was true, in Viet Nam there were some very poisonous snakes. I don't know what kind of snakes these were because now they were totally destroyed.

The other guys could see I was still shaking. One guy said, "You don't have to be afraid of snakes, you can always out run a snake."

That's when either Carden or Jonas piped up. "Well, that's not exactly true. You know up in the hills of Carolina we got a snake called a 'hoop snake' and nobody can out run them."

And of course, I had to ask, "What the hell is a hoop snake?"

He continued his story and said, "Well, like I said, they live up on the tops of hills and when anybody comes near them they bite themselves in the tail and roll themselves up in a hoop. Then they roll down that hill faster than you can out run'em."

Then some other hillbilly jumped in. "Yeah, well we got us a stranger critter than that. We got us 'snollygosters' up in the mountains where I'm from.

And of course, someone had to ask, "What the fuck is a snollygoster?"

He explained, "Well it looks a lot like a goat, except one side of its legs are longer than the other side. That way it can walk around the side of the hills without falling over."

Someone had to ask, "What does it do when it has to walk around in the other direction? Does it have to walk backwards?" The answer was the bullshit punch line, "No you see it turns itself inside out and then it can walk in the other direction. That's what makes it so unusual. And that's no shit!"

The good part was by then I was laughing, and the shakes were gone. I don't know if they told those stories to help settle me down or if it was just part of the bullshit and who they were. Some people would call these guys 'retards' or 'D' Wingers. Some would call them Hillbillies or Windbags or just plain Bull-shitters. All I know is, I called them friends.

Chapter 20

GOOKS, GRUNTS AND NON-COMBATANT PUKES

I REMEMBER WHEN my two sons were in elementary school. The people in the house across the street from the school bus stop had an incident. Apparently, the husband and wife had a rather heated discussion. Some would call it a domestic dispute. The husband had thrown all the furniture out into the front yard. He didn't toss the items out the front door, instead they went out through the closed windows. It must have created quite a scene at the bus stop. I didn't see the damage but heard about it at our dinner table.

When I asked my next-door neighbor, she explained the whole situation by simply saying, "Well, you know he was in Viet Nam!"

For her that was the reason he had gone 'bonkers.' I never told her I was also a Viet Nam Vet. She might have had a whole different opinion of me.

The attitude of a great many Americans was, if you were in Viet Nam you must now have some sort of mental problems. I believe the myth has been perpetuated by Hollywood, the press and American culture in general. After the Viet Nam war ended, America began to have a huge drug problem, which was blamed in part on the war. Many believed that American Veterans became drug users in Viet Nam. I believe the opposite was true. They used drugs before they ever went to Viet Nam and simply continued using drugs along with many thousands of people who never set foot out of the U.S.A.

Another stereotype about Viet Nam concerns the term 'Veteran'. My wife and I joined a V.F.W. in Maryland because it was right next to where we docked our small boat. We figured the VFW had a bar and restaurant and it would be a good watering hole and a nice place to eat before we drove home after a day of boating. The first time I walked into the place I noticed two overweight men about my age sitting at the bar smoking and drinking. They each wore their rank and insignias from the Air Force. They immediately asked what branch of the military I had been in. I told them I had been in the Marine Corps. All they said was 'humm!' and went back to their drinking. My wife and I never spent much time in that place. There were too many war stories being told. For me those stories were in the same categories as fairytales and bullshit stories. They not only brought back bad memories, but I also didn't believe much of what I overheard. You see, there are different kinds of Veterans as I will explain later.

In previous chapters I used the word 'Gook' which has come to be an unflattering, racist term. I feel I should explain my reasoning. That term was used by every American soldier and Marine in Viet Nam. Whites were called 'chucks', Blacks were called 'splibs' and Vietnamese were called 'gooks'. These terms were acceptable and expected. In just about every war that has been fought the enemy has been given different nicknames. During World War II, G.I.'s didn't kill Germans and Japanese. They killed

'Krauts' and 'Nips'. Nip was short for Nipponese the name the Japanese called themselves. And Kraut was short for sauerkraut, which the Germans were famous for making and eating. Psychologically it's a lot easier to kill someone with a slang term which dehumanizes them. In Viet Nam we killed 'Gooks' and we didn't kill them, we 'blew them away'. The only exception to this rule was the American Civil War where brother fought against brother. They killed 'Billy' Yank and 'Johnny' Reb. That must have made that war even more unbearable. So, as I write these stories I mean no disrespect to the Vietnamese soldiers or people when I use the term Gook. It was what we called them and that simply made it easier to kill them – if killing is ever easy! Today the American soldiers and Marines kill 'towel heads' and 'jihads' short for jihadists. Ironically, it makes war a little more tolerable.

Another term I used for some Marines was 'Grunts'. This was the infantrymen's nickname because of all the gear they carried. Marines have had lots of nicknames over the centuries, some flattering, some not. The Marines were first organized to fight on board naval ships in the Revolutionary War. In the 1800's, while fighting against the Barbary Pirates, the Marines wore leather collars to help prevent the pirates from cutting their heads off in battle. They got the nickname 'leather necks' a term they still use with pride. Some other branches of the services think Marines are so dumb that they screw their heads off and on like a jar, hence the unflattering nickname 'jar head'. In return, Marines refer to all sailors as 'swabbies' because they mop the decks of ships. Airmen are called 'wing wipers'. Marines don't have nicknames for regular soldiers except for 'dogface'. The Marines respect the airborne divisions and rangers because of the additional training they get and therefore they have no unflattering nicknames that I know of. Marines didn't have much respect for the draftees in the regular army.

There are many occupations in the Marine Corps needed to support the infantry. I have heard it takes about 600 men to support just one infantryman, whether he is a Soldier or a Marine, if you stop and figure in the clerks, (office pogues) mechanics, drivers, cooks, supply personnel, hospital workers, and engineers not to mention the 'cannon cocker', and air wings... the list goes on and on. Most of those personnel including, some Women Marines, think of the grunts as the stupid ones who weren't smart enough to train for a decent job. All they can do is walk around in the mud and sleep in the mud and dig holes in the mud. The grunts are considered the lowest rung on the military ladder. They are also called names like, 'ground pounders', 'ammo humpers', and 'mud marines', all terms that the grunts accept with a certain amount of pride. I know for a fact that the grunts don't have a whole lot of respect for the non- combatants, who provide support but do no actual fighting or killing. Grunts call them non- combatant pukes.

We, as MP's used to stand guard duty and direct traffic at the west gate of Da Nang Airbase. There were two roads that surrounded the base. One road encircled the outside of the gate and another encircled the inside. Two MP's directed traffic at the gate to prevent accidents and keep the endless lines of vehicles moving. During the course of a day, we saw just about every type of vehicle and every type of military occupation coming in or out of the base.

The grunts were the easiest to spot. They wore different clothing than everyone else. They wore jungle utilities which were lighter weight and camouflaged. As MP's, our utilities were plain olive drab. Their trousers had strings at the bottom for tying the cuff around their boots which they only tied when they were walking in 'leach' territory. The grunts' boots were also different. Theirs were brown and had canvas-like sides and were lighter than our black leather boots. They called their utilities 'jungle ukes' and their boots 'jungle boots'. However, the thing everyone noticed about the grunts was their attitude. They had an 'I don't give a shit' attitude about them. They were unshaven, hadn't showered in days or weeks and smelled. Riding in 'six by' trucks, they wore their helmet unbuckled John Wayne style. No one else would dare wear a helmet like that. Of course, the grunts didn't wear their helmets unbuckled in combat either. Their attitude was, "What are you going to do about it? Are you going to put me in 'the grunts' and make me sleep in the mud, make me eat shit all day and shoot at me all night? Oh, you're already doing that!" They just didn't give a shit. As a matter of fact, that's what they used to say, "Give a shit, give a shit, ten thousand gives 'a shit'!"

In a way we all respected them for what they were going through, even though at the time I had no idea just how bad the grunts had it. They certainly did not respect the other non-combatants. After all we got to sleep in a tent, and take a shower every fourth night, something they could only dream about. We also got a beer ration. They would spend four to six weeks in the jungles and rice paddies, and then come back for a few days or maybe a week. During that time in camp they got a shower, food from a mess hall and some beer. Then it was back to the jungle. The official casualty rate for grunts that spent 13 months in country was between 50% to 80%. That statistic is misleading when you compare it to all casualties in Viet Nam. The chances of someone dying in Viet Nam were 1 in 185. However, 83.5% of all casualties were grunts. It's no wonder the grunts called everyone else 'non-combatant pukes'.

To this day I believe the 1st M.P. Battalion was formed by military bureaucrats to put infantrymen in Viet Nam and disguise the total number of 'combat troops'. The war was becoming very unpopular in America and the civilian population didn't want to see more and more combat troops being sent to Viet Nam. So, the M.P.'s were designated as non-combatant troops even though we were all 0300's (infantry). Each month as regular grunt outfits suffered causalities, men from the M.P.'s were sent as replacements. Some guys volunteered for combat, while guys like me waited to be forced to leave. Eventually nearly all the guys in 'D' Company would be sent to the grunts.

On Saturday, July 2, 1966 our platoon and one other came off the line but instead of being assigned work details we had a big inspection. We had spent the last three days either on guard duty or work details. We were told we were going to be an honor guard for General Westmorland, who was the general of all operations in Viet Nam and had four stars on his uniform. We were told to polish our boots and put on starched utilities and of course clean our rifles. One hundred degrees outside and we had not showered in three days, but our uniforms, boots and rifles all looked great for the general.

We climbed aboard six-bys and were taken to the airbase. It was hot probably well over 100 degrees. We stood on the edge of the runway in platoon formation with the American flag in between the two platoons. There aren't too many shade trees on an airport runway and the black top reflected the sun and made the temperature at least 20 degrees higher. We stood at attention and practiced the manual of arms and using the rifle for the command 'Salute Arms' for when the general's plane arrived. Several guys started to collapse in the heat. Sergeant Deluca told us to bend our knees, so the blood would flow through our bodies to help keep cool. Of course, the plane was late, and it became another instance of 'hurry up and wait'... only this time we were standing in 120-degree heat. Finally, we were allowed to stand at parade rest which is slightly less uncomfortable than at attention.

Kreh sneaked a peek over his shoulder at the rest of the Air Force Base. When he turned around again he whispered out of the corner of his mouth, "What are those things behind us?"

Several other guys took a quick glance around also. Mac replied, "Those are barracks, you dumb shit. Don't you remember sleeping in barracks?"

Sergeant Deluca warned us, "Knock off the 'grab ass', you're supposed to be at parade rest."

After a brief pause Kreh continued his whisper, "I know what barracks look like, but what are those things sticking out of the windows?" This time several more guys turned to see.

Then Carden said, "Damn, those are air conditioners!"

At that point everyone in both platoons, including Deluca and Lt. Evans, turned to look. I think it was little ole' Garcia who said, "Fuck, I knew I joined the wrong branch of the service".

The general's plane finally landed about a quarter of a mile away. The stairway was put down as we stood at 'salute arms'. The General and one other guy scampered down the steps and into a waiting car and then drove off. I don't think the general even saw us. He certainly didn't return our salute. It was over, and we were grateful to finally get out of the sun.

Sergeant Deluca gave the command to stack arms (stand three rifles together to form a pyramid) so we could go eat chow. We were told we would eat noon chow in the Air Force mess hall. The mess hall was air conditioned! We ate on real china with silver ware! There was more of a food selection than at any mess hall I had ever eaten in. I had been in the Marine Corps for nearly a year and this was the best food I had ever eaten. All of us walked out of that place in stunned silence. When I finally left Viet Nam I would spend two more years at Henderson Hall in Washington D.C., which is the headquarters of the Marine Corps. The Commandant of the entire Marine Corps' office was right down the street, but even then, we did not have air-conditioned barracks. We all felt we were seriously getting screwed over.

As Mac and I departed the mess hall we both had to make a head call. We bumped into two Airmen. I asked them, "Where is the head?"

They looked at me like I had just landed from Mars. I asked again. This time I thought the Airman was getting smart with me. He gave me a dumb look and pointed to his skull.

I repeated my question, "Hey, asshole where..."

His buddy interrupted and said, "I think they want to know where the latrine is located."

This time he pointed and said, "It's right around that corner."

"Oh, okay," we replied. Then we remembered the Army and Air force call them 'latrines', the Navy and Marines call them 'heads.' As we walked away I heard one of them say something about 'jarheads' and stupid.

I turned to walk back. I was already pissed at the inequality and suffering from sleep deprivation and was itching for a fight. Mac grabbed my arm and pulled me back. He said, "Come on Dixon. Don't worry about them. They're just non-combatant pukes." He said it loud enough for them to hear.

To this day I respect any man or woman who served in any branch of the service. I do get frustrated though when guys tell me they are Viet Nam Vets, and then I find out they never set foot in country. I have a good friend who was drafted into the Army during the Viet Nam War. He spent two years guarding the border between North and South Korea. He spent many months standing outside in all kinds of weather and it couldn't have been any fun. But at least he never claimed to be a Viet Nam Vet. I have two other buddies who do claim to be Viet Nam Vets. They were both on board ships and never set foot in the country of Viet Nam. I know other guys who served in Viet Nam. One was a mechanic and the other worked in the Saigon post office. Both volunteered to extend their tour of duty because they automatically got a promotion and continued to collect the extra $120 per month combat pay. They were non-combatant pukes, but they got the same combat pay as the grunts.

Even today most people don't recognize the difference between a Viet Nam Era Vet and a Viet Nam Vet, much less the even rarer Viet Nam Combat Vet. There is a huge difference between the three. Only a small handful can claim the latter title.

Chapter 21

GOOD TIMES AND BAD TIMES

I T HAS ALWAYS BEEN my habit to take the memories of bad times and stick them in the back of my brain. Really bad memories I put in the basement of my mind and lock them in a secret room. Any good memories I keep handy and easily relate those stories to friends. Many of my experiences in the Marine Corps and in Viet Nam I never shared with anyone. As my wife read these chapters for the first time she exclaimed, "I never knew that before." Or she would say, "You never mentioned any of this before."

There are several reasons for my never retelling any of these stories until now. After my tour in Viet Nam I flew into California. I remember walking through the Los Angeles Airport and having people spit at me and call me "baby killer". When I was finally discharged from the Marine Corps, I went to college. During my second week of school there was a National Moratorium on the Viet Nam War. Many colleges closed their schools down and held protests and demonstrations. I remember sitting in some voluntary classes listening to professors explain why we should not be in Viet Nam and how this war was evil. I made it a habit to never tell any of my classmates, I was a Veteran, let alone a combat vet. The war had torn the country apart and was becoming more and more unpopular. I found it best to keep my military experience a secret.

I discovered later, when I tried to explain about the war, people already had preset prejudiced opinions. I didn't want to discuss the merits of the war, just explain what happened. Also, whenever people found out I was in Viet Nam, they always asked one of two questions. Did you ever kill any babies? Or, what was it like? Neither question can be answered in a word, a sentence, or a paragraph. I figured it would take a whole book to explain my experiences and I was too busy with college, work and raising a family to write the book. 50 years later, I am now writing these stories as kind of self therapy. It's time to open the basement door of my mind and clean things out.

There were some good things I experienced while in Viet Nam and we did find time for fun. As soon as we arrived in country we began receiving combat pay. Anyone in the military, who does dangerous work like pilots, paratroopers, or bomb disposal, receives 'hazardous duty' pay. Everyone in Viet Nam was in a combat zone, so they received combat pay. It was an extra $120.00 a month. It doubled my pay. Everyone who set foot in country for even one day got a month's combat pay. Guys who flew cargo planes into the base and then flew out again got the extra pay for the whole month. We were paid in military 'script' which we called 'funny money' because it looked just like monopoly money, same size and colored yellow instead of green. Even the coins were printed on paper at 5, 10 and 25 cents, each. We all had enough money; we just never had any time to spend it. I sent back $100.00 each month to my father to put in a savings account for me. I would have sent more back home but...

Early in June, on one of our so-called days off, we lined up in platoon formation to await our work detail assignments. We hoped when the jobs were done we might have a chance to go to the P.X. and buy some much needed goods. The Company First Sergeant addressed us. "Men, the United States Marine Corps is holding their annual U.S. Savings Bond drive. We here in Company 'D' are hoping to have 100% participation in the bond program. Every one of you who wants to sign up for either a 50-dollar bond or a 100-dollar bond will form a line over at the bar tent. After you sign up you will each get your two cans of beer. Anyone who does not wish to sign up for a bond will form a line over by those shovels and will commence digging until you decide to sign up for a bond. Are there any questions?" Company 'D' had 100 percent participation in the bond program.

Everyone serving in Viet Nam could go on five days leave for R. & R. to places like Hong Kong, Bangkok, Taiwan or Okinawa. The R. & R. stood for rest and relaxation. The military would fly us to and from our destination, but we had to save up and use our money to pay for food, a hotel room and other items. Kreh and Garcia were the first to go and went to Bangkok or as they called it, Bang Cock and they went on I. and I. (intercourse and intoxication). On November 8th I went on R & R to Japan. I knew I would never have a chance to see another foreign country, so I saved up my money and did some sightseeing on paid tours. I went with a guy named Davenport who was drafted twice, once by the Cincinnati Reds and once by Uncle Sam. Uncle Sam took precedence over baseball.

I got to experience the culture and the people of Japan. I rode on the Tokyo subway. In Japan it's so crowded the subway hires college kids to be 'pushers' and 'pullers'. They literally pull you out of the cars when they stop and push you in when you get on. I would say you felt like a sardine in a can, but I think sardines have a little bit more room. I was impressed with how clean and neat the Japanese people are. Cab drivers would be fined if the outside or interior of the cab was dirty. Davenport and I went to a 'geisha house' which is not a whore house. It's a place where Japanese women entertained us and served Japanese 'sake'. It tastes great, but boy will that stuff sneak up on you. I went to a bath house and was bathed by a beautiful Japanese girl. Afterwards she gave me a massage with a happy ending!

On the American airbase in Japan we ate real hamburgers and drank real milk shakes. We stayed in a very nice hotel for $9.00 a night. In the evening we went to bars and talked to women. The last night I took one back to my room. In the morning I discovered she had found the $40.00 I had hidden under the night stand and stole it. I considered it money well spent. I returned to the M.P.'s with a smile on my face, and good memories.

As I said before, everyone was supposed to get five days of R & R, however for the five months I spent in the grunts no one ever received R & R. We also only had one beer ration. We were always in combat or on stand-by and short-handed, so we received neither. If no one claimed the R & R, some other guys from another outfit were able to go more than once. Some went numerous times. As for the beer, if everyone was allotted two cans a day and someone couldn't drink theirs, then that beer was reallocated to some other outfit. Some guys had all the beer they could drink. And I'm sure some supply officers sold beer on the black market.

One time around the fourth of July, 'D' company had a steak dinner cooked over an open flame. We were served baked potatoes with real butter. We had an extra ration of beer and afterwards had the afternoon off and played football. It was a great day. They told us that a Vietnamese cow or bull had accidentally stepped on a land mine. The government paid the farmer and we got to eat steak. What I think really happened was the Marines had allocated steak dinners for the grunts returning from a thirty-day operation. The grunts were on standby and had to skip the meal, so we got it instead. I do know for a fact that one night a water buffalo the farmers used to plow rice paddies, walked over one of our trip wires which caused the tin cans with small stones to rattle and sound an alarm.

Several bunkers fired hundreds of rounds into the poor beast thinking they were under full attack. In the morning the engineers loaded the carcass into a six by with a front-end loader. The engineers ate well that night.

Each week we still had our field day and collected an unbelievable number of garbage bags from inside and outside of our tents. It took several guys most of the morning to load up a 'six-by'. We filled the truck to the hilt. One day I was assigned to ride in the truck to the dump and unload all the garbage. I knew the dump would be hot and smelly and I wasn't looking forward to spending an hour unloading the truck. The driver told me not to worry, "This truck will be empty in minutes". As we approached the dump, hundreds of women and kids swarmed the truck like Indians attacking a wagon train. I never got out of the truck cab! The women and children completely emptied the truck bed in a matter of minutes. They were looking for scraps of food or anything useful to recycle or sell. It was unbelievable. Later, I received a movie camera from home and filmed the scene as proof, when I witnessed it again.

The civilian Vietnamese were a 'hurting' people who lived in unbelievable poverty. Whenever we went on patrol, men, women and children would run up to us and beg. If they had a cut they would beg for a band aid, which we always handed out. Children would ask for "chop chop", which meant food. At first, we enjoyed giving them candy, but realized after a while the more we gave the more they wanted. Eventually dozens of kids would be hanging all over us. We ended up walking through villages and saying over and over, "No chop chop. No chop chop." Occasionally we would go on "People to People' programs where our Captain and other officers would meet with villagers and village leaders. We would hand out supplies and cameramen would take photos. It was part of winning the hearts and minds of the Vietnamese people. The whole time I kept thinking, "Are we giving supplies to the Vietnamese or to the Viet Cong?"

I also experienced many bad times. On Wednesday, August 17th one of our jet fighter planes took off from the DaNang Airbase, and only got a few hundred feet in the air, when its engine conked out. The pilot ejected safely but the plane belly flopped into one of the many nearby villages killing a dozen or more civilians. But the bad part was to follow. With a valuable ten-million-dollar plane in the middle of their village hundreds of Vietnamese scrambled to the wreck to see what they could salvage and steal. That's when jet fuel and the two, 500-pound bombs onboard exploded.

One of the many things Hollywood always gets wrong is the sound effects of battle and explosions. In the movies you hear a gun fire and then you hear the bullet hit or whiz by. The exact opposite is true. We heard the bullets long before we heard the gun shot. The same is true of an explosion. When looking in the right direction, a cloud of smoke will appear long before the explosion is heard. With the jet explosion we heard the earth-shaking explosion, and then turned to see a huge plume of black smoke already towering in the sky. We didn't know exactly what had happened, but we knew it couldn't be good.

Two platoons of 'D' company boarded six-bys and drove to the scene. We spent much of the day pulling dead, burnt bodies out of the rubble. It was horrible and disgusting. Carden said, "It was enough to gag a maggot." That night was the only night I couldn't eat evening chow.

If standing guard duty was boring, going on patrol was just the opposite. Four-man, day time patrols weren't too bad, but six-man night patrols could get hairy. On Saturday, August 20th and again the following Sunday, two of our patrols were ambushed. Saturday two of our guys were wounded. I was part of Sunday's night patrol. About 23 to 25 rounds were fired at us. We were pinned down for almost an hour until the entire reactionary team arrived and rescued us like the cavalry rescues a wagon train in the movies.

A week later our nerves were still on edge. At night we walked on patrol and had to pass near a small bridge that was being guarded by men from the 7th Marines. They had just returned from a month-long operation. Their nerves were really strung out. Word was supposed to have been radioed ahead to warn the 7th Marines that one of our patrols would be passing nearby. They never got the word. When they saw troops moving in front of them they opened-up. We dove behind a rice paddy dike. Machine gun tracer rounds passed over our heads like lasers at a rock concert. The outfit from the 7th Marines could not hear us shouting because of all the gun fire. The signal for receiving friendly fire was to set off a yellow flare. But Sergeant O'Leary was laying face down in the mud trying not to get killed and laying on top of the yellow flare. We began yelling as loud as we could to stop firing and for O'Leary to fire the fucking flare. No one could hear anything. O'Leary finally got the flare out from under his flak jacket and set it off. Immediately the firing stopped. The 7th Marines invited us to come up on the bridge and take a break. O'Leary was radioing back to base and giving them hell. That's when one of the 7th showed us how lucky we had been. He pointed to a 106-recoilless rocket launcher they were about to fire at us. In another second or two, we all would have become 'mince meat'. I was reminded of the horrifying statistic that perhaps half of all casualties in Viet Nam were caused by 'friendly fire'. Sadly, that fact is probably true of all wars.

Early in July 1966, I was part of another night patrol into the village of 'Dog Patch'. We were supposed to stay off the main street and walk behind the hooches in the back yards. There were of course six of us. It was a very dark night. We were taught to walk eight paces behind the man in front of us in case they stepped on a booby trap or land mine. It was so dark I could hardly see the guy in front of me, let alone the guys in front of him. As we walked I suddenly heard a muffled choking sound from somewhere ahead. I froze as did the guy in front of me. After a moment's pause we continued walking on. After about seven more steps I heard another choking sound. Again, we paused. No one said anything. We began to walk forward again. And again, I heard a louder choking noise followed by an, "Oh Fuck!" Still no one said a word. As we continued walking I began worrying that some Viet Cong commandoes were picking us off one by one. After another few steps I felt a sharp pain in my neck which forced a grunting, choking noise out of my throat. I had walked into a Gook's wire clothesline and caught it right in the Adam's apple. I started to turn and warn the guy behind me, but then figured...The other guys had not warned me so... The next guy was little Garcia and he caught the line on the top of his helmet. He also said nothing. I met up with the other four men in the patrol as we huddled together and waited for the last guy to catch the line in his throat. Afterwards, we all had a good laugh, because we had all shared in each other's misery.

Each month Company 'D' received a quota of men to go to the Grunts. Today, I firmly believe the NCO's and officers treated us horribly, so guys would volunteer to go the Grunts, and they wouldn't have to pick guys who they knew would more than likely become causalities. I think that's why we had work parties doing things that really were not necessary.

In August and September of '66, we learned the engineers would build permanent bunkers to replace the fox holes that most of us stayed in when we guarded 'the line'. Bunkers offered more protection from enemy fire and from the rain. The bunkers were made of 4 by 12's. Yes, there were stocks of lumber four inches thick and twelve inches wide and eight feet long. The engineers built the frames and placed them along the line facing the land mines. A four-inch thick piece of wood however will not stop a bullet. A round will go right through and continue through you. The bunkers only stood about five feet high. We had to dig down two feet inside the bunker to give us more protection and standing room. Then we had to dig dirt and fill hundreds of sand bags to place around the bunkers, two bags deep staggered like bricks. Each bag had to face outward from where the bag was tied. The roof of the bunker had three levels of bags to protect us from mortars. It was brutally hard, hot work in the tropical sun. It was necessary, so we did it without complaint.

What pissed us off when we finished, a lieutenant would come around and pretend to study the structure and then leave. We would be told that the bunker did not face the minefield in a perfectly straight line. We would then take each bag off the wooden bunker and ten of us would turn and move the whole bunker two inches to the left or right. Then of course all the sand bags would have to be placed back on the bunker. Also, several of us had suggested that a large piece of plastic be placed on top of the roof and then position the sand bags on top of the plastic to make the bunker waterproof. Suggestions from enlisted men were not taken seriously. Instead the bunkers all filled with two feet of water during the monsoons.

After the monsoons began not only did the bunkers fill with water but so did the fields around the bunkers. Some places the water became two feet deep. If we wanted to walk to the next bunker to shoot the shit before going on duty we had to walk through the water. We piled sand bags into small towers and then placed 4 by 12's on them as planks to create a series of bridges from bunker to bunker. Before it got dark each night we would move a corner of one of the 4 by 12's off to the side of the sand bag tower so that it hung by only a few inches. Then when an officer tried to walk across the bridge, they and the wooden plank would tumble into the water. We loved to hear lieutenants curse like us!

James M. Dixon

Chapter 22

THE DEATH OF LANCE CORPORAL DIXON

E VERYBODY HAS A STORY about something dumb their parents
did which caused them embarrassment or worse. I'm sure my two
sons have plenty of those kinds of stories.

Our lives in Viet Nam continued to get worse. In October '66, Garcia,
Flores, and Kreh left for the grunts. It was the first month they picked
guys to go because no one was volunteering. By November it was raining
about every other day. Each day our treatment from the officers became
worse. One day we stood in line to receive booster shots given to us in the
ass. No one told us what they were for and no one asked. All we knew was
the next day our butts were sore. The shots made us sleepy and extremely
difficult staying awake on guard duty. Three guys were caught sleeping
and were given two choices. They could have Office Hours and be busted,
or they could volunteer for the grunts. Two chose to volunteer and the

other became a private. Carden, McDonald and I were the only ones of the original M.P.s left. It was obvious that we would leave for the grunts in December.

I began to prepare myself mentally for the change and began getting my gear and possessions ready for the transfer. I had received many letters from all my relatives warning me about my mother's nervous condition. She continued to worry about me and had developed sores on her forearms from a habit of scratching herself even in her sleep. The doctor had given her bandages for the arms and prescribed tranquilizers to help her sleep. I too worried about her. How would she react if she found out I was being transferred to the infantry? I decided to write and tell her I was going to be getting a new address, which was absolutely true. The new address was because I was going to be transferred to Okinawa which is part of Japan, which was the 'white lie'. Hopefully that would relieve her anxiety.

I should also mention that my mother was not well educated and very gullible. Every night she would watch the evening news with Walter Cronkite and try to catch a picture of me. There was lots of fighting on the border between North and South Viet Nam which was called the De-Militarized Zone or the DMZ. She saw film clips of the soldiers fighting and getting killed at the DMZ and looked each night for me. She wrote me a letter and told me to try and stay far away from the D S M. Yes, I was puzzled at first when I read it, but I knew my mother and figured it out.

I got the idea of the address change and the white lie because of Dochterman. In September, Doc was on a work party to burn the waste from the heads (shitters). The fire had exploded severely burning Doc on the arms and head. When he got out of sick bay they transferred him to Okinawa. He spent the rest of his tour teaching Marines how to repel out of helicopters into the jungle. He of course had to learn how to do it himself. It was dangerous work, but he was not in combat in Viet Nam.

I also wrote all my other relatives telling them what I was doing and to make sure my mother never heard the truth. I wrote a letter to my mother that I would be sending a box of my belongings home because I would be getting new clothes in Okinawa. I told her not to worry about me, that I would be safe and far from any danger. In the mean time I gathered up my civilian clothes that I wore on R & R along with some other gear I would not need in the grunts. I packaged it all up in an empty 'C' ration case. Because Christmas was coming C-ration boxes were hard to find. I finally mailed the box of clothes several days after I mailed the letter. I figured Mom would get the letter long before the package arrived.

I decided to write other letters as well. I mentioned before that there were three girls back home I considered friends and had written to periodically. Gracie was the only one I felt I might be able to date when and if I got home. I wrote to Annette and Becky first and then started a letter to Gracie.

Monday November 20th was my birthday and the 23rd was Mac's. Wednesday was our day off, so several of us drank our two-beer limit, and then Mac and I finished off a bottle of whiskey someone had brought back from Japan. I had never really drunk much hard liquor and not being used to it, I got good and plastered. When I woke up on Thursday I felt horrible. It was the first and last time I would ever be hung over. We were supposed to go out on the line for 24 hours of guard duty. It is common knowledge the best thing for a hangover is food and lots of water. On the line we only ate 'C' rations. Our two canteens of water and Kool Aid had to last 24 hours.

Before I boarded the truck, I looked around for the letter I had started writing to Gracie. I asked the other guys if they had seen my letter. They said, "Yeah, you finished writing that last night. Man, you sure are funny when you're drunk."

"Yeah, well, where's the letter now?" I asked.

"Oh, you mailed that last night. You could barely walk, but you staggered over to headquarters and put it in the mailbox."

It took awhile to process that info before I asked, "What? You guys let me write a letter to a girl back home while I was drunk? And then you let me mail it?" The answer seemed unanimous.

"Yeah, like we said you really are funny when you're drunk!" I figured I would owe Gracie a long explanation and an apology. However, when I got home I discovered she had moved away. I have never, ever heard from her again.

As Mac, Carden and I waited for our transfer to the grunts, I made sure all my gear was in working order. I got two new canteens because I felt the old ones might be contaminated with germs. I went to the armory and had a selector placed on my M-14 rifle. This would allow me to fire it in automatic as if it were a machine gun. I tried to prepare myself mentally for the grunts. I would find out later there really is nothing one can do to fully prepare for that.

Nearly a month went by with our normal routine. Wednesday December 21st, however became another day I will always remember. It started out like any other day on the line. I was catching a few minutes of sleep in a French bunker while the other guy stood watch. Sergeant Deluca suddenly pulled up in a jeep and began yelling for me to get in. I grabbed my gear and jumped into the passenger seat and off we sped.

Deluca's only comment was, "I don't know what you did Dixon, but you fucked up big time!" I had no idea what I was supposed to have done. I knew I hadn't deliberately tried to fuck up. It seemed like an extra long drive back to "D' company headquarters with Sergeant Deluca saying nothing.

We pulled up in front of the company headquarters tent and I followed Sergeant Deluca inside. Inside the tent the normal office pogues, or clerks were sitting at their type writers. The tent also contained my platoon lieutenant, the company captain, and a full bird colonel, whom I had never seen before. They were all standing in the tent waiting to greet me. Sergeant Deluca spoke first.

"This is Lance Corporal Dixon." I stood at attention.

"Why aren't you dead?" asked the colonel. I really had no response to that stunning question.

What I did say was, "I uh, I uh, I'll get right on it, sir." This was the first time a full bird colonel had ever spoken to me, a lowly E-3.

"I have in my hand a letter from the Commandant of the United States Marine Corps," shouted the Colonel. With those words the two office clerks stood up and everyone in the room snapped to attention. There is a saying in the Marine Corps that in heaven, Jesus sits on the right-hand side of God. The Commandant sits on the left side.

"When was the last time you wrote to your mother?"

"Sir, I write to my mother every week. I wrote just a few days ago, sir".

"Well, for some reason your mother thinks you are dead. She has contacted her Senator and wants to know why the Marine Corps has not notified her of your death!"

I was dumb struck. Again, I tried to speak but all that came out were some vowels, "Ah, Eh, E, I. I don't know, sir."

The colonel finally came to the point and ordered me, "Lance Corporal Dixon, you will retire to your tent and you will write a letter to your mother. You will inform your mother that you are currently alive and well. You will hand deliver said letter to your captain. This letter will be mailed home by special delivery. **Do you understand?"**

For a moment I thought I was back in boot camp. I replied in a loud voice, "Sir, yes sir." The colonel's last words before I scurried out of the tent were, **"Now Lance Corporal!"**

I hurried back to the empty squad tent. Everyone else was out on guard duty on the line. I quickly wrote a letter to my mother. I was pissed and probably said some things no one should ever say to a loved one. I asked her to please stop worrying about me. I again explained that I was going to be transferred to Okinawa and would be as safe as I would be in the United States. The letter was hand delivered to the captain and witnessed by the lieutenant and Sergeant Deluca. I was returned to my bunker and that night I had to explain to all my buddies exactly what had happened.

The whole incident would remain a mystery until I returned home and got the whole story. Apparently, my mother received my package of clothing long before the letter that I had written, even though the letter was sent three days before the package. I assumed the letter explaining the box would arrive first. Upon opening the box of clothing, Mom thought these were my last personal effects and that I had been killed. Even though my brothers, grandparents, aunts and uncles said not to worry, she thought the worse had happened. At the time she held a part-time job working for the Delaware State Government at a local armory. Across the hall was a general in the Delaware National Guard. She kept pestering him that she thought she had received my last personal effects and knew I must be dead. He finally suggested she contact her Congressman. Delaware only has one Representative and of course two Senators. She called one of the Senators thinking they would not be as busy as the single Representative! As everyone who has ever been in the military knows, shit flows downhill and it always builds up speed. From Senator to Commandant and all the way down to Lance Corporal Dixon, it built up speed and size and landed squarely on me.

Between Christmas and New Years, promotions for corporal were handed out. Both Carden and McDonald became corporals. Even though I had a very clean record and had never fallen asleep on duty I was passed over. I could think of only one reason. The next month the three of us would head to the grunts. Both Carden and Mac would become squad leaders. I would not. Looking back now, my mother probably did me a big favor. As squad leaders Carden and Mac had to worry about the lives of all the men in their squad. I would only have to worry about my life. Of course, I also had to worry about my mother. If I got killed I knew she would have a heart attack.

1. My original marine dog tags showing service number and religious affiliation: Quaker

James M. Dixon

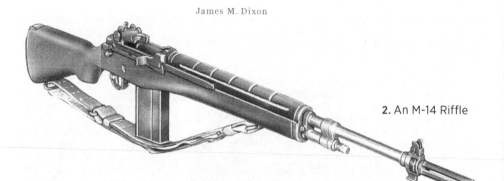

2. An M-14 Riffle

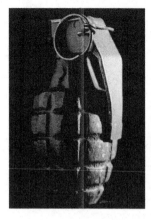

3. Above: The MK-II "pineapple" grenade
Below: The M67 "baseball" grenade

4. Standard-issue gear, including: M-16 rifle, ruck sack, poncho, canteen and mess kit

5. The U.S.N.S. Upshur (1968)

6. A "6x6" standard three-axle truck

7. 2nd Batalion, 5th Marines on patrol

8. Burning Man: This is what the job of burning the "shitter" looked like. (Photo Credit: Randy Barnes)

9. A water buffalo commonly found in Vietnam

10. From 1964 to 1973, Martha Raye (AKA: "The Big Mouth" or "Colonel Maggie) traveled from camp to camp in isolated areas throughout Vietnam for a total of eight visits during the war

11. FROM LEFT: Pfc. Jonas and Pfc. Carden at D. Company, 1st MPs, Camp Pendleton, California

12. Lance Corporal Florez

13. Abel Garcia (RIGHT) and friends

14. FROM LEFT: Mac and Jonas on liberty

15. Jim Jonas "D" Company, 1st MPs

James M. Dixon

16. Photographs of the author in uniform and "in country"

154

Chapter 23

A CHRISTMAS IN THE RAIN

THE OTHER DAY an acquaintance of mine tried to commit suicide. The attempt was made five years to the day after her husband passed away, just a few days before Christmas. I believe she just couldn't bear to face another Christmas alone. It's my understanding that a lot of people have a tough time coping with Christmas. There are more suicides at that time of year than any other time. Some say it's because the days are so short. December 21st is the shortest day of the year. Humans are not instinctively nocturnal. People who suffer from depression have the toughest time. I think Christmas itself can be very depressing. We all remember the great Christmases' of our past and we want this Christmas to be just like the others. So, we over-shop, over-decorate, over-bake and generally "over-do" everything to make this Christmas better or at least as good as any we remember. When things don't work out, our disappointment turns to depression. At the last minute we discover a loved one can't make the visit, or some relatives aren't getting along, or the weather turns terrible... and it seems to ruin everything.

I too tend to get depressed at that time of year, probably for all the reasons I've mentioned. However, I am lucky in one respect. Whenever I get depressed at Christmas, I just think back to the worse Christmas ever. That would have been 1966 in South Viet Nam.

Our outfit was guarding the Da Nang air base. In the six months we were there no one had died from an attack. Occasionally there would be a mortar or rocket attack, but the V.C. were trying to hit the airplanes. All we had to worry about was a *'Short Round'*. Our company had only one non-fatal casualty during a mortar attack. That occurred when a guy was sitting on a bar stool in his flip-flop shower shoes. The bar stools were the metal holders for a jet plane fuel tank. We used them to sit on because they made perfect bar stools. At the first sound of mortars he jumped off the stool, caught his small toe in one of the braces of the stool and cut his baby toe clean off. He was awarded a Purple Heart, because technically he was wounded during enemy fire. He lived the rest of his life with only 9 toes. He bled all over the plywood floor which left a permanent stain. That toe was the only thing our company lost in those mortar attacks. We had a couple of other guys wounded on night patrols, but for the most part we were safe at our duty location.

What made that time horrible wasn't the danger, it was the working conditions and the drudgery of living outside in the weather. In June and July, the temperatures were downright unbearable. By August either the temperatures began to drop, or we had to adjust to them. Sometimes we would have a summer thunder storm just like we do here in Pennsylvania. The old timers would warn us, "Do you see how hard it's raining now? Well this is nothing. Wait until the 'Monsoons' come." By October we started to get some cloudy days and it would rain all day. We thought that was the monsoons. But we were wrong. By November we hardly ever saw the sun. Some days it was just cloudy. Some days it would rain off and on. Some days it drizzled all day. We thought that was the monsoons. We were still wrong. The real monsoons hit in December through February.

Thanksgiving came, and we were all promised we would be getting a full turkey dinner. Yes, indeed we got a full turkey dinner which I still remember every Thanksgiving since. The chow hall was a series of three platoon tents. We got our food in one tent and then walked (or if it was raining we ran) to one of the other tents to eat. We ate out of mess kits. A mess kit is about the size of two small plates. Each is smaller than a dinner plate but a little bigger then a saucer. We stepped through the chow line and each part of the dinner was slapped into your mess kit. First came a slice of turkey, and then came stuffing, mashed potatoes, corn, sweet potatoes, and even cranberry sauce. All was piled one on top of the other. Next gravy was poured over everything. Finally, a slice of pumpkin pie and ice cream was added on top of everything else. By the time we walked to an empty seat in another tent the ice cream had completely melted. As we sat down, Mac said, "Now I know why it's called a 'mess kit'." We didn't complain. The guys on 'day one' spent 24 hours on the line. They ate C-rations outside in the rain. Yes, I think of that meal every Thanksgiving Day. I just smile to myself when others complain that the turkey was kind of dry, or the mashed potatoes weren't mashed enough, or the gravy got passed around before they got their stuffing. After that Thanksgiving, it rained nearly every day.

One nice thing about guarding the Da Nang air base, we were the ones who also guarded all the U.S.O. shows that came to the base. So instead of filling sand bags and building bunkers we would stand guard duty. I got to see lots of performers. The biggest show was Bob Hope. It was a good show with lots of funny gags, beautiful women, and music. Normally, the only music we listened to was Armed Forces Radio, and the military didn't approve of Rock and Roll. So, we heard lots of classical and oldies music from the 40's and 50's. When I was a kid my family always watched

Bob Hope's Christmas Specials on TV. Now I was seeing him in person! I was disappointed in Bob Hope himself. He came out on stage and tested the microphone (which worked) but the cameras weren't ready to film. So, he just stood there and said nothing. After two or three minutes of silence he turned around and left. Later someone signaled him that they were ready, so he came back out and began his show. I thought, 'Was he here to entertain us, or was he here to film a TV special?' When I finally got home I never watched another Bob Hope Special.

I was fortunate to see other entertainers as well. That year I saw the Gold Diggers and Nancy Sinatra sing 'These boots are Made for Walking' as well as Arthur Godfrey, the famous radio and television variety show host. Godfrey's show was OK, but he sat on a chair in the back of the stage and never got up. Someone else was the 'M.C.'. I thought, 'what a jerk'. Later, I felt really bad when I learned he had just gotten out of the hospital. He had one of his lungs removed and was still recovering from the surgery. He had paid for the trip and the entertainers out of his own pocket. He died a few years later from cancer.

The best show turned out to be the least expected. Two days before Christmas, when all the other entertainers had left, and it was raining all the time, we got news that Martha Raye was doing a show in our Chow Hall. We were on Day 4, so our platoon was able to see her. It was pouring rain and standing room only in the Mess Hall. She was older than my parents, well into her 50's. She stood on top of a table, sang songs, told off-color jokes and stories. She drank alcohol and seemed to be a lot happier than we were. She entertained 30 guys for over two hours. After the show she signed autographs and stood for photos. The only cameras were the ones we Marines had. To me she was a real hero.

Dec. 24, 1966 arrived, and it was our 'so called' day off. The holiday was treated like a Sunday and we didn't even have to stand for inspection or go on work parties. We could go to the P.X. The ten guys in our squad decided to exchange names and buy gifts for whoever's name we drew.

We rode in a truck to the P.X. It was one of those days when it was either 'spritzing' rain or a fine mist hung in the air. After shopping, instead of getting back on the truck, I decided to hitch hike out to where my friend from back home was stationed. I had not seen Dave since boot camp. I guess I just wanted to see a familiar face from home. Hitch hiking was easy. All you needed was a thumb. Anyone in a vehicle and a spare seat would give you a ride. After finding his outfit I got the bad news. Dave was on guard duty. Dave was an 'Ontos' repairman, which meant he was a mechanic. He slept in a tent every night and only had to stand guard duty when it was time for a one-hour fire watch. There were only two reasons guys were given guard duty on Christmas Eve. Either they were guys like me who's only job was guard duty or because they had screwed up and faced punishment. My guess, knowing Dave, was the latter. I was disappointed. There would be no familiar face from home this Christmas. So, I hitch hiked back to the base in the misty rain, feeling not only wet, but lonely. This would be my first Christmas away from home.

I got back to base in time for 'chow'. Luckily it wasn't turkey but at least it wasn't C-rations. We returned to our tent, showered and decided to exchange gifts. Of the ten guys in the squad, of course I had drawn Corporal Edwards's name. I hated him. And I know he hated me. As luck would have it he had drawn my name too. We exchanged gifts and wished each other a "Merry Christmas". I don't remember what I gave him, but he gave me a very nice wallet made from elephant hide. He bought it in 'Dog Patch', the Vietnamese village just outside of the base. I kept that wallet for years until it wore out. At Christmas, it would seem even enemies can be nice to each other.

It was drizzling rain outside so by 2100 (9:00 pm) we either wrote letters back home or tried to get some shut-eye in hopes we would forget where we were. I remember trying to fall asleep, thinking, 'What a miserable Christmas this was going to be.' Little did I know that it was about to get a lot worse; more so than I could have imagined.

Around 2200 (10:00 pm) I had just dozed off, when I heard shouting outside. At first, I thought, *mortar attack*, but I quickly realized we always heard mortars and then people yelling. So, it wasn't a mortar attack.

Then we heard the sergeants screaming, "Drop you cocks and grab your socks! Fall-out for formation: full combat gear." None of us knew what was going on, but we all knew it couldn't be good. We were in formation barely a minute when we received word there had been another plane crash. I remembered the one in August and how ghastly it was picking up bodies and parts of bodies. *'Don't tell me we're going to do that again,'* I thought. Soon trucks pulled into our compound and we jumped on board. Four trucks, each with four squads, headed out through the south gate. We tried lifting the canvas flap looking for the wreck, but it was too dark and too rainy, we could see nothing. Mac and I were the last to get in the truck, therefore when we arrived in a field near a village, we were the first to get off.

Our platoon Lieutenant pointed to Mac and me, and said, "You two stay here. There will be trucks and ambulances arriving soon. I want you to set up a place to line up any bodies we find and a place for the ambulances to pick up the injured."

In unison came the reply, "Yes Sir!" The rest of the squads were to spread out shoulder to shoulder in a straight line. When the rest of the platoons from the other companies arrived, they too would continue the line which would eventually surround the entire village. Then, just like the last time, they would walk towards the crash and pick up the injured and help them to the ambulances which were already arriving.

Mac and I looked at each other in bewilderment. Neither of us knew what to expect next. Soon Air Force ambulances pulled up. The military ambulances were really a 4-wheel drive pick-up truck with a place in the back to place four stretchers. They were also covered with a canvas top and had no blinking lights or sirens. These Airmen or "wing wipers" as we called them, probably had never seen Marines in full battle gear. And for some reason they started to salute Mac. I guess it's kind of a reflex mechanism when someone salutes you, you naturally salute them back. So, Mac naturally followed suit. The Airmen were calling him Lieutenant and asking him what to do as we looked at each other in bewilderment. Mac and I had done this before, so he told the Airmen to park the ambulances off to the side and back up so once they were loaded they could pull right out. It was obeyed like a command from God. Another truck arrived. It was a Marine Corp truck with wooden pallets filled with plastic body bags. They too exchanged salutes with Mac and asked where he wanted the bags. Mac and I helped them unload the pallets from the truck. Then they interrupted Mac.

"That's all right Sir. You just tell us where you want them, and we'll put them there". I thought, 'What the hell is going on'? Mac and I were both just lance corporals. These guys were treating Mac like an officer.

The Marines from the supply area drove off after the delivery. The Airmen, who I guess were our version of 'Corpsmen', or as they called them, 'Medics', stood beside their ambulances. Soon Marines began bringing out the first bodies and told us what had happened. A civilian passenger plane had crashed just after take-off. It landed belly up in the middle of a large village a mile outside of the runway. It burst into flames and then, being full of jet fuel, exploded. Not only were all the passengers probably killed, but many people in the village, as well. Survivors were probably civilian Vietnamese. These Marines were from another company and they too addressed Mac as "Sir" and "Lieutenant."

I looked at Mac trying to figure out what was happening. Then I noticed his helmet. Many guys would clip their C-ration can openers to the front or side of their helmet. The can opener was stainless steel and looked silver. It was also the same size as a Lieutenant's silver bar. In the dark and rain Mac looked just like a Lieutenant. We had been told to attach the can opener to our 'dog tags' to avoid this confusion from happening. But the opener was on a hinge and would often swing open allowing the sharp edge to dig into our chest or get caught on our hair and when you leaned over it would pull out chest hair. Mac, for one of these reasons had left his can opener on his helmet. I tried to pull him aside and explain what was happening. He was busy answering questions and directing Airmen and Marines how to lay the body bags in lines and how to place bodies in the bags. I decided to wait.

Soon individuals began bringing us charred parts: hands, arms, legs and what was left of a torso. All were burned beyond recognition. The smell was enough to gag a billygoat. Even the rain couldn't wash the burnt flesh smell from the air. After awhile the Airmen and their ambulances left. They were told the injured were being taken to a different spot closer to the road. The body bags were filled and lined up in rows. Body parts were placed together in bags until the bag was full. I went around pushing the bodies in, so they lay straight in the bag and then zipped them up. This continued for hours. Eventually grabbing hold of what used to be a human being became like picking up bags of anything else. By about 0300 (3 am) things began to slow down. The rain also slowed to a fine mist. Mac and I finally had a chance to talk.

"You know why these guys think you're an officer?" I asked.

"No, but ain't it great!" He answered.

"It's your can opener on your helmet," I explained.

He took off his helmet and checked it out. "Well, I'll be. I forgot all about that."

"You better take it off while you have a chance. If a real officer sees you, you'll be in deep trouble for impersonating an officer."

Mac gave me a strange look, like he wasn't the least bit worried. What he then said were words I would remember forever.

"Really, Dixon? Deep trouble, huh! What are they going to do to me? Cut my hair off? Send me to Viet Nam? Make me pick-up dead bodies in the pouring rain on Christmas? Dixon, this is as bad as it will ever get. They can never do anything to us worse than this." I had to laugh out loud in agreement. But I still worried and continued my warning.

"Impersonating an officer, they'll court martial you and send you to Leavenworth." Again, he looked at me in distain.

"Yeah, Leavenworth," he replied. "At least in Leavenworth you get three hot meals a day, you don't have to sleep out in the rain, and I doubt they make you pick up corpses on Christmas."

"Yeah, but what about the gang rapes in prison?"

He smiled and said, "Yeah there's sex in prison. It's just not the good kind of sex. But there's probably lots of sex. By the way when was the last time you got laid around here?" Again, I couldn't keep from laughing.

By 0400 we had not seen any other victims. Another lance corporal brought word that they were going to stop looking for the injured and just continue picking up bodies once the sun came up. Mac went over to the pile of body bags and grabbed two. He handed one to me and I looked at him puzzled. "What are you going to do with these?"

He answered quickly, "I don't know about you but I'm going to try to get a little shut eye."

He unzipped his bag and I said, "You're kidding?"

"You do what you want. These bags are brand new. They're water proof and dry inside. We have no ponchos. Well, if you want to sleep on the ground, good luck finding a dry puddle." As he crawled into his body bag, I stood there contemplating my options. The trucks had departed. It was just the two of us and a field with rows of dead bodies.

I questioned him, "Well lieutenant, don't you think one of us should be on guard duty?" He looked up at me from inside his bag. "Do you think someone is going to steal bodies? I don't think they are going anywhere on their own." I agreed with his logic and unzipped my bag.

Before I zipped up, I asked one final question, "What are we going to do? The sun will be up in less than an hour. When they come around to relieve us, what are they going to think when we crawl out of these body bags?"

His response defied argument. "They'll think it's a Christmas miracle".

I tried to sleep but couldn't. The inside of the bag had an antiseptic smell and the thought of being in a body bag gave me the 'willies'. About 50 minutes later we heard voices yelling, "Hey, who's guarding these bodies?" Together Mac and I sat up and unzipped our bags. Standing in front of us were 3 Airmen, all with their mouths wide open and their eyes looking like ping pong balls. One was an Air Force lieutenant. The other two were enlisted men.

As we climbed out of the zippered bags, Mac spoke first, "That would be us, sir."

We stood at attention and saluted the lieutenant. The airmen all followed suit, still thinking Mac was also a lieutenant. Then the real lieutenant spoke,

"Well, you are officially relieved. The Air Force will be taking over from here on."

Almost immediately we heard trucks approaching and the voices of the rest of our platoon coming. As the Air Force lieutenant began to give orders, Mac quietly took off his helmet, placed it under his armpit and wiped his forehead. While no one was looking he took off the can opener. As Mac stood there with the helmet still under his arm, the Air Force lieutenant walked back toward us. I thought, *'Oh boy, here it comes'.* The only thing the lieutenant said to Mac was, "You really shouldn't sleep in those body bags. It's bad for my men's morale."

Mac's only reply, "Well, at least we were dry for a few minutes." The lieutenant walked away as I gave a sigh of relief.

We soon boarded the trucks and headed out. Instead of going to 'chow' for a hot breakfast the trucks began dropping us off 'on the line'. For us it was Christmas, but it was also our day of 24 hours on the line. As they dropped us off we were each given two boxes of 'C-rations' and walked towards our bunkers. It was still raining off and on as it had been for several weeks now. The bunkers were built on top of what was once a fox hole. Now after weeks of rain the water had seeped down through the bags and between the wood and dripped on our heads like 'Chinese water torture'. Water had also seeped in from the sides, so the old fox hole was now filled with water. By October the water was ankle deep. By November it was knee deep and now in December the water level came up to just below our waist. Therefore, we never went into the bunker unless we were under attack. And we were never under attack. In front of each bunker were 25 feet of landmines that stretched completely around the base. So, we stood guard duty outside. We did everything outside. Two to a bunker, while one was on duty the other could sleep. As we used to say, "If you could find a dry puddle, you could try to sleep."

I ate my Christmas dinner of C-rations as rain water dripped off my helmet into the can. All that day and night we listened to Christmas music on Armed Forces Radio. Even today I can't listen to Bing Crosby sing 'White Christmas' or Perry Como sing and 'I'll be home for Christmas', without feeling like I'm being thrust back in time to that Christmas in the rain. The next time you hear either one of those songs just close your eyes and listen closely to the words. As you listen, picture a lonely G.I. in a fox hole. Perhaps it's a paratrooper in Bastogne or a Marine on some South Pacific Island, or in Korea on the Chosin Reservoir. You must imagine that they have not had a shower or change of clothes in weeks. They probably can't remember their last hot meal and who knows when they had mail from home. Listen to the words to those songs carefully. And remember some Soldier is listening to those words as he hunkers down behind a berm in Iraq or a Marine hiding behind some rubble in Afghanistan. Those men are thousands of miles from home and just as lonely as I was. I'm not talking about the guys in some barracks or base far from the front. I'm not talking about the guys and officers back in the rear with the gear and the beer. Picture the 'grunt' in the fox hole. I suppose guys like me and other grunts may be the only ones who can truly appreciate Christmas at home.

No, I don't feel sorry for myself. Actually, I feel lucky to have experienced that Christmas. It allows me to really appreciate the Christmases I have experienced since that horrible one in 1966.

The other day at work I rode up on an elevator with two women. It was three days before Christmas. I overheard the following conversation. One said, "I hear they're calling for rain on Christmas".

The other lady added, "Oh, I hate it when it rains at Christmas. It's so depressing."

I chimed in, "Yeah, but at least we don't have to pick up any dead bodies." The two women looked at me like I had two heads.

When I got off at my floor I heard one lady say, "What's the matter with him?" I just smiled to myself and continued, on my way.

I remember what Mac said. "This is as bad as it will ever get." I know that no matter how bad Christmas gets, there is no way I can ever get too depressed. It will never be as bad as that Christmas in the rain.

CHAPTER 24

NEW GUY IN THE GRUNTS

MOST PEOPLE, I'm sure have experienced being the new guy at one time or another. We change jobs, move to new neighborhoods, get transferred to different departments or in my case, transferred to a different school. Sometimes we are met with open arms but usually we're met with skepticism. At the inter city school where I taught, each year we would get several new teachers fresh out of college with their heads filled with hopes and dreams. By Christmas, if they made it to Christmas, most teachers developed a whole new attitude. I remember one young, new female teacher who brought a guitar to school the first day of classes, so she could sing 'Getting to Know You' from the musical The King and I. She spent that first afternoon in the Principal's office crying her eyes out because she wanted to quit. No matter how much knowledge we have, the new guy always has a lot to learn.

The night before we left for the grunts, Mac, Carden and I had a short conversation with a former grunt. As guys were pulled from the M.P.'s to go to the grunts, we usually got replacements right off the plane. Some were draftees, and some were enlistees, but all were boots with no experience. However, there was one guy who had been in the grunts and had been wounded. After getting out of the hospital he was sent to our M.P. Company. The night before we left for the grunts we asked this guy to step outside and give the three of us some advice about this next phase. I don't remember his name because I only saw him that one day. After he asked how much time we had left in our tour, he paused to think. His answer would haunt me to this day.

"Well, one of you will probably get killed, one of you will be wounded, and one of you should be okay". His other advice was, "Stay low!" After he returned to his tent, the three of us looked at each other and wondered. And then wondered some more.

The next morning Mac, Carden and I boarded a truck with guys from the other M.P. companies. The truck headed south. We drove for well over an hour and arrived at the base camp for the 5th Marine Regiment. We were told, "Welcome to Chu Lai." (pronounced 'Lie') Carden and I were assigned to 'K' company. Mac went to 'L' company. Carden was put in first platoon and I went to the second. I would see a lot more of Carden than my good friend Mac.

I walked into a squad tent and was met with looks ranging from disgust to skepticism. I wore the uniform of a 'non-combatant puke'. Everyone else wore jungle utilities and jungle boots. Even though I was a lance corporal and had been in country for seven months these guys couldn't tell if I just stepped off a plane from Okinawa or if I had just been court-martialed and sent to them from a supply hut. I was not one of them.

The squad leader was Corporal Dunkin. He introduced himself and asked, "How short are you?" Short was the expression used for how long you had to go in country before you returned to the 'World'. He was surprised when I replied, "Five months to go." I was surprised when he said, "I got one month." Therefore, second squad would need a new squad leader. I looked around and there were several PFC's and lance corporals, but Dunkin was the only corporal.

One guy did most of the talking, ain't it always that way? His name was Benson (not his real name). He was your typical 'know it all', which is what I called him. He gave me no advice but handed it out to everyone else like a senior student imparting knowledge to freshmen. He had some college experience but dropped out and then got drafted. I had met lots of draftees in the M.P.'s. Some were very 'gung ho' or at least they pretended to be. Benson looked at me with suspicion. He wanted everyone to know how smart and experienced he was.

Corporal Dunkin assigned me to a fire team with two black guys. One was named McCray. His first name was Myers. I only remember it because his first name was so unusual. The other guy was named Wilson. They were the only two 'splibs' (a term used by blacks to distinguish themselves from 'chucks' or white guys). McCray was a southerner from Florida and Wilson was a big city northerner. They couldn't be more different but because they were of the same race they were inseparable.

There were two Spanish guys named Martinez and Gonzales. They seemed to be the friendliest because like me they were new. Another guy, Walker, was from California. He was big, with a baby face which made him look very young.

The last guy was six-foot five and weighed about 140 pounds. He was a long, tall, drink of water. The other guys teased him by saying, "Hey, Drucker, turn and face me so I can see you. When you stand sideways, you kind of disappear."

Drucker would answer by saying, "You laugh now but when the gooks start shooting at us, you better believe I'll be standing sideways." The 'D' wingers are everywhere in life.

I was the ninth guy in this squad. Usually a full squad would have twelve men or more. I would soon find out that the grunts were always shorthanded.

The next day Carden grabbed me and said, "Come on. We're going to get new clothes."

It had never occurred to stupid me because we were now in the grunts all we had to do was ask for jungle utilities. We went to the supply tent, which was guarded to prevent marines from stealing supplies, I guess. Without any questions, we received two pair of jungle boots, two new sets of jungle utilities and trousers. The clothes weren't camouflaged like some I had seen. However, they were a lighter color green and a much lighter weight. Now at least we looked like grunts.

The 5th Marine base was far different from the M.P.'s. The camp was in a hilly area and spread out over many acres. None of the squad tents were in a row. Dirt roads weaved their way up and down and around hills. No zipper trenches could be seen. Extra large holes with sandbags piled around them were strategically located, to jump into in case of a mortar attack. A set of tents for a mess hall were located near the center of the camp. There were also tents with hot showers nearby. Of course, they had a sick bay, the supply tent, and as we found out later, a large ammo dump built partially underground. Everything seemed to be randomly placed and nothing was in a straight line. My old 'D' company first sergeant would have had a nervous breakdown just looking at the layout of the camp! At the foot of one of the large hills was a stage with a giant movie screen just like we had at Camp Lejeune. To my surprise, we got to see the 'Gold Diggers' that Saturday night. At first, I thought; This base may not be as bad as I thought! The problem was we would only be there a very short time.

The grunts had work details like the M.P.'s. But the work in the grunts was necessary. I unloaded trucks full of needed supplies. I filled sand bags, but they were to replace old torn or leaking bags. We never had to flip sand bags, so the grass wouldn't grow. The grunts didn't have 'make work' details just to keep guys busy. We had more free time to hang around our tent.

At night we had guard duty on the perimeter. They didn't have French-built concrete bunkers, just good, old, fashioned fox holes with sand bags piled around them. Instead of two men to a hole, the grunts at this base camp had three to a hole, which allowed us a little more sleep. I was assigned fire team leader and put in charge of McCray and Wilson. They were not pleased. I don't think they were racist or prejudiced, but they assumed that I was. Their opinion would eventually change over time as I earned their respect.

The night after we were issued our new uniforms, a fire mysteriously started in the ammo bunkers. The fireworks show was spectacular and lasted most of the night. Carden and I watched in total wonderment. To our surprise most of the grunts looked at it as if it was nothing and happened often. I guess they were used to explosives going off.

James M. Dixon

Chapter 25

POW'S, MIA'S AND KIA'S

I SUPPOSE most have seen the POW and MIA flags flying from flag-poles everywhere. They are especially prevalent around Memorial Day and Veterans Day. POW of course stands for 'prisoner of war'. Most of the American Viet Nam prisoners were pilots who had the misfortune of being shot down over North Vietnam. But there were a handful of infantrymen who were captured. Infantrymen were not considered high value prisoners. They were mistreated even more than pilots, who were all officers. All of us who are old enough, remember when the Viet Nam POW's were finally sent home in the 1970's to a hero's welcome.

To this day there are many unaccounted-for MIA's 'missing in action' from all wars. Many times, in past wars men were missing because of desertion. During the American Revolution and the Civil War, soldiers would desert and simply go home. No one ever deserted in Viet Nam. If you were MIA, it was because you were truly missing in action.

In the second Rambo movie Sylvester Stallone (Rambo) was supposed to go back to Viet Nam to search for and rescue some prisoners of war. It was a fun action movie but like most Hollywood movies, should never be confused with reality. I was working part time in a department store when the movie opened. A guy in the shoe department, who was well educated and reasonably intelligent, made a comment about the movie. "You know we should go back over there and bring all those MIA's back." The statement struck me as odd.

"What are you talking about?" I asked.

His next statement nearly knocked me over. "Well you know all those MIA's are really POW's and are still over there, working as slave labor."

Still dumb founded, I could only reply, "What?"

"You should know the Communists are keeping those guys in prisons, because they might need them as bargaining chips someday."

I nearly lost it.

"No, I don't know any such thing. Viet Nam is one of the poorest countries in the world. They have all the slave labor they want. It wouldn't make sense to pay two men to guard a prisoner and watch him work. They would send the prisoner home and have the two guards do twice the work. The war has been over for 20 years, what kind of 'bargaining chip' are they waiting for? Besides, the communist country of Vietnam wants American tourists to come over and spend their American dollars."

No, there are no MIA's still in Vietnam sitting around in a prisoner of war camp and working in a rice paddy. The MIA's are truly missing.

After five easy days at the 5th Marine base camp, the first and second platoons of 'K', aka, 'Kilo' Company were told to get ready for a patrol. I had been on many patrols while in the M.P.s. We ran four-man patrols during the day and six-man patrols at night, usually lasting two to four hours. But this time I would have to prepare for something all together different. No one told us how long we'd be out on patrol. We could be gone for days, weeks or a month or more.

We were each given two C-ration boxes and if we would be gone for more than one day we would have to be resupplied. I watched the other guys and followed their lead. We tore open the C-rations, threw away the box and stuffed cans into extra socks. Socks wrapped around cans of rations prevented noise. A knapsack filled with loose cans made way too much noise when moving. Some personal items like soap, a tooth brush and a small tube of toothpaste were also rolled into socks. Our poncho was folded into a square, laid flat in the knapsack and placed to fit against our back. There was no room for extra boots and utilities, meaning the same trousers and shirt would be worn for the duration of whatever we were doing.

After the knapsack was packed we prepared our cartridge belt. We carried the required 120 rounds in six ammo magazines. If more ammo was needed, then it was issued. We each picked two grenades out of a box and attached them to the shoulder harness that held up our cartridge belt. The cartridge belt also held two canteens, a first aid kit and our bayonet.

We filled our two canteens at the water buffalo. The water tasted terrible and we needed to add an iodine tablet, so we didn't get diarrhea, which we called the "screaming shits". You can imagine what the iodine tablets made the water taste like. We packed as many pre-sweetened kool aid packs as we could get our hands on. Kool aid packs were worth their weight in gold.

Every other man got a fifty-round belt of machine gun ammo to carry. The other guy received one mortar round. With our flak jacket, helmet, pack, and cartridge belt with two canteens, we were each carrying at least forty pounds of gear. Adding the extra machine gun or mortars added way over forty pounds. No wonder the other service branches called us, 'ammo humpers'.

The patrols while in the MP's were nothing like this one. This was two full platoons plus an interpreter, several corpsmen, a couple of scout dogs and their handlers, plus a two-man team of artillery spotters with their own radio. This patrol was led by a lieutenant who I had not had the privilege of meeting. In all there were more than 80 of us. 1st platoon was in the lead, and no one in 2nd platoon complained. We walked single file, eight paces apart and weaved along like a giant serpent going up and down small hills, heading into the jungle.

The weather during the five days I spent at the base camp was always cloudy, but it hardly rained at all. I was beginning to think the worst of the monsoon season was past. Boy was I wrong! The day we left on patrol the cloudy weather continued, but the weather changed that night. It began raining and continued raining harder each day. At night it was so wet, and the ground was so rocky and overgrown with trees, that digging fox holes was totally impractical. Each night we set up a perimeter but used trees and rocks for cover and concealment. The expression, "Find a dry puddle to sleep in", was used constantly. If you can picture the worst cloud burst of a thunder storm, try to picture that amount of rain for three or four days in a row. That's what we faced.

One-night McCray, Wilson and I snapped our three ponchos together to form one large cover to put over us. It didn't help much to keep us dry, but we couldn't help but become friends when sleeping elbow to elbow. We were lying in two inches of water and the rain was beating on top of our ponchos so loud that we could barely hear ourselves think. They were starting to accept me as a grunt.

Each day, the platoons rotated position, so neither platoon was always in the lead and therefore in the most danger of an ambush or a booby trap. Also, each day the squads within the platoon rotated. When 'baby face' Walker explained the procedure, I knew sooner or later I would be the point man. Everyone dreaded being on point because it was so dangerous. I guess Walker could see the concern on my face and explained further, "We're lucky. We have Weeocky. He's our platoon point man. He's an Indian and the best point man I've ever seen." It turned out to be true. It seemed every other day when 2nd platoon was in the lead, Lance Corporal Weeocky volunteered for point. One day he found a land mine planted in the middle of the trail. At first, he spotted suspicious foot prints and stopped the whole patrol as he crawled around and located the mine. He carefully pulled the pin of a grenade and placed it next to the mine with a flat rock on top, so the handle stayed in-tack. He had attached a string to the end of the grenade then slowly walked away from the mine to a safe place. With the other end of the string he gave a gentle tug, which released the handle. Seconds later the grenade and mine both exploded. Yes, we were lucky to have Weeocky.

Of course, we worried about land mines, booby traps and ambushes. However, our biggest problem was food. We left the base camp with only two boxes of 'C' rations each. Therefore, every day we had to be resupplied by helicopter. We had to find a clearing or a rice paddy, so the choppers could land or drop off cases of food. Some days we found a spot for the choppers and some days we didn't, meaning some days we went hungry. We ate what we could find which is known as 'living off the land'. Raw peanuts were plentiful. We also picked green bananas and carried them hoping they would ripen. Eventually several of us tried eating a green one. It sucked all the moisture out of our mouths. It took me an hour before I was able to make my own spit and swallow again.

I later learned that this so-called patrol was really a 'search and destroy' mission. We were supposed to walk around and find the Viet Cong or evidence of them. We would go into villages where people had been ordered to leave and relocate in safer areas. Pamphlets had been dropped warning villagers to leave. We came across one village that was completely deserted. We searched the entire area and found nothing of importance. In a second village we could tell the residents had left minutes before we arrived. Campfires were still burning, chickens still running around, and wet clothing still hung from lines around their huts. We searched and found communist propaganda pamphlets written in

Vietnamese. We found no weapons but did find ammunition and some Viet Cong equipment. The company first sergeant and others warned us not to try and pick up any souvenirs, because they might be booby trapped. It was obvious to everyone that this village was being used by the V.C., our enemy. We were ordered to burn it to the ground. I stood there looking and wondering, *what if the people in this village were being forced to help the V.C.?*

The platoon sergeant looked at me and said, "Burn it!"

I didn't smoke and therefore replied, "I don't have a lighter."

He tossed me his. I got to work setting fire to the grass roof of a hooch. After we began walking out on to the trail I tried handing the lighter back to the sergeant. He said, "Keep it. You'll be needing it again." The lighter was one of the cheap Bic's sold in the P.X. On one side of the lighter was the Marine Corps emblem with the globe, anchor and eagle. On the other side were inscribed the words, 'When I die, send me to heaven, because I've spent my time in hell.'

When I finally got home I gave that lighter to my Mom as a souvenir. When she passed over my brothers and I cleaned out her house. I was hoping to find that lighter. Today those lighters are valuable as collector items.

On the morning of the fifth day we were walking along a trail in the jungle. It had finally stopped raining. I think the sun was out but in a thick canopy covered jungle we really couldn't see much sun. I was in the middle of the second platoon, in the middle of our squad. Suddenly an explosion rocked us. We didn't hit the deck as much as we were thrown to the ground. I had no idea what had just happened except there had been a big explosion. I knew the gooks didn't have artillery and we could always hear mortar rounds when they were launched. Then Lance Corporal 'Knowitall' said, "Somebody stepped on something!"

It was true. The point man had stepped over a land mine without setting it off. The second man, eight steps behind him had also stepped near but not on the device. The third man had stepped on it and instantly blown himself up. The explosion killed the man in front of him and the man directly behind him. The point man was wounded along with the fifth and sixth man in the column. Corpsmen were called, first aid administered, and evacuation helicopters were called. Guys scrambled to carry the wounded back to a small clearing where choppers could land. The bomb had killed three and wounded three others. From then on no one had to remind me to stay at least eight steps behind the man in front of me.

When the first chopper arrived, the three wounded men were placed on board, and three body bags tossed out. When the second chopper flew in we only put two Marines in body bags with their dog tag in each of their mouths. We couldn't find the guy who stepped on the bomb. I was part of the search party who went looking for his remains. There was a huge hole in the ceiling of the jungle where the explosion had ripped open the foliage, allowing plenty of sunshine in. I wondered what kind of bomb he had stepped on. Some guys surmised that it was an unexploded 500-pound bomb that the V.C. found and wired to detonate when someone stepped on it.

Our platoon spread out over the whole area and looked for any sign of the poor guy who triggered the explosion. At first, we looked on the ground. Finding nothing we began looking in the trees. I thought for sure we would find his helmet or parts of his flak jacket, but we found nothing. Olive drab uniforms were colored that way for a reason. We searched for an hour, and then had to move on.

To this day I don't know that Marine's name, nor can I even picture what he looked like. His parents would receive a form letter from the Marines, saying ... "We regret to inform you ..."

In 1966 all the form letters read the same. If someone was wounded parents or next of kin received a letter saying ... "We regret to inform you that (fill in the blank) has been wounded fighting against communist insurgents in South East Asia" ... blah, blah, blah. If someone was killed the letter began ... "We deeply regret" ... They were very impersonal but more appropriate, if that's possible, than the Western Union telegrams people received in World War II, Korea and the beginning of Viet Nam. Just the sight of the telegraph delivery man sent chills down parents' spines. After 1965, letters were hand delivered by volunteers from the local National Guard and usually accompanied by a church representative. If a Soldier or Marine were missing in action (MIA), the letter stated such. In the case of the guy who stepped on the bomb, they added the words... "...and presumed dead." I can think of nothing more unsettling to a mother or father than those words. The never knowing for sure must wear on a person's soul like an unforgiven sin.

I only know the poor guy who stepped on that bomb was never found. I have often wished I could have informed his parents that he was indeed, killed in action (KIA) and not MIA.

Chapter 26

MONSOONS

I HARDLY EVER carry or use an umbrella. Maybe if I'm with my wife and she is dressed up I'll carry one in case she needs it. In the 50 years since leaving Viet Nam I have never felt it was rainy enough for an umbrella. Now don't get me wrong. Here in south central Pennsylvania we get our share of rain. We've had floods and terrible rain storms. We've had two tornadoes damage our house. If you look around Lancaster County, where I live today, you will see signs marking the incredible flood heights left by Hurricane Agnes in 1972. Those signs show a flood of near Biblical proportions. I sometimes wear a rain coat or a jacket, and maybe a hat but I have never felt I needed an umbrella. None were used in Viet Nam and I've never seen it rain in Pennsylvania like it rained over there.

After that first search and destroy mission we were picked up in trucks and driven to a new location. The new base camp was just for our 'K'

(Kilo) Company and a few support troops. Obviously, this camp was much smaller. The whole area was marked with dozens of bunkers and foxholes. There were tents for a mess hall and a tent for hot showers. Of course, it had the typical tent for officers and tents for all three platoons. However, our platoon was only there for two days and then we left. We were able to get one hot shower and a couple of hot meals and then we boarded trucks again.

We drove about one mile as the crow flies or one and a half miles around a narrow winding road heading up into the hills. We were not really in a jungle any more, just wooded rough terrain. This wasn't rice paddy land because it was too hilly. No rice paddies meant no farmers and therefore little or no population. We were out in the middle of nowhere, just us and the V.C.

Our platoon passed a narrow trail which was just wide enough to walk on but too narrow for a jeep. This trail circled its way up a very steep hill that overlooked the entire area. From that vantage point we could see for miles, if it wasn't raining. We drove past that hill for about another half mile where our truck stopped at the foot of a second hill, to let us off. Once again, a narrow trail led to the top of this rocky mound. We unloaded and started walking up as another platoon, passed us walking down the same path. They were leaving the area and they looked exhausted and beaten. The top of the hill was rather flat with only bunkers breaking up the landscape. The other platoon had not 'policed up' the area so it looked like a pigsty. 'C' ration cans, boxes and other garbage were scattered everywhere. We were assigned bunkers and foxholes around the perimeter. After dropping off our gear we began policing up the entire rocky top of that hill.

No one told us why we were there, and no one asked. It was clear to anyone with half a brain that this was an outpost meaning the military higher ups could now point to a map and say we control this area. The terrain of the hill top and surrounding area made it a strategically excellent location to defend. The steepness of the hillside was more like the side of a cliff than the side of a hill. Enemy V.C. coming up any of the four sides would have to climb rather than walk. The top of the hill was rather flat and rocky, which made placement of bunkers and foxholes ideal for defense. Several rows of circular, concertina barbed wire encircled the entire outer rim of our perimeter. This barbed wire would ensnare anyone trying to sneak up to the hill top. Chemicals had been sprayed on the sides of the hill to kill the vegetation and allow for a clear field of fire. One rifle platoon of Marines with machine guns and mortars could hold off hundreds of Viet Cong, unless they had artillery, which they didn't. The mortars and rockets they had were our only real danger.

The day we arrived it began drizzling. Then the rain steadily increased. It would rain steadily for four or five days then stop for a day. Then rain for five or six days and then stop for two days. On the few days it didn't rain the sun never showed its face, so nothing really had a chance to dry out. This was the dreaded monsoon season that we heard so much about. We spent forty days on that God-forsaken hill. It rained 35 of the 40 days. Five more days and we could have tied Noah's record! It was impossible to keep our rifles dry, so we re-oiled them frequently to at least keep them from rusting.

The top of the hill was not labeled on any map. We nicknamed it Rocky Top, which had nothing to do with the University of Tennessee fight song. I suppose each new platoon that had the misfortune of holding that hill top gave it a different name. We just happened to be the unfortunate ones who held it during the height of the monsoons.

We fell into a boring routine of: work, guard duty and patrols all accomplished outside in the soaking rain. Each morning a single truck would drive up the road to the bottom of the hill. One of the three squads in second platoon would walk down and unload supplies, mostly 'C' rations. Then those same guys would climb into the truck and drive the mile and a half back to the company base camp for a hot meal. The other two squads still on the hill ate 'C' rations in the rain. In the late afternoon the procedure was repeated for one of the other squads. The next morning the third squad would rotate for a hot meal. However, many days it rained so hard the road was washed out and the truck could not come. That meant no mail and no more 'C' rations. Usually once a week on Saturday or Sunday, we were allowed showers at Kilo base camp, after morning or evening chow.

Everything was done in the rain. Try taking a crap outside in the pouring rain. Toilet paper, or 'shit paper' as it was referred to, would instantly become a soggy mess. But it didn't really matter because all we had to do was wipe our ass with your fingers and then hold our hand out and the rain would wash it off in a few minutes. The soggy shit paper was good for cleaning under your finger nails. The constant rain also made heating 'C' rations with a 'heat tab' (a small, compressed, trioxane tablet about the size of quarter, which when lit would burn at a high temperature for about 15 or 20 minutes) difficult or impossible to light. Many times, we consumed the food unheated.

The C-rations came in a cardboard case with 12 small boxes of rations. Most were packaged in 1944 or 1945. We used to joke that the only reason we were fighting this war was, so we could use up all the left-over C-rations from World War II! I guess the two and a half years in Korea wasn't a long enough war. Each case contained four different meals with one soup-size can of the following:

TURKEY WITH DUMPLINGS

BEANS AND WIENERS

BEEFSTEAK, POTATOES AND GRAVY

(The dreaded) HAM AND LIMA BEANS (always referred to as Ham and Mother Fuckers).

I even heard a lieutenant colonel call them ham and mother fuckers. The name comes from the fact that the ham was over cooked and dry, and the lima beans were not cooked enough and therefore very dry and hard. At first some guys would throw the cans away rather than try to eat them. If we were hungry enough we simply gagged them down. Necessity being the mother of invention, someone came up with a recipe to improve them, which I'll explain soon.

Each box also contained an accessory pack: a plastic spoon, salt and pepper, instant coffee, sugar, non-dairy creamer, gum (two Chicklets), a small box of 4 cigarettes, and a small roll of toilet paper. We also received two small cans of the following:

CRACKERS AND CHEESE OR PEANUT BUTTER CRACKERS

FRUIT CAKE, POUND CAKE, OR PECAN CAKE

A CANDY DISC OF SOLID CHOCOLATE

COCOA BEVERAGE POWER

A third small can contained fruit: applesauce, fruit cocktail, peaches or pears, which all sounds kind of yummy! The cans of fruit were very tasteless. Four choices for 40 days got old real fast.

Each box of C-rations was supposed to provide 1,200 calories so three meals would equal 3,600 calories per day. Two problems arose. First, we only received two meals each day. The critical name of the meals was 'ration', as in rationed out. We never knew when the truck would not be able to come, and we would be short on meals. God forbid they issued too many meals. The second problem was that work parties, going on patrol and standing guard duty at night burned up lots of calories; much more than the 2,400 we were issued. We were always hungry, and I lost about ten pounds, and I was already skinny to begin with. Later, when we went on operations and ate only C-rations for 30 straight days I lost even more weight.

One good thing about eating all those C-rations, we became experts at trading and cooking them. One day a guy who had been in the grunts for six months asked me if I wanted to trade meals. I said,

"Sure, but I got ham and motherfuckers!" He shocked me when he said,

"Yeah, I know, I like ham and motherfuckers." I thought he must either be joking, or he lost his mind. I made the trade.

He set to work and instructed me, "Here, let me show you something." He bent one of the old empty small c-ration cans that were laying everywhere. By bending the small can you could set the main can on top of the small can to heat the bigger can. He placed a heat tab in the bottom of the small can and lit it. I had done this myself hundreds of times. He took his C-ration opener and cut three fourths of the lid off the main can of ham and motherfuckers. After flipping the lid partially off he bent the lid to form a handle. Again, I had done the same thing hundreds of times myself. In the drizzling rain he placed his helmet minus the liner over the burning flame and propped it up with a small stick. This prevented rain from putting out the fire. Soon the contents began to warm. He pulled the can out and stirred it several times.

None of this was a mystery. I asked, "So, what are you going to show me?"

"This," was his answer. He then took out another small can that contained cheese and crackers. He scooped the cheese out and into the ham and motherfuckers. He cooked the contents a good long time. The cheese melted, and the ham soaked up some of it. The lima beans heated until they were cooked, and they too soaked up some of the cheese sauce. Finally, he began to eat. He gave me a taste. Damn that was much better! Ham and mother fuckers became a tolerable meal.

During the 40 days on top of those rocks we ran lots of patrols and set up ambushes. One day we got a new guy in our squad. He had been in country for about three months and had somehow screwed up bad enough that he was sent to the grunts. He had been in the Marine Corps for one year still an E-1 private, not a private first class. Private Meatball (obviously not his real name) was a complete shit bird. He was five foot-two and weighed 200 pounds. He was a splib, round and brown. I doubted he could even do a push-up.

Our squad was sent on a patrol over night to set up an ambush. We were to walk about 15 miles up and down and around another hill, set up the ambush at night and then return to our hill the next day. Staying awake all night waiting to ambush some Viet Cong, then walking 15 miles back the next day, was tough on anybody. For Meatball it was impossible.

During this patrol Meatball became a huge embarrassment to everyone. He simply could not keep up. He complained he couldn't breathe, because he had asthma. He kept falling further and further behind. Several of us, had to carry his gear.

McCray and Wilson refused to help him. McCray told him, "You are an embarrassment to the black man."

Wilson asked, "How in the world did you get through boot camp?"

I asked him, "Why did you even join the Marine Corps?"

He replied, "I didn't. I got drafted!"

Ever since I teamed up with McCray and Wilson, the other two black guys in our squad, all I heard from them was how superior the black man was to the white man. How the black man had a deeper voice, a bigger dick, was a better athlete and if they had swimming pools in the ghetto they would win gold medals for swimming. On and on they went, trying to convince me not to be racist. Me, a Quaker, who were the original equality pushers, and the original abolitionists. I just said, "Yeah, Yeah, Yeah!"

Because of Private Meatball, we were late setting up the ambush, which was unsuccessful, and very late returning to Rocky Top. The sergeant, McCray and Lance Corporal Knowitall went to the platoon sergeant to complain about Private Meatball. Two things resulted from that patrol. Meatball was transferred again. Rumor had it that he was given a discharge for 'physically unable to perform'. That was good for him and us. Sooner or later he would have gotten someone killed. The second good thing was I never heard another word about the superiority of black men.

Two other patrols, which we carried out during the monsoons, stood out in my memory. One night it was pouring rain so hard that you couldn't see more than a few feet in front of your face. We were ordered to go out in the dark and set up a typical ambush. There were six of us. A two-man machine gun crew would aim the M-60 down a trail and four of us would hide along the side of the road and hope some Gooks would come along to maybe set up a booby trap or try to launch mortars. We could then blow them away. The problem was it was raining so hard, no respectable Viet Cong in his right mind would be out on a night like this. They were all at home in their nice warm hooch, sleeping high and dry and laughing at the Marines standing outside in the pouring rain. The corporal in charge knew this as well as we did.

At the foot of our hill stood an old abandoned hooch that was probably used by the Gooks in good weather to sell stuff or do laundry for the Marines up on the hill. The corporal suggested that instead of going on this stupid patrol that we go into the hooch for six hours, to sleep and dry out. We all agreed and swore to keep it a secret. Otherwise if somebody found out we would all be court-martialed. I remember what McDonald told me on Christmas Eve, 'What are they going to do to me? Cut my hair off, send me to the grunts, and make me stand out in the rain for days?' We stayed dry that one night and I got the best night's sleep I had in weeks.

The other patrol involved the wettest I have ever been. Eight of us were picked to walk a wide circle around Rocky Top. We would be gone for three days. Our goal was to walk along a small stream, now a fast, moving river which ran down between several hills. It was believed the Gooks might try to cross the river and attack our hill or the company base. We would follow that stream and eventually make our way back to our hill. It really poured hard those three days and we literally walked in foot deep water most of the time. We found no sign of any place the gooks or the NVA (North Vietnamese 'regular' Army) could cross.

When we finally returned to Rocky Top we had missed the evening chow truck and had to eat C-rations for the umpteenth time but that wasn't the worst part. I went into our squad bunker where we kept some of our gear and clothes, in an attempt to keep them dry. As I took off my soaking boots and socks to change, I noticed something scary. Have you ever been swimming all day and when you finally come out of the water, you notice the skin of your finger tips, are all pink and wrinkled? Some people call it pruning! Have you ever imagined what those fingers would look like after several days or weeks in the water? Your feet will do the same thing. My feet had been in foot-deep water for most of two weeks.

My foot was hideous looking. It was as white as a sheet of typing paper with pink wrinkles of extra skin. The dark tough pad of skin that protects the bottom of the foot and covers the heel and toes had moved from under the heel bone. That skin was supposed to be under my heel but was now up near my ankle bone. I slowly tried to dry the skin and massage the pads of the heel and toe all the way back so that they were again under my heel and toes. I did the same with my left foot which was not quite as bad. I then put on dry socks and my second pair of dry boots. I carefully placed the wet socks and boots on a wooden shelf and hoped they would dry in a few days. Then I walked outside in the pouring rain and hopped down into the fox hole which had a foot of standing water already in it. This is where I would stand guard duty half of the night and then sleep on the other side of the sand bags the other half. I had not received any mail, had not had a hot meal in days and had not been dry in weeks.

I remember that night every time I get caught in a rain storm. The acting platoon sergeant came over to my hole where I was standing in a foot of water and asked if I wanted to extend my tour of duty for another six months. There I was standing in over a foot of water, in the pouring rain. He squatted down next to the hole and waited for my answer. I just stared at him and said nothing. I don't know if I was in shock or if I simply couldn't think of an appropriate smart-ass response. I just stared at him.

After what seemed like two minutes he continued, "I have to ask, and then I have to record your answer. Down at head quarters they want to keep a record." I continued to stare at him, saying nothing.

Then he stood up and said, "I'll put you down as a no."

As he walked away I finally thought of what I should have said. 'You have got to be fucking shitting me!"

James M. Dixon

Chapter 27

THE DRUDGERY OF ANY WAR

MANY A YOUNG BOY have wanted to become a fireman, policeman, cowboy or soldier when they grow up. Children play cops and robbers, cowboys and Indians and army because they believe those are exciting jobs. However, those jobs can be as full of daily drudgery and boredom as any other occupation. Any police officer will tell you that for every police chase and arrest, there are hundreds of hours of paper work and endless days of uneventful and boring patrolling. But as kids we all still play those games because we don't realize the truth which is those jobs can be dangerous, yet boring.

The same is true for any war. On Monday, December 8, 1941 my father joined the army. He was gone for nearly four years. He was never in actual combat. He worked loading and unloading photo reconnaissance cameras for the Army Air Corps. He spent a year and a half in the North

African desert. Up to the day he died he still hated going to the seashore because the sand reminded him of the desert. So even though he was not in combat, the war still left bad memories.

In World War II the average infantryman was in actual combat for 40 days during the four years of the war. In Viet Nam the average infantryman was in combat 240 days during a 13-month tour of duty. The reasons were simple. Helicopters improved transportation. Marines in the South Pacific waited weeks and months before 'island hopping' to the next slaughter beach. We didn't invade Normandy until the last year of the European campaign. Soldiers trained for years before the invasion. In between battles G.I.'s went through the drudgery of war.

We went through the same drudgery in Viet Nam. On that rocky hill top, in the rain, we still had work parties. They weren't 'make work' parties, the work was all necessary. Sand bags still had to be replaced. Only now instead of sand, the bags were filled with mud. Mud had to be shoveled out of fox holes. We tried to devise different methods of draining the water out of the holes, but nothing worked. Shit holes and piss holes still had to be filled and new ones dug.

Toward the end of February and the beginning of March 1967 the Monsoons came less frequently. The sun came out occasionally. When it wasn't raining we tried to improve our communication with Kilo Company base camp. We had only a battery-operated radio with an eight-foot antenna. When the weather was too rainy, or the battery went low we had no communications. At some point the engineers set a telephone pole on top of our hill and another one on the next nearest hill heading back toward the base. There was no phone wire connecting the poles. Either the engineers never ran the wire, or the gooks found a way to cut it before we arrived. If we could run a phone wire between the two poles, then we could use the crank powered phones like we had at DaNang.

One day in March the sun came out and I was selected to help run a wire to the next hill. The task had many problems. The biggest was the steepness of our hill. We couldn't walk down the side of the hill we had to practically climb down. After the first 50 feet, the dense vegetation took over. We would have to cut a path through the jungle which would take forever. Several ideas were bantered about by the lieutenant, staff sergeant and squad leaders. They thought about firing a mortar shell with the end of the wire attached, over to the other hill top. No one could figure out how to attach the wire and still fire the mortar. The staff sergeant said if we had an M-7 rifle grenade attachment like they used in Korea it would be easy. Those attachments could fire a fragmentation (pineapple) grenade just by putting it on the end of a rifle and placing the grenade on the attachment. They worked but were terribly inaccurate. Trouble was we didn't use them now. Our units were issued the M-79 grenade launchers, which used a special 40mm shell loaded into a shotgun-style weapon and fired from the shoulder. They were much more accurate but attaching a wire was impossible.

The only workable solution was to climb down the embankment, cut as much brush away and try to toss the wire over the top of the rest of the trees. We knew we couldn't simply lay the wire on the ground, because the Gooks would surely cut it. That's probably what they had tried in the first place. Six of us, McCray and Wilson, who were the two splibs, along with 'baby face' Walker, 'skinny' Drucker, Knowitall and I, started hacking our way down the cliff with machetes. It was hard work and we had to take turns with the machetes because we only had two. The farther down the hill we went the thicker the vegetation became. Two thirds of the way down, Wilson and McCray were working the machetes. Drucker and I were trying to throw the wire up and over the trees. It wasn't working.

Suddenly we heard screams from the guys chopping with the machetes. They came scrambling up the hill yelling about fire ants. As they rushed to take off their utilities, Knowitall and I figured they were just being 'shitbirds' and were trying to get out of work. We called them pussies and started down to replace them. We hadn't gone more than three steps before we started getting bit. Those little bastards would take a bite out of us and a hunk of flesh. I must have had a dozen bite marks in two seconds. We evacuated that side of the cliff, climbed to the top of the hill and stripped. As we reached the top, other guys were laughing at us, calling us pussies. The name calling ended after we undressed, and they saw the tiny blood marks left by the ants. McCray and Wilson, who had stirred up the nest, had the most bite marks.

Other guys tried different routes to run the phone wire. All ended with the ants driving them back. It must have been a huge nest. 'Time out' was called until we could think of another method. In the end we never finished laying the wire and left the job to the next platoon.

Also, while we were on that hill Corporal Dunkin left for home. There was no cake and ice cream, no farewell party, not even a goodbye. After morning chow back at the base camp, he was ordered to report to the company HQ. We climbed aboard the truck to go back to Rocky Top and Dunkin was gone never to be seen again.

One day later we got a new corporal from another platoon in another company. His name was Crumb or Krum which was short for Kruminoski, or something like that. I was no longer keeping a journal and now my memory fails me on this detail. We just called him Krum. I do remember a lot about him. He was a likeable guy, always joking and his favorite expression was, 'A happy Marine is a bitching Marine.' It was kind of hard to complain when he put us on a work party. If we complained, he simply said. "Well, you must be secretly happy." I learned a lot about being a leader from him.

For months before arriving at this hill top outpost, I had developed terrible sores on both of my arms. They began as cuts from walking through the high elephant grass and jungle in our short sleeves. The cuts became open sores and then scabbed over. The scabs would weep puss from the sides. When I showered, the scab would fall off leaving a pink sore, and the whole process would begin again. I couldn't get rid of them and they began to spread to other parts of my body. I feared I had contracted 'Leprosy' or something. We called these sores 'jungle rot'. Mostly the white guys got them, but some black guys suffered too. The worst places to get them were on guy's feet. Those guys usually had to be hospitalized. I fought with the rot for several months all during the rainy season. Several different Corpsmen told me there was nothing that could be done until the dry season came.

Also, while on the hill we were issued new rifles. A truck pulled up after evening chow and we unloaded the new rifles. We tossed our old M-14's into the back of the truck. The new weapons were black, lighter, and made of plastic. We all had mixed feelings about the new M-16 rifle. Yes, they were lighter, but I wouldn't want to fight someone in battle with a bayonet on a plastic rifle. They were all equipped with selective fire which meant we could fire them just like a machine gun. The rifle and ammo were both lighter. Anything that would lighten our load was welcomed. The ammo was lighter because it was a smaller caliber. We worried that a 5.56mm caliber would not have the stopping power of our old M-14s. Our worries would prove correct.

We test-fired the weapons by standing on Rocky Top hill and shooting down the sides of the hill. They worked fine and were fun to shoot. We were issued new ammo pouches for our belts, to hold the new magazines. Because they were lighter, we were issued two extra magazines, so the weight would still be the same. Now we carried 120 rounds instead of 100. No break there. We had no idea at the time that these new rifles were not yet ready for combat. We would find that out later at the cost of many Marines' lives.

I mentioned that each day when we rode back and forth to the mess hall for either morning or evening chow we passed another smaller hill with one bunker on top. That hill might not have been as high as ours, but the sides were even steeper. Sitting on top was a single 106 recoilless rifle. It was called recoilless because it fired a 106mm rocket. For the novice who reads this, the cannon fires a shell and rocks the barrel and chassis back-wards with a terrific recoil. A recoilless rocket looks like a cannon. How-ever, when it fires the rocket roars out the muzzle and the flame from the rocket blasts out the back. God help the person standing behind the 106 when it fires. Many a Marine and soldier have died when it accidentally went off, or it fired when they weren't clear of the back.

Two poor grunts were stationed up on that hill with the 106. They were trained on how to operate it and trained in calculating range and distance. However, those two guys had to be relieved for meals and showers period-ically. Also, two other Marines were sent up there each night to help stand guard duty. It turned out to be a 'gravy' job, once you did it everyone vol-unteered to go back. Since it was impossible to climb the steep cliff, the only way to walk up was by using the winding narrow trail which circled the hill on its way to the top where the 106 was located. Each night the two 106 operators set out several trip flares on the trail in case any Gooks tried to sneak up on them. A trip flare is a thin wire, almost impossible to see at night, strung across a path and attached to a flare. When someone tried to sneak up the path they hit the wire which set off an illumination flare which lit up the whole area. It acted as a warning and allowed us to see and shoot the poor bastard who set it off. In the nine months that the guys had been there not a single trip flare had ever gone off, not even by accident. Why would any self-respecting Viet Cong want to risk his life going up that hill to kill four Marines and capture a weapon they had no idea how to fire? They could however take the shells which weighed three pounds each and turn them into booby traps.

For nine months one guy sat up there in all kinds of weather and had not ever fired a single shot. The guy he relieved had spent twelve months up there with the same results. When two of us went up for 24 hours, it meant a good night's sleep in a dry bunker and only standing guard duty for one and a half hours. There were no work parties just plenty of time to write letters. We loved it.

As the weather continued to improve, the Marine Corps decided to pull us off Rocky Top and move us back to Kilo Company base camp. The 106 stayed put. I had a chance to talk to Carden and we exchanged notes. He had been on patrols and work parties just like me. However, several guys in his platoon had been killed or wounded, mostly by booby traps. Rumor had it that Kilo was soon going on another search and destroy operation.

One day our platoon corpsman, who we called, 'Doc' came up to me and said, "There is a real doctor who comes to the base camp once a week. He's here today and he can do something for your jungle rot." I went to see him, and he gave me a shot in my arm and a piece of paper called a 'chit' to give to my commanding officer. The chit said I couldn't stand guard duty that night because of the shot I received. The sergeant wasn't pleased but understood.

That night I got to sleep in a tent for the first time since I left the M.P.'s. I slept hard in that tent and it wasn't even raining. I woke early in the morning only to go take a leak and then went back to bed without even going to morning chow. At noon I awoke and ate and then went back to sleep until evening chow. I stood guard duty that night and after, had no trouble falling asleep. To this day I have no idea what was in that shot. All I know is I slept for nearly 24 hours and within three days the rot on my arms finally began to clear up.

A week later we began to get our gear ready to move out. The rumors were real. It was a sunny day, my arms were healing quickly, we were off that horrible hill and I was in a good mood. I had finally gotten some mail from back home and some much-needed Kool Aid. Walker and I were eating a hot meal in the mess hall tent and joking around. Rumor had it we were going to get a beer ration. We got up from the table, washed our mess kits out and headed back to our tent as we continued to joke and laugh. We hadn't walked more than twenty paces when we both stopped dead in our tracks. Simultaneously we both realized we had left our rifles back in the mess tent. We turned around and took about two steps when we had that, 'Oh shit' moment everyone experiences in their life. We froze as we saw the company gunnery sergeant standing in the entrance of the mess hall tent holding two rifles. We approached with serious looks on our faces that didn't quite match the gunny's look. We both knew better. That rifle had not been more than arms length away from me for the last nine months. If we took a shit the rifle went with us. If we went on a work party the rifle was either on our shoulder or within two steps of us. We slept with that rifle beside us. The gunny, a 'lifer', who fought in Korea treated us like we were both 'boots' just out of boot camp, who had just stepped off a plane from the States. His only words were, "I want both of you two shitbirds to report to my tent after evening chow." Walker and I had all afternoon of work parties during which we had time to wonder what our punishment would be.

After evening chow, we headed over to the gunny's tent. I told Walker, "We'll just show up and say nothing. Maybe he will have forgotten, or he is just going to chew our asses out. Whatever he says just say you're sorry and it won't happen again."

No such luck was in store for us. Sitting just outside his tent were four sand bags standing upright. He walked out of his tent to greet us. He didn't lecture us. He just pointed to the sand bags and said. "You see these four sand bags?"

"Yeah." We replied together.

"Well they need to be taken up to Hill 106. You're then going to replace them with four old bags and bring them back here. Do you understand?"

"Yes, gunnery sergeant." The hill where the 106-recoilless rifle stood was three fourths of a mile away as the crow flies and more than a mile away if we walked by road. We looked around for the jeep or truck that would take us to the foot of the hill.

"Well, get going!" Obviously, there was no jeep or truck to drive us. These sand bags weighed about forty pounds each and we were going to hump them to the hill and then up the hill bringing back four old bags.

"And I hope you noticed the white 'X' I marked in paint on each of the bags. That's so you don't walk out of sight and try to return with the same bags." The gunny had thought of everything.

We picked up the bags, along with our rifles and headed on down the road. Walker carried his in each hand. I slung mine over each shoulder. As we walked out of camp we could see the other guys unloading cases of beer and looking at us with curious eyes. We had to stop several times to rest and we each tried different methods of carrying the bags. No one way was easier than another. Lucky for us the gunny had radioed ahead to tell the two guys with the 106 that we were coming. I guess he didn't want us walking up that trail and setting off any trip flares. Those guys were nice enough to have carried four bags down the hill for us. When we got to them they asked, "How did you two fuck-up?"

"Never mind," we replied. Carrying the bags back was even harder. We finally got back about an hour and a half later and set the old bags down next to the gunny's tent. He was standing there with a beer in his hand.

"You going to forget your rifle again?" was all he said. We were both exhausted and the only chance for a beer ration we had in three months was gone. We had learned our lesson.

Two days later Corporal Krum said he needed two guys to go up to the 106. I jumped at the opportunity for an easy job. When would I ever learn? A truck drove tall skinny Drucker and me back over to the 106 bunker. Only this time we weren't going to be spending an easy 24 hours on that hill. We were pulling out of the area and the 106-recoilless rifle had to come down off that cliff. The rifle itself weighed over 400 pounds not including the metal tripod on which it stood. Carrying that beast down the winding trail was going to be a bear of a job! One the 106 operators suggested we simply carry it down the side of one of the cliffs. I thought you have got to be kidding me. His reasoning though made sense.

"The rifle doesn't have to go as far and if it should fall so what. It's less we have to carry." They had already taken the tripod legs off. All that was attached was some built-in bolts and part of the platform that it sat on.

So, each of us grabbed a quarter of that monster and began walking and sliding it down the steep hill. It was heavy, and parts of the platform kept getting caught on tree limbs. We kept lifting it up, but it would get away from us and slide farther down the steep hill and into more brush and tree limbs. After about an hour we began to realize it would have been easier to carry it down the trail. We eventually reached the bottom and laid that 106 down in the road. We made several more trips up and down the trail bringing down ammo cases. Each shell weighed three pounds and there was a dozen in each box. On the last trip down, the guy who had spent nine months in that bunker left a hunk of wood behind. It was a one-foot piece of 4 x 12 on which he had carved a message. He wouldn't let us see what it said. I guess it was his goodbye. Getting the 106 off that hill was pure drudgery.

Soon we all said goodbye to that whole area. It was the most miserable time I spent in Viet Nam. Most guys, who served in Nam or in any war, know the kind of drudgery that we all shared. I'm sure most people have seen their share of war movies. In the movies they never show the drudgery just the excitement of combat. There is one exception. If you ever get a chance to see the movie, or the stage play Mister Roberts you should. The story is about the drudgery of men on a supply ship in the South Pacific during World War II. In the movie, Henry Fonda plays Mister Roberts, and he only dreams about ending the drudgery and getting transferred to a battle ship where he can be in the action. I won't spoil the story, but you'll find out what Mister Roberts discovers if you see the movie.

And so, it was with Kilo Company. We were leaving the drudgery and heading for more action than we ever wanted. In hind sight I would have preferred the drudgery rather than what we were about to face.

Chapter 28

DEATH ON THE TAMI TRON TRAIL

THE SUMMER OF 1967, when I finally came home from Viet Nam I decided one Sunday to put on my Marine Corps uniform and go back to the Quaker Meeting House where I had attended prayer service with the 'Society of Friends' as they are officially named. We all prayed in silence, which is something I still believe in. I could never be a practicing 'Friend' because I am not a pacifist and I could never forgive the Quakers for donating blood to the North Vietnamese during the war. I don't know if they also gave blood to American troops or not. While I was fighting for my country and watching my friends die, they were helping the enemy.

When the service ended several members of the congregation, who still remembered me, stepped forward to ask me some questions. They of course were totally against the war as were half of the people on the home front. They were appalled that the Americans were using 'Napalm' as a weapon. I suppose they felt napalm was inhumane, as if blowing some-one's legs off with a booby trap is more humane. I didn't get into a dis-cussion or argument. I only said, "I guess it doesn't matter how you kill someone, whether you shoot them, or drop a bomb on them, they are just as dead." And then I added, "The how is not as important as the why." I walked away and have never been back to a service at any meeting house. I doubt if they understood then or even now. Sometimes the only way to stop evil is with violence. The only way to stop a bully is to fight back. The fighting is not pretty, and some people will never understand the 'why'.

In late March of '67 Kilo Company left our base camp, climbed aboard six by six trucks and headed south, down Highway #1 and then turned right and headed west into the boondocks. We headed past the flat rice paddy areas and up towards the hills. There were still some paddies, but the landscape became more wooded and jungle-like and much less pop-ulated. We disembarked from the trucks, saddled up with our equip-ment and began walking. We each carried our new M-16 rifle using the rifle sling rigged so it hung from our shoulder and pointed forward. The sling had to be turned around and attached to the small web straps used to hold our cots together. The two small web straps were attached, one to the rifle barrel and the second to the rear stock just behind the hand grip. With the rifle slung over our shoulder, this allowed our hand and trigger finger to be placed on the grip and ready to fire in an instant. The weapon was carried in 'condition one', which meant the magazine was inserted, the charging handle had been pulled back, and a round was in the chamber, but the safety was on. Flip the safety off, pull the trigger, and the rifle would go boom. We called it 'locked and loaded'. I also car-ried a black dagger attached to my web suspenders.

We walked most of the morning in single file through the heavily wooded area and eventually we came to a village called Tami Tron. The village was supposed to be abandoned. Leaflets had been dropped telling all Vietnamese civilians to leave or relocate to a safer area. On entering the village, we were met by a single old lady well into her 60's. She spoke to us in French and must have thought we were French troops since Viet Nam was once a French colony. She seemed confused and scared. It was obvious to everyone that the village was just recently deserted, perhaps in the last half hour when word reached the village of troops approaching. The old lady apparently didn't know this, or they figured she was too old to make a run for it into the jungle. We left her alone and camped while we ate noon chow.

Evidently this little village of Tami Tron was labeled on our map, but the next village was not identified. A trail was marked on the map that led to this other village. We called the village 'No Name'. The trail went from Tami Tron to No Name and we called it 'The Tami Tron Trail'. Our new platoon lieutenant estimated that No Name was about 40 clicks away, or 40 kilometers in civilian speak. That would be 40 kilometers as the crow flies. The trail was a winding, twisting footpath that curved around rice paddies, hills, streams and other objects like jungle thickets and thorny vegetation. In places the trail was wide enough for a single ox cart but most places a jeep couldn't traverse it.

Individually, we could probably walk 20 miles in one day. However, a company of Marines walking in single file through the jungle would take much longer. Kilo Company numbered about 160 to 180 men. Walking in a straight line, eight steps apart, the whole company took up over a mile of terrain. Trying to sneak up on a village with that many men was impossible. Any V.C. could spot us miles away, set up ambushes or booby traps. It was decided to separate, and each platoon would head towards No Name village from different directions. First platoon with my buddy Carden, would head around the south. The third platoon would head north and we in second platoon would stay on the trail. Each day we would switch around so that everyone had an equal chance of getting killed.

Extra care had to be taken as we humped towards the village. We were constantly on the lookout for V.C., booby traps and ambushes. As I explain our method of movement, I'm sure some other Viet Nam veterans might be saying, "That's not how we did it." And they would be correct. Each new commander would try a different tactic and as the war went on year after year many new methods were tried. This is how I remember we did it in 1967.

Our method of walking varied. We would walk at least 8 paces from the guy in front of us. The new guys (boots) would try to walk closer and would have to be constantly reminded, to "keep your distance; one grenade will kill you all." The distance we traveled varied from minute to minute. Sometimes we would walk ten feet and stop for half an hour. Sometimes we would walk half a mile and stop for ten minutes. After about ten minutes of standing with forty or fifty pounds of gear we would naturally sit down, take a break and unload all our equipment except the flak jacket.

No one gave us permission to sit, we just did it. The reasons for stopping were many. It could be to inspect a possible booby trap. Or it could be simply trying to communicate by radio with the company commander or one of the other platoons. Platoons were constantly trying to locate themselves on the map. After each stop the word would be passed down the line to, "Saddle up, we're moving out!" That meant slinging all our gear back on our shoulders and continuing our march.

Many times, it was best not to travel on the trail at all. It was easier and safer to cross a large rice paddy. The Gooks usually didn't booby trap rice paddy dikes where the farmers had to walk. It was also easier to ambush a column of troops on a trail than on a rice paddy. All we had to worry about in the middle of a rice paddy was a sniper and for the most part the Viet Cong were terrible shots. The few times they tried to shoot us while we crossed a paddy, we could hear the rifle fire, but never heard the bullet pass by.

Other reasons to get off the trail included checking out other areas or trying to confuse the V.C. as to our true destination and of course avoiding areas that just looked like a perfect place to be ambushed. Sometimes we needed to fill our canteens and took side trips to nearby streams. Also, at night we tried to find an open area where we could set up a defensive perimeter. It took a week to travel the 40 clicks to 'No Name'.

Every other day we would run out of C-rations. We would look for a safe landing zone (L.Z.) for choppers to come in. Whenever we heard the noise of helicopters, or the announcement passed down, "Choppers coming in!" we would dig in and wait for the inevitable gun fire. The V.C. considered helicopters to be prized targets. If we had no dead or wounded to throw on to the choppers, the crewmen would just toss out the boxes of C-rations and then take off without landing. I was always amazed at how much gun fire we took as soon as the chopper arrived. It was proof the V.C. were everywhere! I would not be surprised to learn on many occasions as we made our way along the Tami Tron Trail, the Gooks were only a few feet away. We probably had accidentally run into them and they simply hid until we passed.

It was not unusual to walk by dead bodies, whether along the Tami Tron Trail or off the trail. This was definitely V.C. territory and the N.V.A. (North Vietnamese Army) was probably in the area as well. The NVA would enter a village and try to recruit people to become communists. After a period of indoctrination, the villagers could either join or if they refused, the NVA would take them out to be shot. The dead bodies were hard to recognize at first. It is unbelievable how much a dead body can swell up in the sun in only one day. They take on an ashen color and blow up so much that a skinny Gook would 'pop' out of their black outfit. The first time I saw one I even wondered to myself, *what is that?*

On the fourth day on the trail our platoon had the point. We were truly blessed to have Weeocky as our point man. The days he had the point, we traveled slower than normal, but we were never ambushed or hit by a booby trap. On this day as we walked along the Tami Tron Trail our squad stopped in a rough area. The trail had been washed out with the heavy monsoon rains and we were left standing on the trail with six-foot high embankments on both sides of us. The Sergeant, fearing an ambush, ordered some of us to climb the embankment and check for any signs of the enemy. I climbed up the steep side and quickly reached the top where I was met by waist high grass and some scattered trees. I stood up to see over the grass but saw nothing. Not wanting to be exposed, I squatted down behind the grass. I thought I saw a dark object in the grass directly in front of me. Not sure what it was I used my rifle barrel to push aside the grass to get a closer look. Again, I thought I spotted a skinny black arm moving sideways in the grass. I crawled forward a few inches and moved more grass to the side. This time the skinny arm rose up and I could see it was a snake. It was only inches from the end of my rifle barrel. As I moved the barrel, so I could shoot the snake it moved sideways. Seeing my rifle barrel, it flared its hood. It was a cobra. I moved the barrel again and fired. As the blast from the muzzle flashed, I sprang back and in one movement I slid back down the embankment.

Everyone was yelling and scrambling to prepare for the ambush we faced. "What do you guys see up there?"

"Nothing!"

"Look again!"

"I don't see anything either!"

The sergeant yelled, "Who fired that shot?" I was too shaken to speak so I raised my rifle.

"Well what did you see?"

I swallowed and forced out one word, "Snake."

Knowitall, excitedly questioned, "What kind of snake?"

"A bad kind," I replied. Knowitall scrambled up the side of the embankment to look for himself. I don't know if he wanted to impress everyone with his bravery or his knowledge. Part of me wanted him to get bit in his ass and part of me prayed the snake was long gone. I was still trying to regain my composure and I tried hard not to appear as scared as I was. I focused on not shaking outwardly but every muscle inside my body was quivering uncontrollably.

Within seconds Knowitall slid back down the hill with the long black snake in his hand. I thought I would throw up. He held the snake by the neck. Its head was three fourths off and hung over knowitall's wrist. I don't know if the bullet hit the snake or the muzzle blast cut his head off. He held the neck straight up over his head, with the tip of the snake's tail still touching the ground. There were cries of "Wow!" and "Holy shit!"

"Dixon killed a snake!" At least no one would think I had panicked and shot at nothing.

"Do you know what kind of snake this is?" Knowitall questioned me and anyone within the sound of his 'all knowing' voice. Without waiting for an answer, he announced, "It's a Black Cobra, one of the deadliest snakes in the world."

I finally had a chance to get my little dig in on Knowitall. I replied, "Yeah, and now it's a good snake!"

"What do you mean good? Man, if this snake had bit you, you'd a' been long dead before we medevaced your ass out of here." Someone else replied for me.

"I think he means it's a good snake because now it's a dead snake!"

The snake's body was laid length ways along the trail, so each passing guy could get a good look at it. I was still shaking inside when we made camp that evening. It was our habit to partially dig a foxhole and then take a break and eat evening chow. Often a squad leader or sergeant would come by and decide to move our foxhole to a different location. There was no sense digging too deep if you were only going to move someplace else. Our squad sat around eating and bull-shitting like we did every night.

hat night's discussion was about the snake. I wanted to talk about anything else. Our squad leader, Corporal Krum, who I liked because of his sense of humor and bullshit, asked a question. "Hey Knowitall, was that a male or a female snake?"

Now, most people would answer that question by saying, "How the fuck would I know?" But of course, Knowitall replied, "Well I never did check."

Old Baby Face Walker asked, "What difference does it make, they're both poisonous."

Krum, always having fun, replied, "Well if it was a male snake I was just wondering where his girlfriend was. And if it was a female snake, I was wondering where her boyfriend was?" Then he added, "Or is?"

We all looked at each other and then we all wondered. I had no trouble staying awake on guard duty that night!

The next morning the platoon sergeant came over to our squad and made a joke.

"I just got off the radio with headquarters and because of yesterday, they are going to issue each platoon a 'mongoose' to take care of any more cobras." We all chuckled and said, "Ha ha!" What occurred next was really, funny.

The sergeant left, and tall skinny Drucker asked, "What good is 'one goose' going to do against a cobra?" This time we all laughed.

Knowitall started to explain.

Corporal Krum interrupted, "Let it go, it's funnier this way." We saddled up and moved out to see what horrors this new day would bring.

That afternoon third platoon had the point and we were right behind them. As a matter of fact, second squad had moved to the head of our platoon. We moved steadily through the heavily wooded area. Suddenly shots were fired at the front of the column. Instantly we moved off the trail and into the jungle to await the impending ambush. We could hear automatic fire from the front of the column, but we could see nothing. It wasn't an ambush. The point man and the first three or four guys in that squad had accidentally walked into a clearing where some Viet Cong were finishing their noon meal. Both sides were surprised and started shooting at each other. This would never have happened if Weeocky had been on point.

Not knowing what was going on, we assumed the worst. The order came back to bring up the mortars. Four guys, each humping the two halves of the mortars ran to the front of the column to set up. The order came back to send up the mortar rounds. Every other man carried one mortar. I carried 50 rounds of machine gun ammo. So, McCray and Wilson ran their shells up to the front. By the time they returned, the firing had stopped, but Wilson was pissed.

"McCray did you see they left one of the 'brothers' lying out in the clearing? He's wounded. We got to go up and get him!" The three of us ran forward. Since I was supposed to be their team leader and I didn't think anyone should be left out in a field, we all ran out into the clearing. I got down on my stomach and began laying down some cover fire into the far side of the clearing while McCray and Wilson dragged the wounded 'splib' back to the column. Mortar shells were fired at the other edge of the clearing. Whatever V.C. had been there were hightailing themselves back into the jungle.

I looked at the wounded black Marine. He was unconscious and covered in blood. He had been shot in the face and the neck. Blood continued to ooze out of the gaping wound on his cheek bone, or where his cheek bone had been. The corpsmen from the other platoons had arrived and were treating the three Marines who were wounded. Helicopters were radioed for medevac. McCray, Wilson and I returned to our squad just in time to be ordered back up to secure the entire clearing, so a helicopter could land.

After the copter left with the wounded, things began to settle down. Wilson was still complaining.

"I can't believe all these 'chucks' left a wounded brother out there to die. Not one white mother fucker would help bring him back!"

Then McCray spoke calmly, "All, except Dixon."

They both looked at me. Then Wilson said, "Yeah Dixon, thank you." A quiet moment of reflection passed and then I spoke.

"You know, I don't think the other men left him out in that clearing because he was black. I think they left him out there because they thought he was dead."

McCray looked back at Wilson and added, "He might have been breathing, but he sure looked dead. I don't think our bringing him out of that clearing is going to save his life. I'll bet he's DOA by the time they get him to a field hospital."

From that day on I not only had the respect of McCray and Wilson, but we became good friends. It's hard not to be friends with guys you are in combat with. The trouble with combat is you can lose friends at anytime.

Somewhere, the powers to be decided to by-pass the village of No Name. Either they wanted to make the Viet Cong think we were going somewhere else or perhaps they felt the village was unimportant. However, on the sixth day some guys in the third platoon accidentally walked up on two V.C. who were taking a 'shit' in the bushes. They had rifles leaning up against a tree but threw up their hands when the Marines stumbled on them. I was not there and can only imagine how surprised both groups were. The captured Gooks were brought to our platoon, which by chance, had the company commander, a captain, walking with us that day.

What occurred next would be burned into my brain forever. The two prisoners knelt in front of the captain. We waited for an interpreter to join our platoon. It was obvious to everyone that these two Gooks were hard core Viet Cong. They were about 18 or 19 years old, the same as us. They wore the black outfit with the straw hat. They were armed with rifles to kill us if they had the chance.

When the Vietnamese interpreter arrived, the captain instructed the interpreter to ask the first man, "Where are the V.C.?" In Vietnamese, the interpreter spoke, and the first prisoner shook his head and replied in Vietnamese.

The translator told the captain, "He says he doesn't know where the V.C. are." The captain pulled out his .45 pistol and shot the man in the top of his head. The bullet exited the lower back of his skull, blowing out blood and brains. His body tumbled backwards and over on his side. This shooting occurred as calmly as someone would swat a pesky fly.

The captain instructed the interpreter to ask the second man. Before he could finish asking the question the second prisoner began speaking too fast for the interpreter to understand. They couldn't shut the guy up. Several times the interpreter had to tell the guy to slow down. The prisoner kept pointing and talking fast. Of course, we couldn't tell exactly what was being said, but even Drucker got the drift of the conversation. The interpreter explained in English that the village of No Name was a kind of head quarters for some NVA who were organizing the civilians and recruiting men and women for the Viet Cong.

The captain radioed a coded message back to the Battalion base and we all waited for further instructions. Our squad and others took a break to eat as we waited. We all knew what was going to happen to the second prisoner. After noon chow we were given the word to "Saddle up, we're moving out!" The interpreter told the second Gook he was free to go. It took some convincing but the scared V.C. began slowly walking away across a field. After he got about 30 yards away several guys opened-up with their rifles and blew him away. I didn't fire. I didn't have the heart. I knew it was necessary. Had we let him go he would have rejoined the enemy and later could have killed one of us. Also, if he returned to his unit, he would have told the NVA what we knew. If we called in a helicopter just for a prisoner, the chopper crew would have taken him up a few thousand feet and dropped him out. Pilots didn't like risking their lives for some prisoner while other Gooks would only try to shoot at their chopper or kill the pilot. Some hard ass veterans would have used this guy as their point man and let him step on a booby trap which I'm sure was done more than once.

This is what war is all about. Horrible decisions made in horrible conditions. Many people who read this will think only about how unjust the death of the captured V.C. was. It's not politically correct or honorable to kill someone that way. The truth is there is no honor in war. If the Gooks had captured any one of us, they would have done the same. Both sides in a war understand that fact, even if civilians don't. War is about killing people. The how doesn't matter. It didn't make me feel good at the time it happened and it doesn't make me feel good retelling the story now.

Chapter 29

IT HELPS TO BE CRAZY

T HEY OFTEN SAY school teachers take on the personality of the students they teach. Elementary teachers act like children who think everything is just too cute. High school teachers are laid back, indifferent, and believe themselves intellectually superior to other lower grade teachers. Junior high or middle school teachers are just plain crazy. I spent over a quarter of a century teaching inner city junior high school, with thirty kids in a class, six classes a day, every work day. That's thirty 13-year olds with no social skills and little or no home support, all going through puberty. Picture Moe, Larry and Curly, times 10, with their hormones raging and no guidance from Mom or Dad! You must be a little crazy to do that. And believe me, there were lots of crazy teachers including me. It helps sometimes, to be crazy. It allows people to cope with hard times.

We left the two dead V.C. behind and continued down the Tami Tron Trail towards the village on the map with 'No Name'. It was the first of the hot weather days after the monsoons and the jungle became steamy. We soon became sweaty and drained, partially because of the weather and partially because exhaustion always followed a fire fight.

That evening Corporal Krum, Wilson, McCray and I were sitting around eating our C-rations and complaining. It was what every Marine did. Krum whispered, "I have an idea on how to get out of here." We all 'daydreamed' of getting that 'million-dollar wound' that would get us out of Viet Nam. The perfect wound was a foot wound where we couldn't walk well any more, but we could still live our life almost as normal. Many of us had thought about accidentally shooting ourselves in the foot. I thought about it but always concluded that I would screw it up and end up with an amputated foot and never be able to walk correctly.

We listened to Krum's plan. He continued to whisper, "The next time we come across a dead body, I'm going to go 'ape shit'!"

"What do you mean?" I asked.

"I'm going to start screaming and empty my magazine into the dead body. I'm going to keep shooting and screaming until you guys pull me off. The lieutenant and staff sergeant will think I've gone nuts and send me back for a *mental discharge*."

"Right!" We all laughed and thought what a crazy, stupid idea.

The next morning, we saddled up and moved out. Right before noon we passed a couple of dead Gooks lying along the trail. They had been dead for quite some time and they smelled overly ripe. I had completely forgotten Krum's crazy plan when he opened-up with his M-16 on full automatic. We all hit the deck thinking it was another ambush. Krum, just like he planned, began screaming and firing and reloading. Everyone stared at him in disbelief. When his rifle jammed, he tossed it aside, dropped to his knees and began stabbing one of the bodies with his bayonet. With each stab a wet gooey fluid splashed out of the body. 'Wow, I thought, Krum really has gone crazy!'

The platoon sergeant yelled, "What the fuck is his problem?"

"He's lost it sarge!" Someone yelled back.

"Some of you guys pull him off there." Wilson and Knowitall pulled Krum off to the side of the trail and held him down in the shade. The corpsman came and gave him some water. The whole time Krum kept screaming, repeatedly, "I'm going to kill all those mother fuckers!"

The lieutenant called in a helicopter as the sergeant found a clearing, so

Krum could be evacuated. When the chopper landed, Wilson and McCray led the still yelling Krum over and placed him in the chopper, then helped to strap him in. I didn't see it, but Wilson and McCray told me later that as they left, Krum smiled and gave them a wink. We continued walking and everyone, including me, wondered if Krum had really gone nuts or had he come up with the perfect plan.

That evening we all sat around and quietly whispered among ourselves about how this would all play out. Several guys planned on doing the same thing themselves the next day. Other guys warned that the same plan would draw too much suspicion. Other scenarios would have to be dreamt up. Still others wondered how long it would take before some doctor figured out Krum was faking it. I wondered what would happen when they did figure it out.

In the morning, we saddled up and headed down the trail. I knew Krum's 'secret' was currently spreading throughout our platoon and probably other platoon's as well. I spent the day thinking about how I could try something similar. That evening it seemed everyone knew what Corporal Krum had pulled off. Other plans were hatched, and pros and cons discussed. I should mention and remind readers that Krum was a corporal or E-4, which is the same as a specialist or corporal E-4 in the Army. A sergeant or E-5 is considered non-commissioned officer (NCOs). Lieutenants, captains and on up are called commissioned officers.

The next morning, we approached a clearing and received word to set up and dig in because choppers were coming in with supplies. One chopper came in to the usual sound of small arms fire from Gooks hiding nearby. The chopper didn't land but only tossed out cases of C-rations and one new guy. After every fire fight it was not unusual for us to get new replacement or 'boot' from boot camp. When the chopper took off several guys ran out to retrieve the food.

As they walked back we all noticed that the new guy was Krum, who headed toward the Lieutenant. We were all pleased to see him and wanted to know what had happened. A group soon gathered around him. He walked up to the lieutenant, set down the case of C-rations, and saluted.

"Lance Corporal Krum reporting for duty, sir."

'Lance Corporal?' I thought? Sure enough, I looked at Krum's collar and the corporal chevrons were gone, replaced with lance corporal chevrons. The lieutenant saluted back, even though we were taught never to salute officers in the field.

The sergeant spoke first, "So, they busted you back to lance corporal, huh?"

Still looking at the lieutenant, Krum replied, "Yes sir. They said I wasn't crazy, so I couldn't be a non-commissioned officer."

Krum then walked back to say hello to us, his old friends. He continued talking, "Yeah, I guess you have to be crazy to be a corporal.

Someone jokingly asked, "What do you have to do to be an officer?"

Krum, who was always a joker, continued, "Well the way I figure it, if you follow military logic, you have to be a nut job to be a sergeant. And you have to be really insane to be a lieutenant."

I took a quick peek over at our sergeant and our lieutenant who were both smiling. I asked Krum, "What about other officers."

"Well, I'm glad you asked that. I figure you must be completely out of your mind to be any kind of officer. And to be a general you got to be a stark raving lunatic." We were all laughing and even the sergeant and lieutenant were trying not to but were unsuccessful.

Later Krum explained that he got a hot shower, a hot meal and got to sleep in a real bed, not a cot, but a real bed. He met some hot nurses and got to eat a real hamburger. So, all in all it was well worth it. A doctor who was a captain examined him and asked him some stupid questions, like do you want to go back in the field?

Krum said, "I told him no way!" The doc replied,

"Well you must not be crazy then." So, it's like we already knew. You must be crazy to want to be here.

Chapter 30

THE LAST MARINE
ON THE TAMI TRON TRAIL

I F YOU ARE a baseball or football fan I bet you can remember the very first professional game you ever saw. You can probably remember walking through that tunnel into the stands which opened to a view of the field. It was lush, plush and greener than you ever imagined from seeing it on television. In between my memories of many games I've seen, they kind of run together. I can remember seeing my first pro football game when John Brody and the 49er's taught the Philadelphia Eagles how the game is supposed to be played. And I remember the last Eagles game I saw when Peyton Manning carved up the Eagles' defense. I've seen many memorable pro games, including the baseball World Series championship game in 1980. Other games were not as memorable or as enjoyable, but I can still remember most.

The same is true of killing people in combat. I remember the first time I killed someone, the last time I killed someone and all the ones in between. I remember all the details of each kill. However, the ones in between become blurred and confused as to the order in which they occurred. I bet most air plane bombers in WWII remember their first mission and their last mission but all the ones in between kind of run together.

After the new information or 'Intel' as the military calls it, which the scared prisoner gave up, Kilo Company headed for 'No Name'. We walked single file along the Tami Tron Trail. The trail became wider as we approached the village. The trail paralleled a small stream which was about twenty yards wide in some places. We walked for several hours.

We stopped to rest and to 'De-leech'. We stripped naked and helped each other burn the slimy two headed blood suckers off our bodies. These leeches were one to two inches long and fat from sucking blood. Leeches just can't be pulled off because part their two heads will remain under your skin and get infected. Some guys used salt to force the leeches to pull their two heads out and then flicked them to the ground and stepped on them. Most guys used a lit cigarette to force the heads out of their skin. Some tried the insect repellant that many had strapped to their helmets. Cigarettes worked the best. I was amazed at how many leeches we each had picked up. I counted 20 on me. They would get inside your clothes and slink up and down your body without you ever feeling their presence. They loved to go to the warmest parts of your body to suck blood. The warmest part is of course your genitalia. Guys would help each other burn the suckers off our back where we couldn't see them. But when it came time to remove them from your penis, you were on your own.

By the time we reached the village of No Name it was deserted. It was a small village of only eight to ten huts. There was a fenced in area where pigs were being raised with some chickens running around. Guys found some spent shell casings and a North Vietnamese flag, but not a single person. It was clear people were living here moments before we arrived. I got my lighter out and waited for the word to 'burn'. I was surprised when we were instead ordered to move out and walk back the way we came in, right back along the stream with the thousands of leeches. When we were several miles away we stopped to De-leech again. I was surprised that we found fewer leaches on our bodies this time. I don't know if it was because of the time of day or we simply killed most on our way in.

We all wondered why the village was spared, but no one asked. We found a place to camp and spend the night. It was earlier than we normally set up our nightly perimeter. Something was up but we didn't know what. Word of mouth slowly passed down the line. We were going to sneak back to the village at night and make a predawn attack. Some hoped a surprise attack would catch the V.C. and the N.V.A. before they could make a run for it.

Soon after midnight we saddled up in silence and began heading back to No Name. I wondered and worried about this idea. We hardly ever travelled at night. I remembered the trail leading to the hill where we spent the monsoon season. Each night we set our trip flares to warn us of any approaching enemy. I knew the Gooks didn't use trip flares, they used booby traps. Even Weeocky would have trouble spotting a booby trap in the pitch dark. I guess the platoon sergeant had thought of the same thing.

His solution was a simple one. Instead of walking down the trail in the dark, we walked in the stream that paralleled the trail. Both stream and trail led directly to the village of No Name. Yes, this was the same stream that we had walked by, where I had picked up and removed 20 leeches from my body. We walked in the water sometimes up to our knees for several hours. Sometimes water came up to our waists, and even up to our arm pits. The whole time I had the creepy feeling that hundreds of slimy leeches were crawling all over me.

We reached the edge of the village before dawn and began spreading out along a line to encircle the enemy. We took off our packs and placed them in front of us and waited for a signal to attack. Suddenly we heard some Vietnamese yelling a warning. The attack began. I walked into the village to the sound of gun fire, shouts of panic and screams of the wounded. Even the pigs were screeching. I looked into a hooch and saw no one. I quickly walked behind the hooch and up a small hill to check out the other side where the jungle met the village. As I turned the corner I saw a moving dark shadow. I turned and fired from the hip, three shots just as I had been taught in training. The shadow tumbled to the ground. I turned, to look into the jungle where other shots were being fired. I couldn't tell if they were incoming or out going. I looked back at the shadow on the ground. It was trying to stand. I fired three more rounds. Down it went. I checked back into the jungle. Marines were shouting, "Look in that hooch and check behind that hooch! Watch out in the jungle!" By now it was dawn and the sun had just begun to light the village, so we could see clearly.

I walked the few steps toward the body I had just shot. It was a young boy, about age twelve. He wore the same black outfit as the Viet Cong. He was unconscious but still alive. I picked him up and carried him around the hooch and down the small hill towards the platoon sergeant and the corpsmen. The corpsman was treating a Marine, who I didn't recognize, for a gunshot wound in his arm. I laid the boy down next to the corpsmen. He looked at me like I was crazy.

"Get him away from me, can't you see I'm busy."

I replied to the sergeant, "What should I do with him?" With that the corpsman took out his .45 and shot the kid in the head.

The sergeant pointed to another nearby body and said, "Pile him over there so we can get an accurate count.

Later I would have mixed feelings about my first kill. Yes, he was a young boy, but he was wearing the enemy uniform and he was in an area where the Vietnamese had been told to evacuate. If he was old enough to be with the Viet Cong, he was old enough to die with them. Plenty of twelve-year old Gooks had killed American Marines just like the enemy does today in the Middle East.

I counted seven dead Gooks and two wounded Marines. No one will ever know if the Marines were shot by the enemy or by friendly fire. We found lots of Viet Cong clothing and equipment. Some guys even found two rocket shells like the kind the Gooks loved to use for booby traps. We burned all the thatched huts, ate morning chow and D-leeched. To my amazement we found only a few leeches among us. Someone surmised that the leeches don't feed at night. Drucker questioned,

"Maybe the gunfire scared them off us?" Sometimes it was good to have a D winger around to relieve tension. After chow we saddled up and moved out again. We left the village of No Name in smoking ashes.

We walked the rest of that day without incident. I hoped this operation would end with the destruction of 'No Name'. There was no such luck. The next morning some aircraft spotters reported a large group of what looked like N.V.A. moving near us. Somehow, we coordinated with other companies of the 5th Marines and we were able to maneuver ourselves into position to trap them. We had no idea how many of the enemy there were or their exact location. We were told to spread out along a low ridge which ran the length of a large rice paddy. The ridge overlooked the rice paddy that lay between us and the jungle. This rice paddy acted as a giant clearing which allowed us a clear line of fire if the enemy came towards us.

It just so happened four of us ended up on the very far end of this line. It was my fire-team of McCray, Wilson, me and our squad leader, Krum. The ridge was rocky, and we found cover behind some very large boulders. We were the last men on the far, left flank of the entire kilo company. We sat, waited and hoped the N.V.A. would choose a different route. We didn't have to wait long. The four of us had a great view of the rest of Kilo Company to our right. To our left lay the end of the rice paddy and a short distance to the tree line of the jungle. We could hear explosions and see puffs of smoke to our right. The main company was being hit with mortars and taking causalities. We could hear all kinds of automatic rifle fire and see flashes from A.K. 47's being fired from the tree line. This was definitely not a bunch of amateur Viet Cong. These were the well trained and well equipped N.V.A.

The four of us were well protected behind the large boulders. We could see movement in the jungle as trees and grass were pushed aside by men moving. We began firing in that direction even though we had no view of individual troops. Soon the enemy troops began shooting back. Bullets began ricocheting off the rocks like in an old B-grade western movie. Only these were real bullets. Just like Hop-a-Long Cassidy and the Lone Ranger, we would peek our heads up and fire a few rounds and then duck back down again. We could hear the hissing of bullets passing overhead, and some hitting the rocks. Soon one of the rounds hit the rocks in front of me, ricocheted, and sent tiny pieces of debris hitting me on the right side of my face and in my eye. I now had a small cut on my cheekbone, under my eye. Like all face or head wounds it bled more than a normal cut. Blood trickled down my face. Worst of all I couldn't see out of my right eye.

Things began to get worse for us as the rifle fire increased. McCray began yelling, "My rifle is jammed. My rifle is jammed!" Wilson handed me the first aid kit from my belt, so I could hold the bandage on my cheek.

Then suddenly Krum began yelling, "I'm hit. I'm hit!"

Wilson crawled the few feet over to Krum while McCray took the cleaning rod out of the back of his stock and began screwing it together, so he could use the rod to extract the spent cartridge that was jammed in the rifle. Krum had taken off his field pack and was leaning face down against the rocks.

Wilson demanded to know, "Where are you hit?"

Krum in a less panicked voice replied, "In my back. I can feel the blood."

Sure enough, even I could see a large wet bloody spot right in the middle of Krum's utility jacket. McCray was using his cleaning rod to push a stuck cartridge out of his rifle's chamber. He stopped to inspect the bloody spot on Krum's back. The spot of blood seemed large enough but there was something odd about it. We couldn't see a hole or open wound and it didn't seem to be the color of blood.

Wilson took his forefinger and ran it across the wet spot. Then he smelled it and stuck his finger in his mouth. Then he spoke, "I don't think this is blood."

McCray did the same test. "You're right. I think it tastes like peaches."

With that Krum rolled over and grabbed his field pack. Sure, enough the bottom of the pack was wet and dripping peach juice. A bullet had passed through his field pack, ripped through a can of C-ration peaches. Another inch or so and the bullet could have taken out Krum's spine or even killed him.

"I'll be a son of a bitch. Those bastards shot me in my peaches." McCray, Wilson and I were greatly relieved, as bullets continued to fly just a foot above us. But Krum was pissed. "I had been saving those for a special occasion." He dumped the remaining contents of his field pack on to the ground. The inside of the pack was filled with the juices from several cans of fruit with bullet holes punched through them.

Wilson and I continued to fire back into the edge of the jungle. Soon Wilson's rifle also jammed, having failed to extract the spent cartridge. I looked over to our right and saw far fewer Marines. It appeared Kilo Company was moving off the ridge and were taking up positions behind the ridge. I could see several guys carrying the wounded to safer ground. Soon the few remaining men were waving to us and shouting for us to join them. One at a time, beginning with Wilson and ending with me, we ran across the open ground to join the rest of our company.

In life there are events and visions that will stay with you even if you live to be a thousand years old, some things you will never forget. Such was what I saw on that tiny ridge. As I reached the crest of the ridge I saw several dead Marines with cleaning rods still sticking out of the muzzles of their brand, new M-16's. Guys would fire a single round and the rifle would not extract the spent cartridge. The only solution was to punch the spent shell casing out with your cleaning rod. The N.V.A. were armed with AK 47's that fired as automatic rifles or machine guns, while we fired like troops using muzzle-loading rifles from the Civil War. Many a Marine died that day because the M-16 was not ready for combat. Later we discovered that the M-16 had to be cleaned much more often than the old M-14. Eventually improvements would be made to the rifle, including a new chamber that held the round and more gun powder added to each round to produce more gas to extract spent rounds, but it didn't help Kilo company on this day.

Lying close by was the dead corpsman who had shot the dying kid back at No Name. Corpsmen were armed with .45 automatic pistols known as the famous 1911 (nineteen eleven). Those things hardly ever jammed. I crawled over to his body and took the holster and pistol from his cartridge belt. He would not be needing them anymore, so I stuck the holster and .45 pistol into my pack just in case my rifle jammed.

As I had run across the open ground to reach this tiny ridge I had spotted my friend Carden manning an M-60 machine gun. He was laying down cover fire, so the rest of the company could move off the ridge. The M-60 was a belt fed machine gun that had been around since World War II. Two men usually operated it, one to aim and fire and one to feed ammo. I didn't know if he was using the gun because his rifle was also jammed or because the regular machine gunners were hit. I knew he needed help. I told our platoon sergeant my friend Carden was in trouble and needed help, and then I left and went back to help him.

As I reached the guy firing the M-60 I realized it was not Carden at all, it only looked like him from the back. I had arrived with an ammo can full of M-60 machine gun ammo. In front of us lay dozens of dead N.V.A. and dozens of others who were fleeing across the rice paddy. The gunner continued firing and yelled at me to hook my ammo onto the rest of his. Lying to his right was a pile of hundreds of spent machine gun cartridges.

The gunner continued firing and I could see more Gooks being hit. The machine gun barrel was smoking hot. I knew the other gunner always carried an extra barrel so when one barrel got too hot to fire it could be quickly replaced.

I shouted at him, (I never did know his name), "Where is your partner?"

He yelled back between gun bursts, "On a helicopter I hope." Next, he yelled for me to pour my canteen water onto the steaming hot barrel which I did. I also noticed two other empty canteens, probably his, laying nearby. We continued firing until the fleeing NVA disappeared into the other side of the jungle. Several wounded NVA lay strewn among the dozens of dead. He pulled the trigger on the few remaining NVA, then he picked up the M-60 and we high-tailed it back to the far side of the ridge. Together we must have killed two dozen NVA.

As things began to settle down we took inventory of our casualties. All the corpsmen were either dead or wounded. Our new platoon lieutenant, who had only been with us for about a week, was dead. Our radio operator had been killed. Tall skinny Drucker had been medevaced out. I never found out how bad he was hit, and I never saw him again. One of the Hispanic guys was dead, and his buddy had also been evacuated. Worst of all, Weeocky had been hit with shrapnel and flown out on a helicopter. They said his wounds were in his legs and were not life threatening, but until his return we had lost our point man. Wilson had a slight wound on his right shoulder where a bullet had grazed him. He didn't want to leave because he knew we needed 'every swinging dick' in case of a counter attack. McCray and I figured the worst was over and he should leave. McCray told him to get on the next helicopter and at least get a hot meal and a shower.

He would not hear of it. "There are too many guys with more serious wounds than me that need to get out of here."

Eventually I told him, "That small wound could get infected and then they'll have to amputate your arm at the shoulder." With that Wilson left with the last of the wounded. McCray, Krum, Knowitall, and I were all that was left of our squad. A squad was supposed to have ten to twelve men.

That night after all the wounded had been evacuated, Kilo Company set up a small perimeter. It was small because the company had lost about a third of its men. Before nightfall I walked over to first platoon where my friend Carden was supposed to be. I asked where he was. Several guys said he was one of the first wounded and was med-evacuated out, but they assured me his wounds did not look serious. I remember what the seasoned veteran told McDonald, Carden and me right before we left for the grunts, "One of you will probably die, one will probably be wounded, and one of you will probably be okay." I was okay, Carden was wounded. I wondered how McDonald was doing in Lima Company.

When morning arrived, we broke camp and returned to the scene of the previous day's battle. It was not really a battle, only a large firefight. We picked up all types of gear, including rifles, packs, cartridge belts, unused mortar shells, flak jackets and canteens. We left the area littered with empty rifle shell casings and mortar craters. Later that afternoon, helicopters landed, to the sound of very little enemy fire, and dropped off reinforcements and supplies. I wished the new wide-eyed boots, fresh off the airplanes from the United States, had been there in the morning to witness the leftovers from a firefight. Each set of web gear with the knapsacks represented a Marine lost (killed or wounded) in combat.

The boots fell into two categories. Most were wide-eyed and looked scared. They followed us around like ducklings following their mother. The second group, looked and acted like tough guys. I think most were just trying to over compensate for their hidden fears. Both could have benefited from helping us police up the previous day's devastation.

McCray was given a new boot and when Wilson returned with a fresh bandage on his shoulder, McCray instantly became a new team leader. I could tell McCray wasn't too happy with his new responsibility and the fact that his best buddy, Wilson, now had to take orders from him.

Knowitall was given two new boots and was thrilled to tell them everything he knew. Much of what he told them began with, "Now listen up, this is no shit!" and ended with, "I shit you not!" I was given two green boots that didn't even look like they were old enough to shave. Nonetheless the next morning we saddled up and moved out to continue our journey on The Tami Tron Trail.

The following day spotter planes reported movement in another village. We came near the village but pretended to pass by without checking it out. At night we executed another sneak attack on this village, just like we had at 'No Name'. In the pre-dawn morning we encircled the village by walking on a rice paddy dike. This time the attack was different. We entered the village with hardly any shots being fired. It looked like the Viet Cong had been alerted and left. Several old women and children were captured. We were again ordered to search each hooch.

I entered one large hut with my two new boots, too close behind me, and ordered them to "Back up. One booby trap will kill us all!" I noticed boards on the floor. Every hooch I was ever in had a dirt floor. The boards were nailed together to form a wooden cover that was partially camouflaged with dirt. Someone was in a hurry and didn't hide the hatch well enough. I had no desire to open that hatch with two, green as grass boots as my backup. The nearest veteran was Knowitall. I called him over to cover me. I quickly flipped open the wooden cover. Instantly daylight streamed into the hole below. I viewed several bare feet and legs squirming back into the darkness of the hole. It looked like cockroaches running for cover when the light switch is turned on. I yelled for an interpreter to come over. This interpreter was an American Marine Corporal who was supposed to know how to speak Vietnamese. He yelled down into the hole for them to come out with their hands up. I don't know if he said the words correctly or not. It didn't matter, if they were 'of age males' we were going to kill them anyway. No reply came.

Every Marine carried two fragmentation grenades either on our flak jacket or like me on my suspenders that held up our ammo belt. We carried the old fashioned 'pineapple' shaped grenades that were manufactured for World War II. Knowitall and I each pulled the pin and tossed the 'frags' down into the hole and yelled, "Fire in the hole." That was how we were taught. Only this time it was literally accurate. We waited. Nothing happened. There should have been two explosions almost simultaneously. Nothing went bang. Could it be that both grenades were duds? Perhaps this was not just a hole but the beginning of an elaborate tunnel system. No matter what, something should have gone off. Together we threw our other grenades in the hole and again yelled. Again, nothing happened.

By now the platoon Staff Sergeant came over and asked, "What have we got here?"

I replied, "It's a hole or a tunnel but I definitely saw feet and legs moving down there."

Then Knowitall added, "We've tossed in four grenades and none have gone off."

The sergeant handed each of us one of the newer grenades, and said, "Here try these." The old, fashioned pineapple grenades were nicknamed that because the cast iron mold formed indentations that made them look like pineapples. When they exploded each indentation became burning hot shrapnel that would supposedly kill anyone within six feet of the explosion. The newer fragmentation grenades had a smooth surface and were nicknamed 'lemons', this allowed for more TNT inside. Wrapped around the TNT was a tightly wound wire perforated every half inch, so when it went off, each half inch of wire became a burning hunk of shrapnel and could kill and wound over a larger area.

Together we tossed in the new grenades and once more yelled fire in the hole. A few seconds later a huge explosion erupted in the hole, followed two seconds later by another explosion. The timing devise of any grenade was never the same. They were supposed to detonate in six to eight seconds but in fact it was usually eight to ten or even twelve seconds, although some went off in only six seconds. I don't know about Knowitall, but I was pissed. I had carried around two hand grenades for three months and neither one of them was worth a dam. Well, at least we were getting rid of all the old, World War II ordinance.

Now came the hard part. If this was just a hole, anyone down there was now dead. If it was a tunnel all we may have done was make a big noise, well two big noises. Someone had to go down there and determine if it was a hole or a tunnel. Knowitall motioned to one of his two new boots, to come here.

I stopped him. "We're not going to send a boot down there on his second day in country." I remember what Corporal Waters had always said, 'Don't make someone do something that you are not willing to do yourself.' I always admired and respected Waters.

I continued, "I'll go down." To his credit Knowitall volunteered to go first. I'm not sure if he wanted to impress the boots or he was just brave. All I knew for sure is that there were four unexploded grenades down there.

Of course, we had no flash lights, but we all carried cigarette lighters. I helped Knowitall slide down the hole. In one hand he held his rifle, and in the other he held his lighter. He moved the lighter back and forth to view as much as possible. He said nothing. Then the light went out and he motioned me to help him up. It was a good sign. He stepped out of the hole and into the daylight. He still said nothing and walked over to a tree sat down and leaned back against the bark. He pulled his knees up towards his chest. Was it a hole or a tunnel? Something was wrong. Both the staff sergeant and I walked over to him.

"Well, what is it?" the sergeant asked.

Knowitall stared up at the sky and spoke, "It's a hole". He paused as the sergeant and I looked at each other. Then he spoke softly, "Five dead … two women and three kids." He then slowly lowered his head, folded his arms on his knees and rested his head on his forearms. His words hit me like a punch in the stomach.

So far in this small village we captured some old women and a few children. We had also killed some. This little village was not a strong hold for the Viet Cong or the NVA. We found no ammo, no guns, and no weapons of any kind. We found no sign the enemy was ever there. We left but this time the village was not burned, except into the minds of most of us.

The next day we saddled up and moved out. I was numb. The Sergeant yelled at me to keep my men eight feet apart.

I just looked at them, "You heard the man. I can't keep telling you!" However, it was not the last time I or Corporal Krum would have to remind them.

We had been out in the field for well over three weeks now, but it seemed like three months. There was no hot meal or shower out on patrol. I ran out of tooth paste and was brushing with just spit. One morning it was our platoon's turn to be on point. It was also our squad's turn and my fire team's turn. Without Weeocky I would have to take the point. The last thing we needed was some boot leading the way.

We moved out from the trees before dawn walking in a single straight line. I soon came to a rice paddy. I began walking across one of the dikes on the paddy but only went about thirty feet and stopped. I knew our procedure was to divide up and cross paddies in three columns. I squatted down and whispered back through the column to send the platoon sergeant up. As I sat waiting I saw two dark shapes approaching us, walking down the same rice paddy dike we were on. I only knew a few Vietnamese words and phrases from training in the M.P.'s One was turn off your lights which didn't seem appropriate at this time. The other phrase was "Halt, put your hands up!" which is what I yelled in my best Vietnamese. The two figures froze in place. I couldn't see if they had their hands up or not. Just then the platoon sergeant, running up to the point, hollered something about another unit in the area.

Someone fired a shot. The first figure turned to run. I opened with several blasts. The first figure tumbled backwards. The rest of our squad began firing. My rifle didn't jam, and I continued firing until it did. The second figure ran sideways across the paddy. If he had continued running away he might have been safe. The entire platoon fired and even though it was still not quite light outside he went down, got up and was finally blown away. I wondered where the rest of the NVA were. Was this the beginning of another fire fight or a battle? All was quiet. Knowitall whose team was behind me walked out to where the first body lay. I already had my cleaning rod out and was punching out the spent cartridge. Lying on the dike was a woman about 45 years old. She looked to be the same age as my mother. The other body was a man of about the same age. They were carrying no weapons.

All they were doing was going out to the rice paddy to attend to the crop, just like they or others had been doing for thousands of years. Now they were dead. The man was trying to run back into the wooded area where three tiny huts stood. We approached the hoochs carefully, but everyone had heard the shooting and had fled into the early morning darkness. Should we burn them, or should we leave them alone? It was decided to move on and leave these three huts standing alongside the rice paddy.

Nothing of significance occurred the rest of that day. I had the point and proceeded as slowly and cautiously as I needed. I wasn't very good at spotting trouble, certainly not as good as Weeocky. Each time I stopped to check things out I noticed all the men, veterans and boots would stop, take off their gear and sit back and rest. Some guys even took quick naps. We were all both physically exhausted and mentally drained.

We received a radio message that tomorrow trucks would pick us up at the end of the trail and we could ride back to our old base camp. The news was almost too good to believe. We spent a long but uneventful night. We knew the Gooks listened to our radio messages and the night before we were to leave would be a good time for a surprise attack. Fortunate for us, nothing happened. In the morning we rotated platoons and squads as we did every day. Since our platoon was first yesterday, today we would be last. The same for our squad, the first shall be last. I had been the point man the day before, today I would be the last man on the Tami Tron Trail.

It took a long time, several hours, for the entire Kilo Company to climb aboard the six bys. Each truck would load up fifteen or so guys and then take off. Another truck would back down the narrow trail and pick up some more. We waited in a long line spread out eight feet apart. Most of the time we sat or laid down, waiting to be picked up.

Our platoon sergeant walked to the very back of the line and told Krum, "Be very careful. The fuckin Gooks would love to shoot one of us to make a statement that they're not beat."

As I waited I feared the worst. It would just be my luck that some bastard Gook would shoot me in the back just as I climbed aboard the truck. They would make their point and I would be crippled for life. Perhaps I would be lucky, and they would shoot me in the head. When our turn came, the last of our platoon climbed on the truck as I stood staring down the trail as the last guard. Finally, the sergeant yelled, "Hop aboard!" As I climbed onto the back of the six-by, the sergeant closed the door of the truck cab. He would be riding shotgun. Luckily, nothing happened. We quickly drove on.

The sergeant shouted out the window for us to sing the Marine Corps Hymn. Some of the veterans and all the boots began singing. However, no one finished. I don't know if we were simply too exhausted, or too numb. I didn't sing at all. It's a proud song and at that moment I didn't feel very proud. Yes, we killed a lot of NVA and they too, killed a lot of us. Sadly, we also killed many innocent civilians. Such is the cost of any war.

Chapter 31

THE GREEN TEAM

SOON AFTER I finally returned home from Viet Nam, my father purchased a brand-new Ford convertible. I think in the back of his mind he wanted to sell it to me. He knew I wouldn't take it as a gift, but he offered to sell it to me probably for less than he paid for it. I refused. It was a pretty, green Mercury Cougar and had all the gadgets I wanted in a new car. I think he was very disappointed when I bought a blue 1968 Mustang instead. He didn't understand, but by then I really hated the color, green.

After almost four weeks on that patrol, we returned to our old base to reload, reorganize and get reacquainted with the new guys.

We had no sooner jumped off the truck when the platoon sergeant told us, "I don't know if we will be here for one day or one hour or one week. My guess is we won't be here long."

Several guys began complaining. "Damn it Sarge, we spent over three weeks in the field, we should get three weeks back here at base." It was not to be. The rainy season was over. The NVA were on the move and so we would move out shortly. We had time for a hot shower, mail call and an inspection.

It was weird walking back into our old tents and seeing the cots and personal belongings of guys we knew were dead or wounded so badly they would not be coming back. We were ordered to pack up their belongings in their duffle bag and throw the bags onto a truck to be sent somewhere. Some guys picked through magazines and books and kept toiletries and shoe polish and other items for themselves. I doubted the folks back home wanted their son's Playboy magazine or his Crest toothpaste. We got busy cleaning up.

While back in camp we had time to clean up and to get chewed out. We showered, and we dropped off our filthy jungle utilities at the civilian Gook's hut to be cleaned. We were told it would take several days to clean dozens of uniforms. After showering, we put on clean clothes and went to the mess hall for our first hot meal in weeks. After evening chow, we had a formation and the company commander gave a short speech. First, he congratulated us and told us that we, the 5th Marines, were going to be given a Presidential Unit Citation for our bravery and heroism. The 5th Marines were already the most highly decorated Regiment in the entire Marine Corps. The honor meant nothing to us. It was something that went into our personnel file and nothing else. Then the Captain chewed us out for having dirty rifles. He explained that these new M-16's had to be cleaned much more carefully and cleaned more often. The next morning, we would have a rifle inspection.

That night of course we all had guard duty as usual. We were instructed to, "Clean your rifle while you were on duty." The captain was correct the rifle did need to be cleaned more often and kept clean. But it still did not change the problems we experienced with the rifle. The M-16 would continue to malfunction until the ammo and chambers were replaced. But we believed him and set about cleaning them.

That evening as we sat around in groups discussing world issues and movie stars we wanted to take to bed, the new corpsman came around with a clip board. He was making a list of all of us who had minor wounds that would make us eligible for a purple heart. Wilson of course showed his stitches and scab on his shoulder. The corpsman filled out the report. McCray pointed to me and told the corpsman about the tiny scab under my right eye. The corpsman began filling out the form as I sat and thought. I stopped him and said, "No, don't put me down for anything."

I had two reasons for not wanting a purple heart. First, I remembered my mother, who still believed I was 'safe and sound' in Okinawa. If she received a government letter saying her son had been wounded fighting Communist insurgents in South East Asia, she would have a heart attack. I had already killed one 45-year-old woman on a rice paddy and I didn't want my mother's death on my conscience. The second reason was even more important. My tiny scab was not worth mentioning. I could never look at myself in the mirror if I equated this wound with somebody who had lost a limb or an eye or wound up in a wheel chair. It just wasn't right. Many of the other guys including the new corpsman wanted to argue about it. It was my decision and I stuck to it and have never regretted doing so.

The next day, after morning chow, we stood for an inspection and waited for news of when we would return to the field. The Captain didn't show up for inspection, but our platoon sergeant checked everyone's weapon. Everyone passed. After inspection we had mail call. As we sat around reading and dreaming about life back home, a truck arrived. In the truck were supplies that had to be unloaded and with Weeocky riding shotgun. Man, were we glad to see him, especially me. I hated being point man. Weeocky never talked much and I never heard him joke around. He was one serious Indian. He showed us his legs. He had bandages still covering some nasty holes burned into his skin from mortar shrapnel that would leave scars for life. He only asked one question, "Who are these new guys?" After they introduced themselves we all got acquainted. The usual questions were asked about where they were from and did they join or were they drafted. It turned out most had joined, so they said.

With the arrival of Weeocky the sergeant made some shifts in personnel. I was assigned a new guy from first squad to be in my fire team. He was different from the rest of the boots. His name was Cranston and looked and acted older. He was only a PFC (private first class) but this was his second tour in Viet Nam. He had a strange story. Evidently after his first tour in country as a truck driver, he had to finish out his four-year enlistment stationed at Camp Pendleton in California. On a weekend pass he and some other guys went down to Tijuana, got drunk and got into a fight with some sailors from San Diego. The Mexican police arrested him and his buddies, but he got into a fight with the police. The judge sentenced him to one year in a Mexican jail. He only served nine months and was released on good behavior. While he was in jail the only thing he had to read was the Bible and he discovered Jesus. He swore he would never drink again. However, when he returned to Camp Pendleton he had been U.A. (unauthorized absence) for nine months. The Marine Corps busted him down from corporal to private, the lowest rank there was. As a private he hated cleaning heads and doing every dirty job they had so he asked to make a deal. He volunteered to do another tour of duty in Viet Nam and the Marine Corps promoted him to PFC and promised that he could win back his rank of corporal in six months. However, what they didn't tell him was they were changing his MOS from truck driver to Grunt. A lot of his story made sense but as I had discovered before, there were a lot of bull shit artists and con men in the Corps.

The supply truck delivered C-rations, ammo, and some personal items like soap, toothpaste and tooth brushes to our camp. I was kind of disappointed with the personal items. It meant we would not have a chance to go to a real PX and buy other items like paper and envelopes, or snack food. The truck also contained towels and I hope I don't have to tell you what color they were. Here's a hint. Our underwear was green. Our socks were green. Every bit of clothing we wore was green. Even our helmets were covered in green camouflage. The towels looked like the typical bath towel from a cheap motel. The sergeant ordered a work party to cut each towel in half and hand one half to each of us. Because the temperature was getting hotter each day these towels were issued to wipe sweat off our face and eyes, so we could see better and shoot straight. In the jungle and rice paddies we soon discovered they were best used when soaked in water and wrapped around our neck to help cool off our bodies.

On guard duty the next night, McCray, Wilson, Walker and I sat around talking before jumping into our fox holes for the night. The new guys formed a group of their own. The conversation was always the same. What are you going to do when you get home? We hadn't been paid in months and we all had savings and back pay that would add up to over a thousand dollars. I figured I would go home with nearly two thousand dollars. A brand-new car only cost three thousand dollars. So, we discussed cars, specifically Fords and Chevys. I wanted a Ford Mustang and McCray wanted a Chevy Camaro. We were dreaming about what color to get. I wanted blue and McCray wanted yellow. I asked Wilson, who was playing with the scab on his shoulder, what color car he was going to get. I'll never forget his response. "I don't know what color it will be, but I know what color it won't be. It won't be green!"

We all had common dislikes and complaints. Our favorite song to sing was, "We Got to Get out of This Place", by the Animals. They never played it on Armed Forces Radio, but we had recordings we heard and had all memorized it. We also complained about the unofficial motto of the Marine Corps. There's the right way, the wrong way and then there's the Marine Corps Way, which was a combination of 'makes no sense' and the wrong way. Everyone would quote, "Eat the apple and fuck the Corps!" and "Any team but the Green Team". Guys would threaten to shoot their own sons if they tried to join the Marine Corps. I have always been amazed that everyone I met in the Corps hated it when they were in but seemed so damn proud of the Corps when they got out.

James M. Dixon

Chapter 32

THE TAKING OF DUC PHU

AMERICA HAS, throughout most of our history been a peace-loving nation. Recently we've gotten involved in fighting in Croatia, Iraq, Afghanistan and other parts of the Middle East. Troops have been deployed and lives lost on both sides. Regardless of the merits of war, some people never want to send in ground troops. They want to win the conflict with air planes. Each time I hear the arguments pro and con of using ground troops or just an air war, I am reminded of a village in Viet Nam called Duc Phu.

Once more we prepared for battle. Word came down right after morning chow that the choppers would come in and we had to be ready to leave in one hour. We didn't know if it was an operation, a search and destroy mission or just a patrol. Of course, the 'where' was also a mystery and never questioned. We were each given the usual two C-ration boxes which meant we would be gone for maybe one day and then we would need to be resupplied. We showed the 'boots' how to stuff the cans into socks and wrap them in layers of socks to prevent loose cans from making too much noise. We also showed them how to fold their poncho into a square to lay flat in their pack, placing it to fit against their back for comfort. None of this advice was taught in boot camp or infantry training. We explained to the boots there was no room for extra boots and utilities. Which meant the same trousers and shirt (utility jack) would be worn for the duration of whatever we were doing. We each picked two grenades out of a box and showed the boots how to attach them to the shoulder harness that held up our cartridge belt. We filled our two canteens and told the boots to write letters home and ask friends and family for as many pre-sweetened Kool Aid packets as they could send. We told them to always add iodine tablets to their canteen, so they wouldn't get the 'screaming shits'. Kool Aid packs were worth their weight in gold. The new boots complained about all the extra ammo they had to carry. We told them 'Now you know why they call us, "Ammo Humpers".

We would each be leaving behind our personal gear like magazines, letters, our extra utilities and extra boots. For the past two days we had use of a cot, blanket and even a pillow. Of course, we spent the days on work details and then guard duty at night. So, the cot was only a staging area for the few personal items we had. We did not realize at the time but none of us would be coming back to this spot. Some would never come back at all.

We straggled to the top of a hill and fell into formation. After a quick 'once over' inspection, each squad was divided into groups of twelve. I had never been in a helicopter before but evidently there were to be 24 of us per chopper. Soon we could see the choppers in groups of three, far off in the distant sky. As they approached the make shift landing zone, the noise and wind from the chopper blades seemed unreal. It all happened so fast. The next thing I knew we were airborne and on our way to God knew where or what.

Aboard the chopper we sat twelve on each side facing one another. No one spoke. We couldn't hear anything anyway. Some guys sat with their eyes closed. Some stared straight ahead. Some prayed and crossed themselves. Even though I had never been on a helicopter before, I knew from training on simulators and landing crafts, that when we landed the back ramp would drop open, but we never knew what would happen next. We had all heard stories of choppers landing in the middle of the NVA. We sat wondering what it would be like. I tried to look out the small window but all I could see was gray sky. Soon we could feel the craft descending. I thought to myself, *'But I'm not ready. I want the trip to be longer.'*

We landed with a thud and the rear ramp dropped open. Out we scurried, fanning out in a semi-circle with rifles pointed at the ready. No shots were fired. The terrain looked much like the hill top we had just left. At first, I thought we had taken off, flew up and around, only to return to the same spot. Had this been a drill? No such luck. To my left was a wooded area. The lieutenant, our new platoon leader, gave the order to move into the woods. As we ran towards the woods those three choppers took off as three more approached the landing zone.

The wooded area was narrow. We could see daylight through to the other side. Sometimes villages separated their rice paddies with small strips of woods. Once we entered the trees we immediately began walking down a small grade and then up to the other side of the trees. This strip of woods grew on both sides of this narrow gully. So this gully in the woods made a perfect staging area. We had both cover and concealment while we waited for the rest of the 100 plus men from Kilo Company to arrive.

We took cover and assessed what stood before us. We could see the next village. As we gazed across a sizable rice paddy we spotted a large village of almost 50 huts, on top of a knoll. It was at least one hundred yards across the paddy to the village. This village seemed to be surrounded by one giant sea of a rice paddy. The rainy season had just ended, and the paddies were still flooded with about six to eight inches of water. The only things not covered in water were the dikes that randomly crisscrossed toward the village. To our left was a concrete bridge that connected the village to dry land. Concrete told us this bridge was built by the French who had once occupied Viet Nam. As I looked closer I could see other Marines to our right and left. I couldn't tell what companies they were but guessed they had to be (India, Lima or Mike), all part of the 3rd Battalion, with usually 150 men in each Company. Apparently, we had this village surrounded!

I could overhear the lieutenant explaining to the platoon sergeant what was happening. This village was called Duc Phu and suspected of being a headquarters for the Viet Cong. Our job was to take the village and destroy any Viet Cong. After the search and destroy missions I knew the phrase "destroy any Viet Cong" meant kill anything that breathed. The lieutenant pointed to a giant hill that he referred to as a mountain off to our right. Duc Phu sat at the base of this hill. On top of the hill we could see a military camp with its tell-tale tents and sand bag bunkers. I figured it must be an artillery base. The lieutenant explained to the sergeant the camp was a base for the Army Special Forces, the Green Berets. Several of us overheard this conversation and simultaneously gave a sigh of disgust.

The sergeant said what we were all thinking, "So, the Special Forces have a Viet Cong headquarters on their door step and didn't even know it."

The Lieutenant's only comment was, "Yep!"

One of the new guys, a "boot" of less than a month, asked a question, "Why don't we let that company by the cement bridge walk across and into the village?"

Cranston, who was the oldest in our squad, answered what the rest of us already knew, "Cause the gooks probably booby trapped the bridge. That's just what they would hope we would do."

The boot then asked, "Why don't we bring in some tanks?"

We all must have rolled our eyes, and gave a group sigh, because the boot asked with a dumb look on his face, "What?"

Again, Cranston answered, "Because, a ten-ton tank would bog down in that rice paddy like quicksand. How long have you been here? Have you seen any tanks?" Cranston was correct. I had been here for over ten months and was still waiting to see my first tank.

As usual we sat around and waited for orders and I guess for other companies to get ready. We knew we had to cross that giant rice paddy to reach the village of Duc Phu. How to cross was the big question. With eight inches of water plus the mud, running across that rice paddy would be very slow. One or two riflemen or snipers could shoot dozens of us by the time we were half way across. We had all crossed hundreds of rice paddies before. The country was nothing but one rice paddy after another. The only practical way across a paddy was to walk on the dikes. Each dike was about eighteen inches wide, just wide enough for one person to walk on. Many a Marine, with full battle gear, had accidentally stepped too close to the edge and tumbled into the paddy. Plunging into the smelly water, which was, in reality the Gooks' bathroom, was bad enough. But of course, the soaked Marine would be met with laughter and comments about his coordination, his intelligence, and probably something about his mother. Falling into the Gooks' toilet was a mistake we hopefully only made once. I slipped in the first month I was in country but luckily only got my boots wet. It took days of airing out those boots to get rid of the smell.

Crossing on the dikes posed several problems. First, we had to walk in a straight line. One bullet from the enemy could pass through two or three men. A single VC with an AK-47 could wipe out an entire squad with one burst of fire. The dikes crisscrossed the paddy in a random pattern. No two distances between dikes were the same. If we walked on the dikes we would in fact be walking back and forth in front of the enemy like ducks in a shooting gallery. The alternative was to try to slog through ankle deep mud and eight inches of water in the paddy. Both would be slow and murderous. We waited for the decision of when to move and what method we would use to attack Duc Phu.

We didn't have to wait long to find out we would walk across on the dikes. As usual the rule of eight paces between troops would be followed. The best we could hope for was that the village contained no VC. If so it would not be the first time that the whole exercise was a waste of time. Several times before we had walked down a trail towards a suspected VC village and found it empty. No VC and no one else for that matter. Either the VC had never been there, or they knew we were coming and left. Those other villages were deserted. Maybe this village would be the same.

Our platoon was divided into three squads which would all begin walking toward Duc Phu on three separate dikes. Second squad, where I was, would be in the middle with the platoon sergeant, and the radio operator. The lieutenant would walk with the first squad and the corpsman would travel with the third squad.

It was common knowledge that the enemy liked to shoot at leaders, and corpsmen. First, they would shoot the radio operator. He was easy to spot with the eight-foot whip antenna. When the corpsman came to his aid they would shoot him. The lieutenant would begin giving orders and then he would be the next to fall.

That is exactly what happened. Just like the VC had scripted it. It all happened in less time than it takes for me to describe it. At the first sound of gun fire everyone jumped into the paddy next to their dike and began returning fire. The lieutenant ran toward our middle squad and gave the order to fall back towards the wood line. That was the last thing he said before a bullet passed through his shoulder. No one had to tell us twice to head back to the woods.

Several guys grabbed the radio operator, the lieutenant, and the corpsman along with two others who were hit. As I headed back the sergeant pointed to me and yelled, "You! Grab the radio!" The last thing I wanted was that heavy radio, but I grabbed it and thought, 'Well, I'll carry it to the woods, but someone else can be the new radio operator.'

As soon as we reached the wood line the firing ceased. Again, the platoon sergeant ordered, "Dixon, get base on the radio. We need a med. vac."

I looked at him and said, "But I don't want to be the radio operator."

His only reply, "Yeah, and I don't want to be the new platoon leader either. Get base on the horn."

I put the radio mic to my mouth and spoke, "Kilo-3-5 to Base, Kilo-3-5 to Base, over."

We immediately heard the reply, "Base to Kilo-3-5, what is your situation, over?" I handed the mic to the staff sergeant. I had now become the radio operator.

We had four wounded and one dead. The lieutenant was the only one hit in the shoulder while the other three were leg strikes. The fact the radio operator was the only one killed was not lost on me. The VC had time to aim at him. The rest were all shot on the move. Again, we thanked God the VC were such horrible shots. Helicopters soon landed, and the wounded and dead radio operator were loaded and sent back to Chu Lai. We waited. Only now we began to dig fox holes for a long stay and for protection. The hope that Duc Phu would be empty vanished with the first assault. We knew other assaults would soon follow.

The staff sergeant, our new platoon leader, called in an artillery strike. Word of the artillery strike was passed to everyone. The older more experienced guys like me began to dig deeper holes. Another boot asked, "Why?"

Again, Cranston was the first to explain, "Have you ever heard of a short round?" Do you want one of them dropping in your hip pocket?" A short round was an artillery shell that fell short of its target. I was reminded that just as many guys died from 'friendly' fire as enemy fire.

The boots began digging deeper holes.

We sat around waiting for the artillery to open-up. Everything moves slowly in the military. Hurry up and wait. It gave us time to talk and entertain ourselves. Four guys got together to play cards, which Cranston always carried with him. Because I had the radio and needed to receive messages I didn't participate in the game. I only watched. The three other guys playing cards were McCray, Wilson and Weeocky.

I remember the first time I went on patrol with Weeocky. He was our platoon's point man. It was a night patrol. We left the perimeter of our base camp and went out in a drizzling rain. We left from one area, walked around the outside of the perimeter looking for the VC, and then returned to a different area. The idea was that if the VC were going to set up mortars or rockets outside of our lines, we would bump into them and either, prevent an attack or at least everyone would be given a warning, when the VC killed us. As the patrol ended and we neared the perimeter, Weeocky stopped and walked back to the squad leader. Weeocky said nothing. As the new boot, I was told to now take the point. I couldn't quite see our lines in the dark and rain but knew we had to be close.

As we approached I heard the scariest sound anyone in combat ever hears. Click, click-click, over and over, again. It was the sound of bolts slamming rounds into rifle chambers and safeties being taken off. I could have shit a brick. I was speechless as I heard, "Who goes there"?

The squad leader had to answer for me. "It's a patrol, second squad. We're returning."

Then a second question came from the line, "What is the password?"

Again, the squad leader replied for us, "Fuck your password!" We never used passwords. Yes, we were given a new password every night. It was two words, the sign and the counter sign. Usually two words with unconnected meaning, like ham and bacon, instead of ham and eggs which might be easily guessed. No one could remember the passwords. It was a system left over from World War II when the Germans spoke English very well. The Gooks all spoke with horrible accents which made passwords obsolete. When the squad leader told them who we were, everyone, unless it was a boot, knew we weren't the VC. And it only took one new boot to accidentally fire his rifle and all hell would have cut loose. That's why Weeocky never took point coming back to our own lines. I remembered when I was in the MP's and our patrol walked in front of the 7th Marines and the 7th Marines had opened-up on us and nearly killed all six of us.

After a while McCray, Wilson and Weeocky were accusing Cranston of cheating. In the meantime, the platoon sergeant called in the grid coordinates to the artillery. The coordinates were "said again". The word repeat was never used on the radio. "Repeat" was the command to fire again. The sergeant gave the order to "Fire Three". They always fired three for triangulation. We dropped down in our holes and covered our heads. We heard three high pitched swooshing sounds as the shells whizzed by overhead. Then three thundering booms as the shells exploded. One landed square in the middle of the paddy. One landed near the bridge. The third fell to the right nearest the actual village. The explosions were easily observed and formed kind of a triangle. The sergeant studied the map and told the artillery to move their aim, so they would zero in on the village. Three more rounds were ordered and fired. This time one landed on the far side of the village, the other two landed on our side of the village. The sergeant gave the order to "Fire for effect". Soon dozens of shells began raining down on Duc Phu.

I lay crouched against the side of the fox hole I shared with Cranston. It felt and sounded like I imagined World War I or II or Korea must have been like. The shelling was intense and relentless. I thought to myself, 'Nothing could survive in Duc Phu'. When the bombardment stopped, and I finally got a peek across the rice paddy at the village, I was shocked. Parts of some of the huts were still standing. Most had sustained heavy damage and some of the grass thatched roofs were burning. I thought, 'Boy, I hope the shelling got everyone.'

The staff sergeant passed the word down the line to the rest of the platoon, to begin the new assault in ten minutes. This time we would walk side by side through the paddy. Those one hundred yards seemed much longer now. When the order was given, Kilo Company stepped out of the woods in a parallel line and began walking toward Duc Phu. There was no sense in running, if, as we hoped, everyone was dead in the village.

If the VC were still alive, when they began firing we could head back to the wood line. I hoped the VC would not be like the Americans at Bunker Hill and wait until they saw the whites of our eyes. They didn't. We had not moved more than fifteen steps when we began hearing the whizzing sounds of bullets passing over head and then the sound of gun fire from the village. A couple of bullets hit the water in front of me and splashed paddy shit in my face. The fire was not nearly as intense as before, but it would be suicide to try a one hundred plus yard assault across that rice paddy. Back into the wood line we scrambled. The VC must have gotten quite a laugh seeing an entire company of United States Marines running like scared rabbits back to their holes.

I don't know about the rest of the guys, but I was pissed and amazed. How could they have survived that bombardment? On the radio I called, "Kilo 3-5 to Base, Kilo 3-5 to Base, over."

I immediately heard back, "Base to Kilo 3-5, what is your situation?"

I handed the radio mic to the platoon sergeant. I heard him speak into the mic, "Those Mother Fuckers must really be dug in." I could tell I was not the only one who was pissed.

Back to our holes we went to wait. Some guys wrote letters. Some played cards, some sat around and 'shot the shit'. Many tried to get some shuteye. Secretly we all worried what the 'powers to be' would try next. Because I manned the radio and could hear what was being said to base and what base was ordering, I had the 'scoop'.

Several times guys would come over to our fox hole and ask, "What's the scoop?" I would whisper what I had heard, and they would pass the word to the rest of the troops. It was kind of like that old game we played in elementary school. The teacher would whisper something in the ear of one student and say pass it on. By the time the secret went around the room and back to the teacher, no one could believe how much it had changed.

It was decided to use naval gun fire. Up to that point, I had never experienced naval artillery.

I found it interesting when I heard the platoon leader tell the staff sergeant, "Well, we may not have any idea where we are, but at least we know we're no farther than twenty miles from the coast."

The sergeant gave a knowing nod and replied, "Yeah, those guns can only fire so far."

As the platoon leader checked the map and grid coordinates the sergeant added, "I'll pass the word to dig in deeper."

I thought to myself, 'twenty miles?'

I heard the sergeant tell everyone, "Those naval shells weigh as much as a Volkswagen and a short round could wipe out an entire platoon. Pass it on!" Everyone began throwing dirt out of their fox holes like they were digging to China, or, given where we were, digging to America.

I thought and feared, *'A one-ton shell being fired twenty miles away, from a rolling ship… I hope they are allowing for windage.'* Every other man carried an E-tool, which was a small folding shovel. Everyone who carried it complained that the handle was always catching on something or would stick you in the ass when you tried to sit back. Now everyone wished that E-tool was the size of a snow shovel.

We were still digging when the sergeant yelled, "Take cover!" The ground began to shake like the beginning of an earthquake. Then it sounded like a giant freight train flying over our heads. It was incredible, and I will never forget it. The explosion was deafening, and I covered my ears, but it was too late. When the noise and shaking subsided I had a ringing in my head that hurt. *'Wow!'* I thought. Then three more rounds roared overhead. When the noise died down, I peeked up out of the fox hole. A huge gray cloud rolled up toward the sky like the cloud from a nuclear bomb. The cloud hung directly over Duc Phu. When the smoke cleared I could see no huts, no trees, no anything. Only burning debris remained. A second naval barrage would not be necessary.

We prepared for the final assault on what used to be Duc Phu. Again, we lined up in the wood line and when given the order proceeded to step out into the paddy and began trudging through the muddy water toward the village. This time after about twenty steps we heard the distinctive sound of automatic rifle fire, probably an AK-47. It stopped us in our tracks. We each looked at each other in disbelief. The shots seemed random, sporadic, but, definitely from an automatic rifle. It was the typical POW, POW, POW, POW, POW followed by more POW, POW... I didn't hear the bullets pass over and couldn't tell who they were shooting toward. We could only see the small tell-tale flash and smoke from where the shots came from. Again, we were ordered back into the wood line. This time I wasn't so much pissed as I was amazed. Several thoughts entered my mind. How could anyone survive those explosions? Also, why would anyone want to defend that village? But then I realized the enemy knew they were surrounded and there was no escape.

Once again, I contacted base and handed the radio mic to the platoon leader and listened as the next option was discussed. Base contacted the Marine Air Wing. An air strike was ordered. At least we would not have to worry about a short round. Our fox holes were plenty deep enough and we could sit in the tree line and watch the Phantom jets fire rockets on what remained of the village. I stayed next to the radio and overheard the conversation between the pilot and the captain, our company commander.

The Phantom jet passed overhead twice and then radioed a question, "Where exactly are your lines and the village?" Even the pilot couldn't tell where Duc Phu had been. Our company captain tried to explain where we were and where the village was. A jet pilot flying three hundred miles an hour and at a thousand feet above us was having trouble locating the enemy. The pilot requested us to throw out some yellow smoke grenades, so as he made his strafe he would know where to fire. Our platoon and the other platoons complied, and several yellow grenades were tossed out in front of our lines.

As streams of yellow smoke drifted up and the breeze carried it across our lines, I heard the platoon sergeant and others yell, "Holy Fuck! The

Gooks have thrown out yellow smoke grenades too!"

We all looked up at the sky and saw the most terrifying thing ever. A Phantom jet was roaring down towards us and we could see the machine gun fire coming from the bottom of the jet. Each round from the jet was a twenty-millimeter grenade that soon landed right in front of us in the rice paddy. The explosions blew water, mud and debris high into air and on to us. Amazingly no one was hurt. I guess because the water and mud muzzled the explosions. However, a lot of Marines had to check their skivvy drawers. I was one of them.

The captain yelled into his radio so loud several of us could hear him on my radio. The pilot apologized and said he deliberately fired into the patty. Now he knew where the village was and would fire on it. This time the roar of the jet sent us into our holes. We peered out from our holes like mice looking for food. The twenty-millimeter shells landed in the village confirming the exact location.

Our commander gave the order to, "Light 'em up". This time, three Phantom jets screamed down and dropped three napalm shells on the village. The explosions were different from the artillery shells. Reddish orange scorching hot balls of fire glowing with black smoke boiled upward. It looked like the bowels of hell. The heat from the napalm was so intense we had to cover our faces and not look directly at the village. And we were at least one hundred yards away. The smell reminded me of burning tires. The heat was so intense it caused a breeze at our backs as the fire sucked the air upward.

The idea was that no matter how deep the Gooks had tunneled, the burning napalm would suck the oxygen out of their holes. I thought, 'What a way to die!'

We waited for the fires to burn out and the heat to subside. While we waited, noon approached so we broke out the C-rations. Each C-ration came with a small box containing four cigarettes. I traded mine for food. Chow time was always a good time to bitch, complain and scrutinize our

---

situation. Questions were thrown out, answers offered, and predictions made. Most were bullshit and even meant to be humorous. Such as, "After the shelling, we will all walk into Duc Phu without firing a shot."

Another added, "And then we'll get back on the helicopters and fly back to Chu Lai and take hot showers."

"Yeah and go to the PX."

"Yeah, and then they will fly us back to the PX in San Diego."

Cranston brought us back to reality. "It depends on how long the VC have been in that village. They could have dug miles and miles of tunnels. It doesn't matter how many bombs and shells our guys drop. Sooner or later somebody with pointed sticks will have to go in."

We all thought about what he said. Then I asked, "What do you mean, 'pointed sticks'?"

He shrugged his shoulders and continued, "Ever since the cavemen, people have been fighting wars. The cavemen used pointed sticks. The Greeks and Romans used spears and swords. Washington, Napoleon and Hitler used bayonets, just like we do. There will always be a hill, a ridge, an island, a village or a city that has to be taken. And in the end, it will be grunts like us with pointed sticks that get the job done." He held up his bayonet.

We all thought about what he said. Most shrugged it off as more bullshit. Deep in our hearts we all hoped he was wrong but knew he was probably right.

We continued to wait for the fires to completely burn out before we began the next assault. This time most of us would slog through the rice paddy while the first squad would walk on the dikes in hope of reaching the village quickly. Once they were in the village the rest of us would also climb on to the dikes. The command was given, and we began walking forward. This time, to our relief, we heard no enemy fire. Just as the first squad was about at the edge of the village a couple of VC began shooting. I was still slogging through knee deep mud and water. Because I carried that extra twenty, pound radio I sank deeper into the water and fell behind. First squad began returning fire and the other two squads jumped onto the dikes and began hurrying towards the village.

When I finally reached the closest dike, that ran parallel to the village, I could not get my leg and foot up onto the edge of the dike. Each time I tried to lift my foot onto the dike my other leg sank deeper in the mud. I could hear the platoon sergeant yelling at me to hurry up. He needed the radio that was weighing me down. Suddenly Weeocky ran across the dike to help me. He held out his hand and I grasped his wrist as he grasped mine. As he began to lift me and the radio out of the paddy, he suddenly let go and I went tumbling backwards into the paddy. I thought, 'Weeocky, this is no time to be joking around!' As I landed on my back the radio buried itself in the mud. Then I realized that Weeachy was lying on top of me! His face laid on my chest. As I lifted his head up and pulled him off to my left side, I noticed the gaping hole in his chest. Blood dribbled from his mouth. He had been shot in the back. The bullet passed through his flak jacket and out of his chest, taking his heart with it. Part of his heart was splashed on my chest. He was already dead.

Several other guys ran to our aid. They managed to get me up and on to the dike. I had to hurry toward the platoon sergeant who still needed the radio. By now the shooting in the village had all but ceased. By the time I reached the village the only thing left to do was find the entrances to the tunnels where the Gooks had been hiding. Grenades were tossed in and then some poor bastard had to crawl into the hole and find what the Gooks had left. The remaining tunnels were permanently blown shut with explosives. What was left of Duc Phu belonged to us.

Helicopters were called in. Weeocky's body and several wounded were placed inside the choppers. Their war was over. The rest of the day and evening we waited to find out where and what would happen next. Eventually we saddled up and headed out toward the next village.

Whoever fired the shot that killed Weeocky was probably aiming for me, the radio guy. Weeocky saved my life that day. He received no medal for bravery. His family got an American flag, a Purple Heart Medal and a form letter from the military, simply stating he had died while fighting Communist insurgents in Southeast Asia. They would never know how he died or what he did in Viet Nam.

You won't find any mention of Duc Phu in any history books. You won't even find it in military history books of Viet Nam. It was not an important event. Even the Marines that fought there never gave it much thought. To them it was just another village that had to be taken, just like the countless hills or ridges or other villages that soldiers and Marines were ordered to capture. Except for the few who died there or the dozen or so that were wounded there, most would prefer to forget it.

I only retell this story because I remember Duc Phu every time I hear a politician, or a reporter say the military is only going to use robots or drones, in some far-off land. They'll say, "It's only going to be an air campaign." I know we took Duc Phu that day. It wasn't done with tanks, or planes or artillery, or even naval gunfire. It was taken by men with bayonets. Or as Cranston said: "With pointed sticks". It's always been that way and always will be that way.

Chapter 33

BECKY'S LETTER

I GUESS WE all have memories of things in our life we regret. I'm not talking about the car you bought that turned out to be a lemon, or the marriage that fell apart or the career path that turned into a dead end. I'm talking about opportunities we had but failed to act on. Maybe we regret not studying harder in school, or perhaps not finishing school, or regretting not asking the girl you had a crush on for a date. I have my own regrets, but I don't include cars I thought about buying one day but they were gone the next or people I should have told to go to hell but didn't. I believe God never meant some things 'to be' anyway.

We left the village of Duc Phu and proceeded down another trail. We didn't know it at the time, but this was the beginning of an operation called "Operation Union'. The object was for the 5th Marine Regiment to find, engage and destroy elements of the NVA who had arrived in South

Viet Nam to attack American troops and installations. We wandered up, down, and around hills for several weeks. The terrain was much the same. There were some rice paddies, but the landscape was far too hilly for growing much rice. Villages were farther apart so we saw very fewer people. It was obvious the NVA was not interested in fighting us unless they had the upper hand. We would walk slowly along trails and across rice paddies, sensing but not seeing the enemy. However, every time a helicopter arrived with supplies, we could hear AK47's being fired from the cover of dense woods. The NVA were all around us.

Our biggest problem continued to be getting food. Helicopters tried to resupply us every other day with C-rations. Most times we could not find a flat, open space for choppers to land. Since I now carried the radio, I knew when spotter planes would tell us they saw movement and we would change direction and investigate. Once we were ordered to 'fix bayonets' and walk side by side through an eight-foot high sugar cane field. We couldn't see more that one foot in front of us. It was scary thinking that at any moment we could be face to face with someone trying to kill us. Our entire company walked all the way through the cane field and saw nothing. I believe the spotter plane mistook a farmer for some NVA troops or the NVA was deliberately leading us away from a good L.Z. (landing zone). Without C-rations we had to live off the land. The only food we could find were peanuts. Raw, unsalted peanuts and sugar cane stalks were eaten far too often.

Getting letters and news from home while on an operation was rare. Helicopter pilots weren't too keen on risking their lives, so we could have mail call. One or two choppers bringing in food, medicine, and ammo didn't have much room for a bag full of letters. We had been in the jungle for almost three weeks when we stopped at a clearing big enough for helicopters to land with supplies and mail.

We were all instructed to write take time to write a letter home. Of course, we had no stationary, so we were told to take a box of C-rations and carefully tear off the back of the box and use it as a post card. On one side in the upper left corner we wrote out our return address as simply 'K-3-5' Marines, Viet Nam. Then we carefully wrote the address of who the card was going to. In the upper right, hand corner where a stamp would normally go, we simply wrote the word 'FREE'. On the other side we wrote a note just like you would a post card.

This whole process posed a problem for me. I remembered what happened the last time my mother got a confusing letter from me. Sending a make shift postcard from a torn-up box of C-rations would send up a whole lot of red flags. Not writing to her would cause even more problems. The solution was to send two postcards, one to my Aunt and one to my Grandparents who both were in on the 'white lie' of my being in Okinawa. I gave instructions for them to contact my mother and tell her all was well in Japan.

The day I wrote those postcards was one I will never forget. Three weeks in the jungle means three weeks without a hot meal or a shower or even a letter from home. On that day we finally had mail-call. I got four letters: one from Johnny Riblett (my friend and neighbor), one from my mother, one from my grandmother, and one from Becky. Becky was not my girlfriend, just a good friend from high school who happened to be a 'girl'. I quickly opened each letter which also contained a pack of pre-sweetened Kool Aid, and stuck the Kool Aid in my pack. I then began reading all of them saving, Becky's for last. All was well at home. Johnny was doing fine in college. My mother was still convinced I was not in Viet Nam, but rather in Okinawa. Becky's letter came as a surprise. She was inviting me to her wedding. I had never gotten a letter saying she was engaged, but I was not shocked, since I knew a lot of mail was lost. As I sat leaning up against a fallen tree, I had mixed emotions. No, I wasn't jealous because she was getting married. I knew she would marry a good man. She wouldn't marry any other kind. I was happy for her, but also jealous because her life was moving forward. She was finishing her degree from the University of Delaware, and her life was moving in the right direction. My life on the other hand was stuck in neutral. As a matter of fact, it might be ending at any moment. I put Becky's letter in my shirt pocket to save the wedding date. The other letters I threw away.

I sat there feeling sorry for myself and wondering if I would make it home in time for the wedding or if I would make it home at all. That's when it began. The NVA we had been chasing for nearly three weeks finally caught us. All hell broke loose. There were mortars, rockets, machine gun fire and unbelievable noise. It was not the first firefight I was ever in, but it was the worst. I was the radio operator, which meant I carried that heavy thing which was our only communication for 'help'. When I was able to reach someone on the other end, I would hand the 'mic' to the lieutenant or to the platoon sergeant. That day I handed it to the sergeant, because the lieutenant was one of the first to die.

A lot of men died that day. But there were a lot more who were wounded, maybe two or three times as many. I remember the sergeant pleading into the radio for helicopters to try and pick up the wounded. The pilots refused to come in because they said it was too dangerous. They were right. It was. We would have to wait for night fall. Once it got dark the small choppers called 'Hueys' could land with their lights off. Lucky for us it was a moonless night and very dark. The NVA couldn't see the choppers. But they sure could hear them. The Hueys were so loud the NVA couldn't tell exactly where they were so they just fired in the general direction of the noise. The choppers would only come in one at a time. Each chopper could haul out four wounded men on each trip. Sometimes four of us would pick up a wounded Marine and carry him to the chopper. Sometimes two of us would carry one, and sometimes one of us would toss a wounded man over our shoulder and run to the chopper. To this day I still cannot look at a helicopter or hear one fly over, without also remembering the hissing sound a bullet makes as it whizzes past you. Or the pinging sound it makes as it pops through the aluminum on a chopper.

The evacuation went on, one chopper at a time, for most of the night. Some guys would only make one trip out to the landing zone. Some made two or three. Some guys got hit on the way to the chopper and we just put them on with the rest of the wounded. I don't know how many trips I made, probably more than I should have. I just couldn't stand to see wounded guys lying there and not do something for them. It was hard work on a very hot night. When we were finally finished I was soaking wet with sweat through my uniform down to my tee-shirt. Afterward, I lay down between the jungle and the grass of the landing zone and waited for dawn.

Just as the sun was coming up, a relief column arrived and secured a much larger perimeter, so it would be safe for larger helicopters to land.

Two of the rescuers came over to me and started to pick me up. I said, "Whoa, what are you doing!?"

"We're putting all the wounded on the choppers" they said.

"But I'm not wounded!"

They looked at me puzzled, and said,

"You must be wounded. You're covered in blood!"

I didn't have a mirror, but they told me I had blood all over my face, probably from wiping the sweat off my forehead when I carried men to the choppers. As I looked down at my uniform it was true. What I thought was 'soaking wet with sweat', turned out to be 'soaking wet with blood'. I was wet with blood all the way to my underwear. None of it was mine!

Whenever people are faced with intolerable horrors, many use humor, as a way of coping. There were comments like: "Hey Dixon, don't argue. Just hop on the chopper and get the hell out of here." And, "They're going to need all the blood they can get back at the hospital. Maybe they can ring some out of your clothes." There were other so-called jokes, too gross to mention here.

Later that morning, bigger choppers arrived with fresh supplies. They brought in more ammo, more C-rations, and of course body bags. They also brought in a complete set of clothing for Lance Corporal Dixon. I dug a small hole and took off my old uniform, which was crusty with dried blood, to bury it. We didn't want the NVA to have a complete Marine Corps uniform; no telling what they could do with that. Before I covered it up I tried to take Becky's letter out of the pocket. As you can guess, it was ruined, and unreadable. So, her letter got buried in that hole with my uniform.

Soon after that we got the word to 'saddle up' and move out. Between K and L companies there were 240 Marines who had walked into that jungle clearing. I stood next to the platoon sergeant as he counted each man as they walked past. Now only 80 of us were walking out. The rest were all loaded on to helicopters, one way or the other. I still had two more months to go 'in country'. There would be other 'bad days' and some terrible nights; but none quite as bad as the day I got Becky's letter.

When I finally got back to the States, or as we called it "The World", I tried to look-up some of my old high school friends. Johnny Riblett took me down to the U. of D. and I met up with some of my buddies from high school. The only thing they wanted to know was, "What's it like in Vietnam?" They were all part of the anti-war college movement. It was almost like they were asking, "What's it like to kill babies?" I remember two of us in uniform walking through the L.A. International Airport to transfer planes and some girls were yelling, "BABY KILLERS". Times sure had changed. World War II vets were met with open arms, as well they should have been. Korean War Vets were ignored. Some Viet Nam Vets were spit upon.

As I mentioned earlier there were three girls I knew in high school who I considered friends and wrote to. When I finally returned home, I only contacted Annette. Grace had moved away. I tried to write to her and even tried looking up some of her relatives, to no avail. 'Nette was married. She and her husband seemed to instinctively realize I didn't want to talk about the war. I was grateful to them for not bringing up the subject.

As a matter of fact, I tried hard to take all my war memories and put them in a locked box, down deep in my subconscious. I carried them down to the basement of my brain and stuck them in a dark closet, so I could forget everything. The truth is I only ever told one other person about some of my experiences. That person was my wife and I never even told her all the stories. She only heard many of these stories when she helped proof-read this book.

They say time heals all wounds. And it's true. Those old memories are just old scars now. I moved on a long time ago. But I have always felt guilty for never trying to contact Becky. I could have. I knew where her parents lived. I could have gotten her new address and sent her a congratulations card or even a wedding present. The truth is I just wasn't brave enough to go down to the basement of my mind and drag that box out. Especially the memory of the day I got Becky's letter. For years I felt terrible about not contacting her. She deserved better from me.

Many years later, after I retired from teaching, I began looking up old friends from high school. Thanks to the internet, I found Annette living in Atlanta. She was still close friends with Becky and eventually all three of us were able to meet. I believe Becky has forgiven me and forgotten the letter and my never staying in contact. However, I will forever remember the day I got Becky's letter.

James M. Dixon

Chapter 34

LONG DAYS AND LONGER NIGHTS

I OFTEN WISHED I had a memory like my wife. She can remember things and details of events I only vaguely recall. She'll say, "Do you remember when we took the kids to Disney World?" And I'll reply, "Yeah." She'll continue, "And John kept walking too far ahead of us and Tom kept falling behind?" I will jokingly say, "Yeah, what was I wearing?" Without skipping a beat, she will say, "You were wearing those stupid cargo shorts and a white tee shirt!" I'm always amazed at her. Who can remember details like that? Nobody!

I certainly can't remember all the details of my time in the Grunts. There are, however, some events from that time which are burned into my mind like a branding iron on the hide of a Texas steer. Some things I'll never forget. I will always remember exactly what I was wearing. It was the same thing thousands of Marines wore. Memories of each day's march along a trail or across a rice paddy, were uneventful and pure drudgery, all kind of run together now. But memories of some days' events I will carry to my grave.

We continued walking down yet another trail. We didn't know it at the time, but this operation was coordinated with the entire 5th Marine Regiment and some soldiers from an Australian Army Unit. We would be looking for the NVA and not some local VC guerrillas. We only found out about the operation when someone accidentally got ahold of a Stars and Stripes Newspaper and read about 'Operation Union' and what the 5th Marines were doing. We found ourselves between the flat lands with the rice paddies and farmers, and the jungle-covered mountains where hardly anyone lived. This day the terrain was mostly hilly, rocky, with scattered trees, many of which were tall pines. There were some farms that grew sugar cane on the hills and some rice in flat paddies.

One morning we found ourselves walking on top of the biggest rice paddy dike I had ever been on. The top of the dike was wide enough for a wagon or cart to roll along. The sides of the dike were steep. The right side dropped down about ten feet to a rice paddy. While the left dropped off about twenty feet to a small gully that ran parallel to the dike. Nothing grew in the gully except grass. I imagined that during the Monsoon season this gully filled up with water and was used as a reservoir.

Standing in the gully, directly below us, was a huge water buffalo. Water buffalos were domesticated by the native Vietnamese and used to plow sugar cane fields and to pull carts. They usually roamed wild and because of their size and enormous black horns could live off the land. No other animal living up in the mountains including tigers, would dare to take on a water buffalo. These animals tipped the scales at over a thousand pounds of solid muscle. I could never understand why the Vietnamese didn't cut those horns off when they tamed them for domestic use. Their neck muscles were well known for their pure strength. Have you ever heard a football lineman described as having a bull neck? With that neck and sharp pointed horns sticking out two feet on each side, they could gore a man and flip him over their back. Seeing them at a distance across a field they looked like Black Angus cattle grazing, but up close their sheer size impressed everybody.

The beast, was tethered to a pole about the diameter of a telephone pole except it only stood about five feet out of the ground. When I say tethered, I mean the bull was hooked to the pole. A person couldn't exactly throw a rope around its neck and expect it to hold him. The water buffalo was so strong it could probably pull that pole out of the ground. No, the Gooks had drilled a hole through his nose and attached a brass ring connecting his two nostrils. A chain held the nose ring to the pole. The nose is a very sensitive part of the body. Anytime I see a young 'Goth' teenager with a pierced nose ring, I cringe and remember that day with the water buffalo.

As our platoon walked along the top of the dike the bull became agitated. We kept eight steps between us. For some reason the buffalo began to stare directly at me. Its eyes followed me as I approached, and as I passed, it lowered his head as far as the four-foot chain would permit and began pawing at the ground. The buffalo made snorting sounds that were downright scary as he paced back and forth as much as the chain would allow. Each of us watched in awe as the bull clearly was disturbed. The guy behind me asked, "Why is he staring at you Dixon?" The guy in front of me said, "It's a good thing he's chained to that post."

Just then the buffalo snapped its head to the side and the brass ring ripped out of his nose causing blood to begin dripping from the wound. Immediately it swung around and headed down the gully still staring at me. As soon as the beast came parallel to me he turned and began charging up the 20-foot steep side of the dike. The three guys behind me and the three guys in front of me emptied their magazines into its side. I fired my entire magazine into its head. Most of my rounds bounced off the skull and horns like bullets off Superman. I remember the blood dripping out of its nose. With amazing strength that buffalo kept coming and got to within two feet of my rifle muzzle. However, it couldn't quite make it up over the crest of the dike and slowly lowered its head and began sliding back down the hill. On the way down, it rolled over on its side and by the time it finished sliding to the ground it lay in a heap, a thousand pounds of dead carcass!

I was shaking and heard voices saying, "Holly fuck! Did you see that? We must have put 100 rounds in that son of a bitch!" It was true, the M-16's with their 5.56 caliber rounds were not meant for killing water buffalos. The civilian version, the M-15 is .223 or a .22 caliber with a magnum case. Not the ideal size for shooting people.

Finally, Krum came along and asked, "Are you okay?"

I wasn't, but I wasn't going to admit it. Knowitall commented, "I don't know what you did to piss off that animal, but you sure did."

"He sure wanted a piece of you!"

At the time I could not figure out why that beast tried to attack me. Many years later, I deducted that perhaps it was the radio antenna on my back, which stuck up in the air eight feet. We called it a whip antenna. Perhaps the bull thought I was going to whip him like the gooks did to encourage him to pull faster. I really don't know why. All I could think about was after all the shit I had been through; I might have been killed by a fucking water buffalo. I dreaded my mother getting a government form letter saying her son had been killed in South East Asia, not fighting communist insurgents, but was gored to death by a pissed off water buffalo!

All the shooting had awakened a gook farther up the hill on the other side of the gully. He was watching us with interest. The staff sergeant, who was the acting platoon leader, ordered some of the men in the last squad to go get him. We all knew what, 'get him' meant. We couldn't allow a possible enemy to hit us from behind or warn others of our size and our movement.

Just then one of the new guys announced, "Don't worry I got this." He raised his rife and took careful aim. I thought, 'Who is this boot trying to impress?' The Gook was up a hill at least 600 yards away. Even in boot camp we only fired at targets that were at the most 500 yards away, and then we fired from the prone or lying down position. This was an impossible shot. He fired, and we all looked towards the Gook on the ridge, who was slowly walking to our left. Suddenly the Gook dropped over like a single bowling pin hit by a ball.

Damn, I thought, that was one very impressive shot! This guy was either awfully good or very lucky. Either way I was glad the new guy was shooting at them and not the other way around. Sadly, we began to hear cries and sobbing coming from atop the ridge. A woman ran toward the man, who we could no longer see. I guessed she was the wife or mother. She continued wailing, but seemed to offer no help to the victim, indicating it was a kill shot. I was impressed with this Marine's marksmanship, even though the results were saddening. We were all reminded of how our loved ones would cry if we were killed.

Carrying the radio had its advantages and disadvantages. Sometime on the last operation, guys complained that carrying the 50 rounds of machine gun ammo was much more difficult than carrying a single mortar round. In typical Marine Corps fashion, it was decided everyone would carry both 50 rounds of machine gun ammo and a mortar round. Problem solved. Because I already carried the extra 20-pound radio I didn't have to carry any other ammo. I was also in the middle of the circle each night which meant I got slightly more sleep. The big disadvantage was the target on my back. Every fire fight we were in began the same way. The first to be shot was the radio operator. Each battle with the enemy always resulted in the loss of all the corpsmen, the lieutenant and the radio man. I had less than two months left in country and I really hated that radio.

On this night I had the last watch. Reveille was always an hour before dawn, which was the perfect time for an enemy attack. One hour before dawn everyone would pass the word up and down the perimeter to "stand by". We were all supposed to be awake and alert. This night I had the last watch from 0200 until the sun would make its predawn appearance around 0400. At dawn I began spreading the word to the platoon sergeant, corpsmen and the guys in Knowitall's fire team. Knowitall awoke and asked what time it was. When he was informed he began bitching like he had overslept. I couldn't understand why he was upset. It turned out I was supposed to wake Knowitall at 0300 so he and his team could scout or recon (reconnaissance) a wooded area on the other side of a large field that we all had to cross that morning. No one passed the word to me.

The Corpsman who woke me to stand guard had not said a word. His excuse was, "I thought Dixon already knew." Knowitall immediately accused me of falling asleep on duty. The platoon sergeant simply said well we'll just have to cross the field but first we'll recon by fire. That meant we would fire our rifles into the wooded area and hope to draw enemy fire if anyone was there.

After morning chow, we moved toward the woods and began firing. No one returned fire, so we continued moving forward. All morning I could overhear Knowitall bitching to other guys that Dixon had fallen asleep and that's why we were all in danger of an ambush. I explained again to the staff sergeant that I had not gotten the word to wake anyone early. The Sergeant said, "Don't worry about it now, it's too late." When we took a break to eat noon chow, Knowitall continued to make accusations. He wouldn't let it go.

I never really liked Knowitall. I thought he was not only a 'know-it-all', but also a bully and would do anything to get promoted so he could be important and order others around. I began arguing with him that I had not fallen asleep. Words were exchanged. He continued making jokes about how I must have been asleep.

Finally, I stood up and walked to within two feet of where he was sitting. I spoke loud enough for the whole platoon to hear. "I have been in Viet Nam for almost eleven months and I have never fallen asleep on duty! And if you say I slept on duty one more time, to me or anyone else..." I took my rifle and grabbed it, so the rifle butt was pointed at his face. "I will take this rifle butt and smash your fucking teeth down your throat!"

He started to speak, "Yeah well..."

I interrupted, "Go ahead, say it one more time I dare you!"

By then McCray, Wilson and Walker stood up to break up a possible fight. I knew there wasn't going to be a fight. I would have jammed that butt stock down his throat. He would leave on a helicopter and maybe I would have been court marshaled. But that's all the fight there would have been. Like McDonald said on Christmas Eve, 'What would they do to me? Cut my hair off and send me to Viet Nam?' Perhaps they would even make me carry the radio?

Just then Krum stepped between us and said, "There will be no fighting as long as I'm the squad leader. Save it for the Gooks."

McCray pulled Knowitall aside and told him, "You know Dixon doesn't say very much, but I can tell he's really pissed. You better drop this if you know what's good for you!"

For several days after this incident Knowitall and I did not speak to each other. But he never mentioned my sleeping on guard duty again. I honestly think he respected me a little more or was a little afraid of me.

I respected all the lieutenants we had, and I felt sorry for them because of their causality rate. Our platoon went through four lieutenants in one month. No, they didn't average one a week, because most became causalities in much less than a week. Usually the staff sergeant filled in as the platoon leader each time one left on a helicopter. I already mentioned how two were killed. Another one literally lasted just a matter of minutes. We were walking in a long line through a heavily forested area. We had just left a landing zone when the lead squad began exchanging fire with enemy troops. The fire was sporadic and the rest of us simply watched the sides of the trail in case of an ambush. A single helicopter had landed back at the L.Z. and dropped off supplies and a new lieutenant.

This poor guy, probably just out of college ROTC and Marine Corps officer training school, heard the shooting and came running up the trail to the front of the line to 'take command'. We all watched him run past us in his brand, new jungle utilities. The shooting continued. It was probably only a handful of NVA trying to harass us and slow our movement, so the other Gooks could have more time to shoot at the chopper. About two minutes later the same poor lieutenant came running back down that same trail. His helmet was gone, and blood was running down his face. A bullet had grazed a wound across his forehead which was not serious. Head and face wounds always bleed the most. One of the corpsmen was chasing after him with some bandages as they both were running back to the L.Z. They made it in time for the lieutenant to get his head bandaged and to board the chopper and leave safely.

Walker, who somehow didn't seem like a baby-faced kid anymore, stated, "That's got to be some kind of record!"

"What was that, about five minutes?" asked McCray.

"More like four minutes," stated Knowitall.

We had another young lieutenant who was very 'gung ho'. I don't know if he wanted to be a hero or he was just trying to impress us or the company commander, but he kept volunteering our platoon to be on the point instead of rotating with other platoons each day. After the second and third day in a row of our being the tip of the spear, guys began to complain. Krum spoke to the staff sergeant. The staff sergeant explained that the new lieutenant was volunteering us each day for the point and we were all upset. Nobody wanted to volunteer to get killed!

Our platoon had the point for seven straight days. On the seventh day as we were walking down a trail we suddenly got the word to about face and double time it back up the same trail. Usually we were never told why but this time word spread that some Marines were in trouble and needed help. It was close to 100 degrees in a steaming hot jungle and we were running with all our equipment. I figured we could run for maybe ten minutes before someone collapsed. I was wrong. We jogged for at least half an hour and I thought I would die of a heart attack or stroke. I was determined I would not be the first to drop over. Later some guys confessed they felt the same way but thought if Dixon could carry that radio and not pass out, they could keep going too.

It turned out we were trying to rescue the crew of a downed helicopter.

It made a forced landing in a semi-dried up river bed. We could tell it was a large river during the monsoons and now huge rocks and boulders lined both shores. When the chopper smashed into the river bed, the crew ran into the jungle to hide and await rescue. By the time we arrived the Gooks were crawling all over the chopper like ants on a picnic basket. They were trying to steal the radio and any other goodies they could find. The first guys to arrive took cover behind the giant rocks and a brief fire fight ensued. The Gooks quickly fled. Luckily, we only had one casualty. Strangely it was the gung-ho lieutenant. He had been shot in the back of his calf muscle, even though he was behind a massive boulder. The staff sergeant explained to him that it must have been a ricochet. The lieutenant was 'medevaced' out and the next day we didn't have the point anymore.

I'm not suggesting the staff sergeant or any of us shot the lieutenant. I would never make such an allegation. However, if I had not been running with that heavy radio, and had arrived at the fire fight in time, I would have had no problem shooting him in the leg myself.

After our run through the jungle and the fire fight we were all exhausted and spent the rest of the afternoon guarding the smashed helicopter. It was hot but the river water running down from the mountains was clean and cool. Half of us took turns bathing without soap, while the other half stood guard. We all filled our canteens and put in the necessary iodine tablets. Lots of us drank some of the clear mountain water right out of the stream.

That evening we left the river and set up a perimeter on a nearby hill. We were in good spirits because we knew we would not be on point the next day and rumor had it because we had been out in the field for over three weeks we would be heading back to base. That meant hot showers and hot meals along with some much-needed rest. I was already counting the days, instead of weeks until I would leave this god forsaken land. The talk that night was about returning home, a favorite topic for everyone. Someone asked what I was going to do when I got home. I explained that I would fly to Philadelphia and take the train to Wilmington and then a cab…

"Wait a minute." McCray interrupted. "Why don't you just fly to Delaware?"

"Because there aren't any major airports in Delaware," I explained. What I should have said was the nearest major airport is Philadelphia. This brought about a slew of questions and jokes from the rest of the guys. "What do you mean there aren't any major airports in the state?" "Just how small is Delaware?" "You mean it's so small you can't land an airplane in the state?" "Damn Dixon, you can land a plane on an aircraft carrier, but not in the state of Delaware?" And on and on it went. Even I had to laugh, even though the Delaware Air Force Base in Dover, Delaware is one very major airport, and Air force installation, it's just not a civilian one.

The next morning, we broke camp and because we had been the lead platoon we now became the last platoon. We sat on a wide trail with rice paddies on both sides waiting for the entire regiment to walk in front of us. They each walked eight paces apart and it took several hours for the 500 or so Marines to pass by. Someone decided to ask each guy where they were from in the hope of finding someone else from Delaware. Each man gave us his home state. Most were from New York, Pennsylvania, Ohio, Texas and California which are the most populated states. However, just about every state was represented in the battalion. When someone was from California, Walker would ask whereabouts? When they were from Florida, McCray would ask and so on. After all had passed we saddled up and moved out following them. Someone, probably Knowitall, had kept a record of all the states. It was discovered that men came from every state except Alaska, one of the Dakotas, Montana and of course Delaware.

Krum commented, "Damn Dixon you might be the only guy in the whole 5th Marine regiment from Delaware." He might have been correct.

That night we formed our circle and made camp as usual. Krum and I found ourselves sharing a foxhole. We had an enlightened conversation that meant little to me at the time. I asked him what he was going to do when he got home. He paused and then surprised me.

"You know I used to be able to picture myself walking down the street where I grew up and going to some trade school. But, lately as I fall asleep, I can't see myself doing any of those things. The truth is I don't think I'm going to get out of here alive."

"Don't be ridiculous. You've just been here so long that it's hard to imagine anything else. It doesn't mean you're not going to get out of here alive."

His reply was haunting, "Maybe you're right, but I don't think so."

After our conversation, while on guard duty, I had to take a crap, something we all hated to do at night. It meant crawling away from our line, digging a small hole, with our E-tool (shovel), doing your 'business' and then burying it like a cat. But this night I really had to go. By the time I dropped my trousers the crap came out very watery. The first thing in the morning I went again. This time it was even more watery. It was the first signs of the 'screaming shits'. After several more movements I couldn't get my skivvies and trousers down in time. I wasn't the only one in this situation. As radio operator I called in a request for several pairs of skivvies and various sizes of jungle utility trousers. I made that request several times and each time the number of items went up. By night fall, my inability to retain fluids caused a fever to begin. The following day I received my skivvies and trousers only to crap my pants again.

I realize reading about this may seem unnecessarily gross, but the seriousness of the situation warrants explaining. Dysentery and malaria, disgusting as they may be, are two very deadly diseases. I was running a high fever and I was shivering cold and it was 100 degrees outside. I ached all over. The second evening I went to the acting platoon sergeant and asked to be medevaced out.

I never liked the staff sergeant very much. He was 'a lifer', and secretly liked being the platoon leader. It was a colorful feather in his military record and would ensure his promotion to gunnery sergeant. Gunnies were usually company first sergeants and had a gravy job, like the gunny I experienced in the MP's. The staff sergeant also expected others to wait on him like he was a real officer. He always wanted me to make him coffee each morning. I didn't drink coffee and really didn't know how to make a proper cup. He used to chew me out for putting iodine tablets in the water when the boiling made it unnecessary. I made my request and I'm sure he could see I was ill.

He sat me down and talked to me like I was a real human being instead of a civilian who had enlisted one day and would be back as a civilian someday soon, not a true Marine. He explained, "Dixon, you had to be listening on that radio every day for weeks. You should know by now from the spotter planes that we are surrounded by the NVA. I got about one third of the men in this platoon down with the shits, and I think I got a touch of it myself. The captain thinks the Gooks are planning an all-out assault on us any day now. I need every swinging dick here. No one is leaving on a chopper unless they are bleeding."

I replied, "I understand Sarge."

He continued, "Tomorrow I'll have one of the boots follow you. The two of you can take turns carrying the radio, but I want you making all the calls. It's time we trained someone else to use the radio, okay?" I shook my head in agreement but was disappointed and wondered how long I could go on.

The next morning, I was as weak as a newborn, but for the first time I didn't have to shit, probably because there wasn't anything left to come out. We left camp and all morning we walked up a steep hill. Still keeping eight feet apart, it was customary to pass official messages up and down the line by repeating the words exactly as they were told to you. Usually it was, "corpsmen up" or "corpsmen back", "Watch out for sniper at 3 o'clock." "Take five" (which meant take a break) but the only one that concerned me was, "Radio up!" On this day the company commander, a captain, was walking only two guys away from me. Some message was passed up the line and I signaled to the boot "to pass it on."

When I failed to yell up the line the captain asked if I was okay. I replied, "Yes sir, I just have a little fever."

He responded, "Yeah, me too!" I don't know how I made it all the way up that hill. I was just determined that I would not be the first to fall out.

I still didn't have to take a shit by nighttime and I think my fever began to break. The corpsman had instructed all of us to keep drinking lots of water and to be sure we put an iodine tablet in the canteen. If there was any doubt, put in two.

In the morning we were told we would be heading to some open ground for resupplies. Open ground was where the enemy liked to set up an ambush. They knew helicopters had to land for the wounded and therefore became easier targets. We began walking and although I was still part of second squad, on this day I was walking back with the captain at the end of our platoon. Suddenly shots rang out, followed by automatic rifle fire. Before I heard the words, 'Corpsman up!' and 'Radio up!', I began scrambling up the trail towards the gun fire. By the time I arrived the short fire fight was over. I had already called, "Kilo 3-5 to Base, Kilo 3-5 to Base, over." I handed the radio to the platoon staff sergeant. I could see the corpsman already bandaging up Cranston's forearm. I was also shocked to see crazy Krum lying nearby taking a break. It looked like he was asleep. His legs were crossed, and his hands folded on his chest. He rested his head on his helmet like we always did when we slept. McCray and Walker were going through his knapsack. Other guys were yelling to watch out for other holes.

I asked the sergeant, "What's wrong with Krum?"

He looked at me like I was stupid, "He's dead."

I stared at Krum, I could see no wound and he looked so peaceful. It couldn't possibly be true. I walked over to him and knelt. Sure enough, there was a small hole, smaller than a dime, just above his right ear. That's where the gook, hiding in a hole, covered up with grass, shot him. On the other side of his head, where the bullet exited, was a hole the size of a baseball. Krum died instantly. The Gook then fired several other rounds but only wounded Cranston before the other guys opened-up on him. The

Gook probably had been shot 20 times. As I stood up McCray and Walker had already unfolded the poncho from Krum's pack and were waiting for me to say my goodbyes. They carefully covered him in the poncho, so his face didn't show. It was a sad day for all of us. Krum was a good squad leader and a fun guy to be with. I remembered when he got shot in his peaches. I remembered when he couldn't be an NCO because he wasn't crazy. I'm sorry to say more sad days were coming soon.

The sergeant was requesting yet another medevac as men searched other holes where gooks could be hiding. I was standing around without my radio. The company captain called me over and said, "You see that hole there? Check it out." He held out his 45 pistol, butt first. You can't go crawling down a tunnel with your rifle. It's too big. I took off my pack and pulled out my pistol.

The Captain asked, "Where did you get that?"

"Off a dead corpsman," I replied. The captain re-holstered his pistol. The last thing I wanted to do was crawl into a tunnel that the Gooks probably booby trapped. We all heard stories how the Gooks would tie a poisonous snake by its tail and hang it on top of a tunnel, so it would bite you in the head or neck. I would much rather die like Krum. Lucky for me it was not a tunnel but just a hole and only went down about four feet with nothing in it but dirt.

McCray became the new second squad leader. Knowitall became the leader for third squad. Wilson, Walker and two new guys each carried a corner of the poncho with Krum in it. They were the only ones left of second squad. McCray commanded four men, in a squad that should have at least ten or twelve men. Knowitall had about the same number in his squad, as did the first squad.

We walked a short distance to the top of a hill. Kilo Company spread out with each of the three platoons taking a third of the circle. This was the perfect place for a defensive position. We were up high with foot tall grass covering the entire area. Foxholes were dug about ten to twelve yards apart which allowed us to see a good 40 yards before the trees blocked our view. On one side of the hill there were no trees at all, just more grass sloping down to a small river stream where we could get fresh water. This hill was obviously used to graze cattle or some other animal. It reminded me of the dairy farms near my home. There was plenty of room in the center of the circle for a helicopter to land and pick up Cranston and Krum. I can vividly remember seeing that chopper leave and the conversation I had with Krum just a few nights before.

We spent the rest of the day on that hill. I worked the radio and could tell by the sound of voices; base command was worried. They talked about re-enforcements and spotter planes seeing lots of enemy movement. Each of our four companies, were not only trying to locate their own position, but also the position of each other. We knew how the NVA would listen in on the radio, so a lot of the messages were simply alpha-numeric grid co-ordnances on a map. But we couldn't be sure exactly where the other companies were unless we had visual contact.

That evening just as it got dark it was decided to send one fire team down the hill to the stream. There was a narrow path that ran along the stream. McCray was to take three guys, Wilson, Walker and a new guy, and walk along the path to recon. They hoped the recon patrol would run into Lima Company that was thought to be nearby. The captain and our staff sergeant discussed at great length whether I should go along with the radio. The captain said yes but our acting platoon leader didn't want to give up our only radio. They finally compromised. I would take the radio and go down the hill to the path where I would wait for McCray to return from the recon patrol. It was ordered and so it was done.

I sat at the bottom of the hill for two or three hours. I heard no gun fire. I only heard the bubbling stream and tried to keep my wits about me and listen for anything else. I had to maintain radio silence and simply listen. A message was to be relayed if McCray was able to make contact with Lima. The sounds of helicopters and planes made hearing any other sounds more difficult. For some reason the sky was busy with aircraft. Finally, at about midnight McCray and his team returned with good news and bad. We walked back up the hill and McCray reported. They had found nothing. The path didn't go very far, and they got lost. McCray's squad found the stream and followed it back. Good news: they found no NVA. Bad news: they didn't find Lima Company either.

Because it was after midnight and the perimeter was already secure the sergeant told us to lie down on the side of the hill and get some shut eye. The tall grass was comfortable to lie on and we soon fell into a deep sleep. Weeks of sleep deprivation doesn't allow time for the mind to have its necessary dreams. Without R.E.M sleep we never got the proper rest our bodies needed. This night I fell sound asleep and dreamt I was back home. All five of us slept hard in the foot-tall grass.

I dreamt that a space ship was landing to take me back to Delaware. Suddenly I could hear men yelling, "Get up!" and "What the fuck!" I looked up and sure enough there above my head was a giant alien spaceship. It was loud and had red and blue flashing lights. There were flood lights shining down and waving streams of lights back and forth on us.

It looked like a flying saucer from a sci-fi movie. 'What the fuck', was exactly what I thought too.

It turned out it was one of our helicopters landing on the side of the hill where we were sleeping. We ran for our lives and I could hear the blades of the chopper cutting through the foot-tall grass. Luckily, we got out in time. The chopper didn't land and took off again eventually landing at the LZ in the middle of our perimeter where it should have landed to begin with. We never did find out what went wrong. My guess, it was a rookie pilot. Choppers never landed with their lights on at night and they never landed on the side of a hill where the blades would cause a crash. Also, someone on the ground was supposed to set off a flare or a smoke grenade so the guy could see where to land. I thought to myself, *'There are lots ways a guy could get killed over here.'*

Chapter 35

THE LONGEST NIGHT

I SUSPECT MANY of us at one time or another have faced a near death experience. Some people will tell you that their whole life flashed before their eyes. I don't know if that is true or not. I know it's not true for me. Several times in my life I have thought I was going to die. I pictured nothing in my mind. Maybe I'm just not smart enough to see my own images. There was one time that I knew for sure, without a doubt that I would not see the sun come up in the morning. All I could think of was the things I would never get to do, like fall in love and raise a family. All I did was pray.

After our own helicopter almost killed us, we spent the next day digging deeper than normal foxholes. Word spread this would be our last night on Operation Union. I heard these comments on the radio, so I was sure the NVA also heard we were leaving. Everyone's conclusion was this would be the last chance for the NVA to mount a major attack on us. That same fear was not lost on battalion headquarters. The sky continued to buzz with spotter planes.

We prepared for the upcoming showdown. The foxholes were dug extra deep but kept narrow and small to make it less likely a mortar would land in one. The dirt was piled in front of the hole facing away from the center of our perimeter. This extra dirt would be used as added protection in case of an all-out infantry assault. We stomped down the tall grass directly in front of the holes, so we could have an unobstructed view. Two recon patrols were sent out during the daylight to find the exact location of the other companies. We knew Lima Company was to our north and believed Indian or Mike was to our south. All day long fighter planes dropped bombs on wooded areas and spotter planes circled looking for any troop movement. We knew from experience, all Marines feared one of our own jets would bomb the wrong target. Finding the exact location of all four companies was imperative. Several times we set off smoke grenades to signal planes of our locations. We also experienced the Gooks throwing out the same color smoke as we did to confuse pilots.

During the day I had the new 'boot' assigned to me, watch the radio while I went around to the other three platoons camped on the hill. I was looking for my friend, Carden, who was in the first platoon. The first guys I found in Carden's platoon were boots and had never heard of a guy named Carden. Finally, another lance corporal knew about him. He explained Carden had been wounded at the beginning of the last operation and had been in a hospital for three weeks. He had returned about four or five days ago only to be wounded again. The first time he had shrapnel in his leg. This last time he had shrapnel in his head. I was shocked and worried. The lance corporal said he didn't think this head wound was too serious. Carden had walked to the helicopter himself. I thought, "So Carden has been wounded twice, and they have come close to killing me on several occasions, and I wondered about my friend McDonald.

I remembered again vividly the grunt in the MP's who told us, "one of you will die, one will get wounded and one of you will probably be all right." We couldn't even find Lima Company where Mac was. I wondered again, how true his prediction would be.

As we ate the last of our C-rations at evening chow we got word for each squad to send four men to report to the company commander. The captain wanted to talk to us. The platoon sergeant sent the three squad leaders and me.

When all twelve of us from the three platoons arrived, the captain began to speak. "It looks like the Gooks are going to hit us hard tonight with everything they have. I want each platoon to set out two 'claymores' after it gets dark." Orders were never questioned verbally, but I guess by the expressions on our faces he knew we wanted to know 'why after dark'? He continued, "I want to wait until dark so any of those little bastards won't see where or what we are doing. I want you to go out about 40 yards from our lines. In other words, about twenty yards into the jungle and rig the claymores. It will take two of you, one to run the wire and one to set up the mine. Don't forget the curved side faces out towards the enemy. Any questions? You guys, I hope, have done this before, right?"

I had done it in infantry training but never for real, in combat. But we all replied, "Yes sir."

The captain finished by saying, "I'm going to have other guys crawl out when you get back to set up noise detectors."

A claymore mine is a nasty piece of death in a box. It's about the size of a rectangular tissue box. It's curved with an explosive charge covered with 700 small round steel balls like ball bearings. It has two small metal screws on the top where wires are connected. Then the wire is run back to a box with a handle. When the handle is turned, the mine will explode sending the steel balls flying toward the enemy. The explosion is about ten times more powerful than a hand grenade. Claymores are easy to set up but we all feared an accidental explosion.

The noise detectors are nothing more than C-ration cans with a couple of stones inside. A wire runs through the can and is strung across two trees or two bushes. Someone crawling or walking along would hit the wire causing the cans to rattle and make noise. If we heard the cans rattle we would open fire and kill whoever was out there. In this case, tonight, if we heard the cans rattle someone would also set off the claymore mines.

One of the guys from another platoon asked the captain, "Whatta-we do if there is an all-out attack on us?"

The captain paused and then said, "The same thing Marines have always done, we'll give'em hell!"

It sounded good, but I believe that is exactly what Colonel Travis and Davy Crockett said their last night at the Alamo. I had a bad feeling about this night.

We returned to finish eating our C-rations and explained to the platoon sergeant what was up.

He paused to take it all in and then spoke, "Well, I'll get the new guy to work the radio then. Dixon you'll have to triple up and get into a hole with two other guys." I had spent much of the morning digging a hole with the other radio guy. The sergeant and the corpsman would be in another hole twenty yards back from the line. He gave us all some last-minute advice and passed the word to everyone about what we were going to do. Our greatest fear was getting shot by one of the boots as we crawled back in the dark.

I walked over to two new guys who had already dug their foxhole. I told them I would be coming back and jumping in this hole. They complained. I simply stated, "Well if you want, I'll switch with you. And you can crawl out there and set up the claymore and I'll stay here and make the hole bigger." They said nothing, so I continued, "Make it bigger!" I left them to go get the claymore.

Knowitall and I were assigned to plant our claymore. Yes, my good friend Knowitall. We managed to crawl out the necessary 40 yards. Knowitall carried the deadly claymore and I strung the wire as we went.

When we finally stopped crawling, he said, "This looks like as good a place as any." Then he asked me a question which surprised me, "Do you remember how to wire this thing?"

"It's pretty simple just attach these two wires to the two screws, and make sure it's facing that way" as I pointed into the jungle.

He wired it up and we began to crawl back to our line as he said, "I sure hope we don't have to set these suckers off."

I agreed.

When we got back two other guys replaced us and crawled out to set up the C-ration cans. Knowitall and I returned to the platoon sergeant's hole to give him the other end of the wires to be attached to the hand crank. I returned to the foxhole with the two boots. I jumped down into the fox-hole only to discover the two new guys had dug the hole deeper, but not wider. It was too late to do any remodeling, so I was stuck lying on top of them as they sat curled up in a ball. This uncomfortable position is where I would spend the longest night of my life. Our position was also ineffec-tive. If an all-out assault came, I would have to climb out of the hole to fire. I thought perhaps I should stand up and try to make the hole wider or perhaps try and crawl around and find the foxhole I and the new radio operator had previously dug.

The final decision was made for me. We heard the distinctive plunking sound of mortars being launched, 'kaponk, kaponk, kaponk, and then baboom, baboom, baboom.' It was the first of hundreds of mortar rounds that fell on us like rain. I knew it was only a matter of time until one landed in this hole and blew all three of us into tiny pieces. We could barely move, and all we could do was pray. One of the guys in the foxhole was Spanish and began praying in Spanish but I could tell the English words were, "Hail Mary full of grace…" The other guy was saying the Lord's Prayer in English. I prayed silently.

In addition to the mortars we could hear helicopter gunships and airplanes flying over head. The gooks were shooting in the air trying to hit anything flying, but the planes and choppers were way too high. The planes were dropping flares which lit up the sky like it was daytime. The gunships fired machine gun rounds into the thick wooded areas. I also prayed that I would die from an enemy mortar and not from machine gun bullets fired by my own guys. The night seemed like it would never end. I wondered if with all the flares lighting up the area, we would even know when the sun came up. It didn't matter. I knew in my heart I would never see the real sun again.

During the night my muscles began to ache because of my cramped position. The guy under me began to complain that his foot was burning. The Spanish guys said, "It's probably a cramp."

"No." he replied, "It feels like it's on fire." For hours we listened to the mortars and the machine gun fire. I realized each time there was a lull in the noise, we might be under a full attack. I would try to peak my head up to see and listen for cans rattling, but each time the mortars would start again.

Somehow, and I will never understand why, we made it through the endless night. I like to think prayers helped, but they had not helped everyone. When the sun finally came up the mortars stopped, and yet there was no attack. The cans never rattled. We all began to look out from our foxholes like gophers, to see who was alive. Miraculously we had very few casualties. One foxhole had taken a direct hit and the two guys were both blown out. At least parts of them were. They too were probably praying just as hard as anyone else. Luckily, the dog tags of the two dead men were found. Several other guys, including the guy lying under me, were hit by flying shrapnel and were burnt. A piece of red hot shrapnel had somehow missed me and had landed on the boot of the guy under me and burned a hole through the canvas and into his ankle. During the night one of the guys hit with shrapnel called out for a corpsman. Bless his heart, the corpsman got out of his hole and ran to help him. The corpsman was also hit by shrapnel in his leg. A hot piece of shrapnel also landed on the platoon sergeant's shoulder, burning him.

I looked around and surveyed the ground. There were hundreds of mortar craters but luckily most had fallen too short or too far from us and had been ineffective. I was probably not the only guy who prayed to God to give thanks for being spared. Helicopters were called in and to everyone's surprise they took very little gun fire from the trees. I guess the NVA had simply given up and left. Some guys cut the wire to the claymores and Knowitall and others went to retrieve them. The two dead guys and the corpsman were evacuated out by the choppers. All the other wounded were able to walk as the 'walking wounded'. We began our trek off the hill, and along the same trail that McCray had followed on his recon patrol. Finally meeting up with Lima Company I spotted Mac and was filled with joy as we walked around a hill and came to a road. There waiting in a field were six by six trucks to pick us up. Somehow, I had made it through the longest night of my life, and I was alive!

James M. Dixon

Chapter 36

SHORT TIMERS

EVERYONE AT SOME TIME in their life has counted down the days awaiting some important event. Little kids count down the days until Santa Claus comes down the chimney. Most school age kids count the days until summer vacation. Believe me, teachers count those days too. I remember counting the months, weeks and days until I got my driver's license. Many an old worker counted the time in years until they could retire. Count downs are a part of most people's lives. However, the biggest countdown of all is waiting to leave a combat zone and be able to return home in one piece.

After the longest night we climbed on the trucks and drove a couple hours to a brand, new location. We all knew it had to be near Chu Lai. This was like no other base camp I had been to. The whole area was flat. The first thing I noticed was a lack of tents. Most camps had tents and cots for nearly everybody. This place didn't even have tents for the officers. The only tents I saw were ones clumped together to form a large mess hall, a good mile or more away from where we were brought. There were tents for showers, but they were even farther away. Everything seemed to be spread out because I guess no one was expecting an attack here. We had a choice of walking two miles back and forth to chow or we could help ourselves to C-rations. I hiked to chow in the morning while it was still, fairly cool, but ate out of cans the rest of the time.

There were several other things that made this camp different. I did not see any of the tell-tale signs of barbed wire surrounding the area. There didn't seem to be a perimeter at all. It looked like this camp was still in the process of being set up. The area was huge, with way more than just the 5th Marine Regiment located here. There were lots of trees which grew in straight lines. We camped out under as many as we could, so we could be in the shade with temperatures again approaching 120 degrees. But this made our whole outfit spread out in a single line instead of a circle. Before we arrived, some Marines had filled thousands of sand bags and made above ground shelters. We took our ponchos and rigged up even more shade. It was late May and I remembered the 120-degree temperatures, when we first landed in country during June of the year before. Each day temperatures rose above 100 but for some reason I didn't mind it like I did a year ago. I also saw my first tank. And I saw several civilians walking around. Some were technical advisers, and some were contractors who worked with the engineers. There were also reporters.

We were given strict instructions not to complain to the reporters about anything. The captain especially warned us about complaining about the M-16 rifles. "Remember if you keep them clean, they work fine." *Like hell, I thought!* But mostly I thought about leaving this place forever in a week or so.

For the first time in months we seemed to have lots of free time. Of course, we cleaned our rifles and went to the supply area and replaced old worn out gear and clothes with new stuff. I say new, but it was fresh out of storage from World War II. So, it was technically new and unused gear. We taught the new guys how to pack a knapsack and the secrets to cooking C-rations.

We all had some complaints. There was no laundry, so we had to wash clothes in our helmet. There was no temporary PX where we could buy soap, toothpaste, brushes and letter writing supplies. We showed the boots how to write post cards on the back of C-ration boxes. I couldn't complain because I hoped to be home before the mail got there anyway. At night we still had to stand guard duty, but it was only for two hours a night. During guard duty I had time to reflect. I cried when I thought about the guys we lost. Dunkin and Krum had never even had a chance to go on R & R, as a matter of fact, neither had Knowitall, Wilson, Walker or McCray. I couldn't believe they had only had a beer ration twice the whole time they were in country. I was lucky to have spent seven months in the M.P.'s. I was luckier still to be going home soon.

Each day Carden would come and visit me, or I'd go visit him. Twice we went to visit Mac in Lima Company. It was fun joking about how short we were. 'Short timer' was the term used to describe how long we had left in country. Some guys would tease the other guys about how short they were. They'd say. "Don't start any long conversations with me, 'cause I won't be here to finish them." Or they would say, "I'm so short I can walk under a doorway and not duck my head." I tried not to tease other guys. I remembered the day we landed and the 'short timer' truck driver told us he was going home in a week. I remember how sick I felt in the pit of my stomach hearing that. It was fun talking about what we would do as soon as we got home. Carden hoped to go to college. Mac had given up his dream of playing college football. He and his fiancé had a wedding planned and he hoped to go to college on the G.I. Bill and just be a married man in college. It all sounded so good.

I will say the Marine Corps was pretty good about following the policy of only a thirteen-month tour of duty. It was also obvious that the 600 of us who had come over on that horrible ship could not leave on the exact same day. Some guys would be lucky and leave a few days early and others like me would leave a few days after our 13 months. Sadly, many of the 600 had already gone home in boxes.

One morning in late May 1967, Carden and I strolled back from morning chow to the battalion headquarters to check on any mail that we could take back to Kilo Company. As usual there was a 'six by' truck sitting in the middle of the headquarters' center. There was always something being loaded or unloaded in this area. Today Carden spotted some guys from our old MP battalion sitting in the back of the truck. They were obviously passengers waiting to be driven somewhere. Carden yelled at some guys he recognized, and they yelled back. These men all seemed excited and happy. They were the first of the men to be heading home. I spotted several guys I recognized but didn't exactly know their names. I did see Coulter and laughed to myself. He was the guy who did the imitations of our MP Colonel. Then I saw my old friend Donald. He sheepishly smiled back, not wanting to rub it in that he was leaving, and I was staying. They all wished us luck and gleefully explained our day was coming soon. We watched as the truck turned around and drove off down the dirt road toward Highway #1. The truck peeled out, stirring up a small dust storm. Carden headed back to first platoon and I headed toward second platoon.

I hadn't walked more than a few steps when I spotted McCray. I figured I'd walk back with him. He looked terrible. He was a black man, but his complexion looked ashen. It was a hot morning, one of those days that was sure to reach above 100 degrees. Though, he looked like he was cold.

"Hey man, how are you doing?" I asked.

"Not good," he replied, "I feel like shit!"

I put my hand on his forehead and felt the heat. "Man, you're burning up. Have you got the screaming shits?"

He answered, "No, I just seem to ache all over."

I told him, "You got to get yourself to sickbay."

"Hey, I ain't no sickbay commando!" McCray was no different than a lot of black guys. It seemed the 'splibs' had to prove they were just as tough as the 'chucks'. In so doing they often went overboard and tried to over achieve. I remember how hard it was to talk Wilson into getting on a helicopter when he was wounded in the shoulder. We told him it might get infected and need to be amputated.

I explained to McCray that he might have Malaria or Yellow Fever. "This might kill you and if they don't treat it quickly you could carry it the rest of your life."

I don't know if it was my argument or the fact that he was feeling worse by the minute, but he asked, "Where exactly is sick bay?"

I pointed toward three of the few tents located in the area. I said, "You can't see them from here, but they have large red crosses painted on the roof."

"Okay, I'll see you later." He walked off and unbeknownst to me that was the last time I would ever see McCray. I don't know what ailment he had but they transferred him to a hospital somewhere. I would be gone, when he returned. To this day I pray he got out all right. I cannot find his name on the Viet Nam Memorial Wall in Washington DC, but I don't remember exactly how he spelled his name. His first name was Myers and he lived in Florida. Also, the Wall doesn't list the names of the wounded, crippled, blind, or maimed. I hope he made it out in one piece.

As I watched him walk off, I started back to our platoon area. Suddenly I felt the ground shake and heard the sound from a huge explosion. I turned and looked in the direction of the noise. There I saw the all too familiar sight of black smoke already rising toward heaven. It appeared like a small atomic bomb; only instead of white smoke it was black. Someone had run over a mine. I thought to myself, 'God, I hope that wasn't the truck that Donald and the other short timers were on.'

Days later I found out it was!

On May 25, 1967 we received word we were going out on another operation, 'Operation Union II'. Because we were short timers with about a week to go we hoped we would be exempt and could stay behind. Carden went to his new platoon lieutenant and explained the situation. The lieutenant understood and assigned Carden to stay back and guard the gear. Then Carden and I went to see my new lieutenant. When I say new, he literally had been with us for two days. As a corporal, Carden could grow a mustache. It made him look much older and perhaps like a 'lifer'. Together we talked to my platoon lieutenant. The new lieutenant explained he didn't have the power to leave men behind. He did have the power, but he just didn't know it. He asked Carden and me about the exact day we had started our tour and we explained about the 600 of us who left by ship on the first Saturday in May. Next week was the first Saturday in June, so our 13 months were up. I however, had to go on this operation. Yes, I felt sorry for myself, but I also felt sorry for the lieutenant, for the new radio guy and the new corpsman. The chances of any of them making it a full 13 months and out in one piece were slim. The best they could hope for was a million-dollar wound.

Carden and I decided to visit McDonald. We walked in to his sand bag bunker and watched as he was packing up his gear like he was going home. He had a serious look on his face, almost sad looking.

I was confused. Carden asked, "What's wrong?" Mac handed Carden a piece of paper, which the military called a 'chit'. It was his orders to leave. This was known as having your orders 'cut'. The orders stated he was to report to Da Nang in three days. I thought wow, there is no way he's going on this operation. I wished I had my orders cut. Still, there was something wrong.

At second glance it looked as if Mac was packing his knapsack for combat.

"What are you doing?" Carden inquired.

Mac simply replied, "We're getting on choppers tomorrow morning." I thought Mac was smarter than that. Perhaps he didn't realize he didn't have to go. When Carden explained, Mac showed him a second piece of paper. It was a single page letter from home. It was a 'Dear John' letter even though it was addressed Dear Gerry. Evidently there was still going to be a wedding, but Mac was not going to be the groom, or the father of the baby his fiancé carried. I could see he was heartbroken. Carden and I tried to explain that the letter didn't change anything. He was still going home and there was no way he had to go on this operation.

I'll never forget his response. He never made eye contact but just said, "I got a lot of new guys who need my help. Some of these boots have never been on a patrol, let alone an operation." Carden tried to reason that the new guys were no longer his responsibility.

"Somebody else will look after them. It doesn't have to be you."

Mac's only response was, "Look, all I know is I can't go home and face my friends and family right now. Maybe I'll extend for another six months. I don't know what I'm going to do, except get on that helicopter tomorrow morning."

As we walked back to Kilo Company, Carden kept going on about Mac and how worried he was about him. I didn't say much. I was too worried about myself. I was getting on those same choppers tomorrow. That evening I made ready for combat as I had done so many times before. I would still be carrying the radio and the new boot PFC would be nearby observing. And he would take over when I got shot. I had been downright gleeful waiting to pass the last few days in peace. Now I had to worry.

The next morning after chow I boarded a chopper with all of first squad and part of second squad. The platoon lieutenant was on the first chopper and the platoon staff sergeant would be on the last chopper. Just like the previous trips choppers departed in groups of three and would land in groups of three. We left with the second group. I was the last guy to board the craft, which meant I would be the first one jumping off when we landed. This time the flight seemed longer. I wondered if we were going farther from base or if it just seemed farther because my thoughts were only of surviving one or two more days. I had a bad feeling in the pit of my stomach.

Suddenly the chopper began to dip and rock to one side and then to the other. I thought, 'Is the pilot trying to make us sea sick or something?' The whole chopper seemed to be moving erratically. Each man began looking toward the pilot and copilot compartment in the front of the craft. There seemed to be a commotion going on up there. Perhaps we were being shot at? Each man would turn down the line and shout something to the next man. The chopper was so loud we had to scream to the guy next to us to be heard. A message seemed to be making its way down the line as I waited to hear what was going on. Each time someone yelled to the guys next to him the man receiving the message would look up at the front and then turn and relay the message. When the guy next to me turned and shouted in my ear, "They shot the pilot!" I also turned and looked toward the cabin. All I saw was confusion as each pilot seemed to be shifting in their seats. One pilot appeared to be wrapping a bandage around the leg of the other pilot. The bad feeling in my stomach just got worse.

The chopper seemed to be descending too quickly. Were we going to land or crash? Then suddenly we landed with a thud. Usually the rear hatch would flip open immediately, but now there seemed to be a delay. Once the hatch did open, I scrambled out into the daylight. I ran forward and fell into line with the others, forming a semi-circle. I could see the other two choppers and guys running off and continuing to form a large circle. I could hear shooting, but I didn't see who or where the firing was coming from. We all spread out in a semicircle in a dried-up rice paddy. As soon as the platoon sergeant arrived, he ordered all of us to move towards a dike and take cover. The new lieutenant followed us, sticking close to the staff sergeant and my radio. The dike ran in a straight line, so our semicircle was of no use.

I immediately called base and got them on the radio. As I looked around I could see our platoon was right next to Lima Company. I handed the radio mic to the lieutenant. As I listened I could hear sporadic gun fire and knew the Gooks were looking for radios and officers. Corpsmen would be next. Several guys in Kilo and Lima were returning fire. It was noisy and scary. I huddled beside the dike and was turned toward Lima Company when suddenly I saw a guy standing straight up in the middle of the rice paddy. He was pointing and yelling at guys to stay down. I thought, is that some boot lieutenant or is that guy just crazy? Then I realized it was Mac.

I jumped to my feet and started to run towards him. I thought I could tackle him to the ground. Suddenly I tripped. It was the platoon sergeant, who grabbed my leg as he yelled,

"Where the fuck, do you think you're going?" I lifted my head just in time to see a single bullet knock Mac backwards and to the ground. The shot lifted him clean off his feet and dropped him backwards about three feet. I knew in an instant he was dead. None of the corpsmen ran to his aid. They also knew it was a kill shot.

I don't remember exactly what I said or what happened next, but I believe I said something like, "That was my friend."

The sergeant said, "Not anymore."

I was numb. A guy I had known since the first days in the MP's was dead. The guy who I helped drive a jeep into the Pacific Ocean, was dead. The guy who helped me pick up dead bodies in the rain on Christmas Eve was dead. My friend who got a 'Dear John' letter yesterday was gone forever.

After we secured a perimeter, patrols were sent out to recon the area. I called in a chopper to pick up causalities and drop off more ammo. The boots, whenever they got into their first fire fight, always seemed to shoot until they almost ran out of ammo. As the chopper lifted off with Mac's body, I cried.

That evening, the lieutenant and platoon sergeant got word that another chopper was coming in to pick up Lance Corporal Dixon.

My tour was up. I remember the staff sergeant saying, "Well, I guess you really are a short timer."

I thought to myself, *'Did you think I was lying?'*

James M. Dixon

Chapter 37

GOODBYES

A FTER I GOT a teaching job and built up a little equity in a starter home, my wife and I designed and built our dream house. We lived there for 28 Christmases, 28 anniversaries, over 100 birthdays, plus proms and graduations. When our two sons left home, we decided to down size to a smaller property and smaller house. The day we moved was far more emotional than I ever expected. Saying goodbye to the house, no, a home, was traumatic. There were too many great memories. When my three-year-old grandson asked if he would be able to come back and sit on my lap and help drive the riding mower, I teared up. Saying goodbye to any memory can be emotional. Every time I see a tree house, or fort as our boys called it, I remember the one we built in our back yard in Millersville. Some memories, you never completely say goodbye to.

I hopped off the chopper back at the same field I took off from, just hours before. I was told to report to Battalion headquarters. The place seemed deserted. The colonel and a captain were studying a map in the back of the tent. A corporal, an office pogue, told me to find some place to sleep and to report back tomorrow morning. It was late evening and just getting dark. The line of sand bag bunkers where we lived for the past ten days were abandoned and lonely looking. All four companies of 3rd

Battalion, 5th Marine Regiment were out on Operation Union II. I found Carden lying alone in the same bunker he had used before. I told him about Mac and how he died. We were both sick to our stomachs. He told me the terrible explosion we heard the day before was indeed the truck carrying Donald, Coulter and the other men beginning their journey to go home. We both felt even sicker. We sat there in silence. Then he filled me in on the scoop and what I would have to do in the next two days.

The next morning, I had to go to sick bay for a physical. There was no way they were going to keep me in Viet Nam even one more hour if I had a cold or even the sniffles. They took my blood pressure, listened to my heart and weighed me. I weighed less than I did as a sophomore in high school. Eating C-rations and having the screaming shits is one hell of a diet.

Carden told me headquarters would place me on work details while I waited to travel back to DaNang. They assigned Carden to loading trucks with supplies that someone else would then load onto choppers. He was a corporal and only had to supervise. The other guys who worked in supply, the other noncombatant pukes, knew what to do so Carden just stood around and watched. He was also in charge of me and sent me on important errands, like to the mess hall for coffee.

That afternoon Carden reported to the supply depot to turn in his gear. He showed them his 'chit' and they took all his web gear except for his cartridge belt, one canteen and his rifle and one magazine. I went along to observe and see how the process went. The corporal asked to see my 'chit' which was dated the day after Carden's. He never looked at the date and just took my gear. We left, and Carden suggested that I get on the truck with him, since no one had asked or studied the date on the 'chit', "You may as well leave a day early." It was fine by me, and that is exactly what we did.

This time it was a half ton pickup truck picking us up. Carden rode shotgun and four of us road in the back. They told us the engineers had cleared the road of mines, but I still worried until we reached Highway #1. When we arrived at the Da Nang Air Base it was like going back home. We drove through the south gate where I stood guard and over to a giant hanger which was a staging area for guys going home. I was a day early, but no one seemed to know or care. Carden was given some paper work to read. It was a list of do's and don'ts. It stated what things we could take home and what we had to leave behind. We had to exchange all our funny money (military money). I had a few dollars and cents of the funny money that I mailed home as a souvenir. We were given a partial pay of $100.00 which we partially used to get our clothes washed. The rest was ours to do with as we pleased. The government still owed us about four months back pay. We were not allowed to take any souvenir weapons home. They showed us a giant wall with examples of things other guys tried to smuggle home, which included: grenades, rocket launchers, mortars, ammo and other really, unbelievable stuff. I still had the .45 pistol I had taken off the dead corpsmen. I found an empty C-ration case and filled the box with old clothes and the pistol which I mailed home to my father. I still have the pistol. I know the statute of limitations has probably expired, but if the government really wants that pistol they can come to my house and take it.

Carden was told to report back in two days to the staging area for his flight to Okinawa. I of course had three days to wait. Carden had a brother in Viet Nam, which was extremely rare. Ever since the five Sullivan brothers all died together serving in World War II, the military would not allow brothers to serve in combat at the same time. If two brothers were sent to Viet Nam, they both had to sign papers and their parents had to sign papers allowing them to both be in country. I remember when Corporal Waters was about to be sent to the grunts. His brother arrived in country and was a cook or some other non-combat role. Our Corporal Waters was sent to Okinawa to finish his tour and his brother stayed in a relatively safe area.

I thought it strange that Carden had a brother in Viet Nam. His brother was also stationed in Da Nang. He had only been in country a few weeks. Carden could have immediately requested a transfer and been pulled out in the middle of Operation Union II. However, Carden was in the hospital and didn't know about his brother until just days ago. We both went to visit his brother who was in a nearby signal corps. His camp was located right along the coast and contained lots of high antennas. His brother stood guard duty each night in an above ground bunker that faced the ocean. I guess he was protecting the base in case the NVA decided to mount an amphibious assault on Da Nang. He was safe as anyone could be in Viet Nam. The whole area looked like a Boy Scout camp. There were tall pine trees and palm trees everywhere. The ground was sandy with little patches of grass growing under each tree. It looked and felt like a resort. I watched the two Carden boys hug and get caught up on family news. Carden and I could have gone back to the Air Force hanger and slept there but this place seemed a whole lot nicer.

I don't know how Carden found out information, but he always seemed to have all the right scoop. He discovered Donald had not died in the truck that had run over the land mine. He was back at China Beach, in the hospital. We decided to pay him a visit and maybe get a real cheese burger and a milkshake. We hitched a ride to China Beach, found the hospital and walked right in. It was a permanent building, clean and air-conditioned. We found Donald without any problem. He was lying on a hospital bed and we recognized his face immediately. That was all we recognized. Parts of both of his legs were gone, one at the knee and the other just above his ankle. One arm was cut off at the elbow and the other was missing a hand. He had a large tube sticking out of his neck and other smaller tubes attached to his veins that ran up to plastic bags on metal hangers. Unbelievably, he was conscious and recognized us. Carden walked right up to him and put his hand on Donald's shoulder. If I live to be a thousand I will never forget how Donald looked away in shame. He didn't want anyone to see him looking like this. I too could not bear to see him like this and I looked away. I glanced over at a nearby doctor who was pointing at us and saying something to a nurse who rushed over and told us we had to leave.

I explained, "He's our friend and he was supposed to go home yesterday." She nodded understandingly but explained about germs and quarantine and led us out of the hospital and said,

"Perhaps you can come back tomorrow, and we'll fit you with a gown for his safety and yours." We started to walk away, and she called back to us, "If your friend was on that truck then perhaps you should go to the tent over there, the one marked 'grave registration'. You might be able to help them."

The tent was a typical platoon tent left over from World War II. We walked into a musty dark tent with a chemical smell I didn't recognize. Inside were a dozen or more tables. A corpse was resting in a plastic body bag on each table. I had filled many similar bags.

Carden announced, "The nurse at the hospital suggested you might need our help. We had several friends on a truck that blew up yesterday."

The corpsman working there began unzipping several body bags while we tried to identify our friends. Carden knew the names of several men. We both recognized Coulter. There were several others that we either didn't know, or their faces were unidentifiable.

The corpsman said, "That's okay; I guess we'll have to use their dental records." We signed some official papers concerning Coulter and the other guys we I.D.'d. He thanked us, and we left. Neither one of us felt like eating a cheese burger or a milk shake. We went back to Carden's brother's camp.

The next morning Carden went back to see Donald. He was a better man than I was. I couldn't face Donald and didn't really think he wanted to see me. After morning chow, I sat in front of Carden's brother's tent. Thinking back, I remembered how Donald showed me the trick in boot camp of how to assemble and disassemble the M14 rifle. I remembered being on mess duty and the sponge fight that hit sergeant 'grumpy' in the face. And I remembered our trip to Tijuana, Mexico. As I reminisced I watched a large lizard run past me. It was being chased by a long black snake. The snake and the sand fleas that ate at me during the night convinced me I wanted to sleep somewhere else. Carden returned with the news Donald had died during the night. Part of me was sad and part of me was grateful Donald didn't have to live the rest of his life without limbs.

Carden was to leave the next day and wanted to stay with his brother. I completely understood. We said our goodbyes and promised to stay in touch. It never happened, although I often wondered whatever became of him. I hitched a ride back to the old 'D' Company of the M.P.'s. It was still located in the exact same place but now looked completely different. There were no tents. The outline of the tents had been covered over with metal roofs and the sides were screened now. None of the original M.P.'s was there. We had all been transferred to the grunts. I found my old friend Fisher and he said I could spend the night in his tent. We really weren't friends anymore because he had moved on in the last six months. He did tell me that Payne, who was one of the first to volunteer, died shortly after going to the grunts. The only other guy Fisher knew about was Private Bill Hilly who had gone to E Company which worked with sentry dogs. He stayed in the M.P.'s but guarded the base with a dog.

I asked if he knew about Garcia and Flores, the two Mexican guys from Texas who would imitate Poncho and the Cisco Kid. Garcia had joined the Marine Corps with the promise from his Marine recruiter that he would play in the Marine Band. Garcia's best friend was Kreh, who supposedly joined for the sex. "He got fucked everyday he was in the Corps." Fisher didn't have any news, but I found out later what happened to them.

On May 8th, 1967, Kreh received word that his friend Garcia and the rest of his company were pinned down on some hill and they were putting together a rescue team to save them. Kreh volunteered. When he got to the hill he discovered it was no longer a rescue mission but a recovery of dead bodies. That night Kreh found Garcia's body. Kreh knelt and found

Garcia's dog tags and placed one in Garcia mouth for identification. He carefully lifted little old Garcia up and cradled him in his arms. Kreh had not noticed the hand grenade that the Gooks had placed under Garcia's body. They had pulled the pin and carefully slid it under the body, so the handle would not spring off until Kreh lifted him up. He didn't hear the handle pop off or notice the grenade roll down the hill and land between his feet. When the grenade went off, shrapnel blew up into both of his legs and groin. The corpsmen of course ran to his aid but there was no way they could stop the bleeding. Kreh died on that hill next to his buddy Garcia.

The reason I know this story is because when I arrived in Okinawa I ran into Flores. We ate chow together and he related the story just as he saw it. I remembered how Garcia 'The Cisco Kid' would always say "Oh Poncho" and Flores 'Poncho' would say, "Oh Cisco." We would all laugh and so would Garcia and Flores. Flores wasn't laughing now, and I wondered if he ever would again.

Two days later, I finally left the staging hanger and walked out onto the runway with a hundred or more Marines and Soldiers. We all waited in line to walk up the steps and board the plane to fly us to Okinawa.

I remember when I reached the top of the steps; I paused and looked back at the base. The soldier behind me said, "What's the matter, didn't you get to see enough of this place yet?"

"Yep, I just wanted to say goodbye to some friends."

"Didn't they teach you in basic that you shouldn't make friends in the military?"

I turned and walked into the big bird as we called it. I replied, but I don't know if he heard me say, "Somethings are easier said than done."

To this day part of me has never completely said goodbye to Viet Nam. Every time I hear a helicopter or get caught outside in a pouring rain storm or hear loud noises like Fourth of July fireworks or a hundred other things, I am reminded of that time (1966-1967) in my life. It's funny how little things will bring back memories. Some good, some bad, but all mine.

James M. Dixon

Epilogue

I NEVER DID anything in Viet Nam for which I am ashamed. However, I never did anything in Viet Nam for which I am proud. Yes, I was proud to serve my country and did my small part to stop the spread of communism in South East Asia. We never did stop communism we only slowed it down. We lost that war, not because of a lack of bravery by our troops who fought there. The war was lost at home. I won't go into all the reasons why and will leave that for another book. I accept the fact and reasons why we lost.

What I cannot accept is the way our returning veterans were treated when hundreds of thousands came home from Viet Nam over more than a decade of war. Today when strangers find out I served in Viet Nam or that I was in the military, they pause and say, "Thank you for your service." I find it insulting and I think to myself, 'It was 50 years ago and now you thank me!' Usually the thanks come from today's younger generation. My generation never thanked us for serving our country. Over time, the liberals were deeply criticized for the way they treated returning servicemen. They learned their lessons well. Today all the people who are against the war in the Middle East will gladly tell you, "Oh I support our troops. I just don't support their mission." That makes no sense to me. It sounds like pandering and not genuine gratitude. Maybe it makes sense to them.

All I know is, the men who fought in Viet Nam were just as brave as the men who fought at Bunker Hill or Culp's Hill, or San Juan Hill or Mount Suribachi. And if you never heard of some of those places, well shame on you; look them up. The men who fought in Viet Nam deserved just as much respect as the ones who fought in any other war. They didn't get that respect when they came home and it's too late now to tell a Viet Nam Vet, "Thank you for your service."

We have a monument in Washington D.C. for the Viet Nam Vets. It's the only monument I know of that is below ground. It lists all the men who died in combat, in that war. Some say the monument is in the shape of a 'V'. I think it's in the shape of a check mark, as in "we can check that off". Many a veteran complained about the monument, designed by a Vietnamese architect. So, the government added a statue above ground, of three Americans in combat gear. Then to be politically correct they added a statue for the women who served in Viet Nam. By adding to a mistake, you don't correct it. I'm not saying any of the monuments should come down. They are fine. I've visited them and am moved by seeing all the names on the Viet Nam Wall. No monument however, will change how the troops were treated when we came home from that war.

I wrote these stories, so readers will understand what it was like to serve in Viet Nam. There are thousands and thousands of men who fought in combat in Viet Nam, perhaps you might know one. Don't go up to them and say, "Thank you for your service". You might tell them you read this book and now you know a little bit about what it was like. And hopefully we will never again show distain for service men and women returning from serving our country in a foreign land!

This book is dedicated to all my friends in zippered bags.

IN MEMORY OF

Coulter – I don't remember his exact name, only his smile. As I searched on the Viet Nam Memorial website, he could be David W. Cloutier, however no picture is available.

Howard A. Donald –Age 19 from Tamaqua, PA. (Panel 21E, Line 73 on the Viet Nam Memorial in Washington, D.C.) I have his picture from my Boot Camp Yearbook, but have not received permission to publish it.

Abel D. Garcia – Age 19 from San Antonio, TX. (Panel 19E Line 58).

Gary H. Kreh – Age 19 from Flint MI. (Panel 19E Line 61) There is a picture of him on the Viet Nam Memorial Website however I don't have permission to use it.

Krum - I do not remember the exact spelling of his name or if Krum was short for some other spelling like Krumly or Krumcowski therefore I have no other information.

Gerald McDonald – Age 19 from Dorchester, MA. (Panel 20E Line 122) There is a picture of him on the memorial website.

Weeochy – His name is Indian and I have no memory of how he spelled it. This is the phonetic spelling of how it was pronounced. I cannot find his name on the Wall.

You can visit the Viet Nam Memorial website at **TheWall-USA.com.** Or visit the monument in person:

National Park Service
900 Ohio Drive, S.W.
Washington, D.C. 20242

Phone: (202) 426-6841 or (202) 619-7225

Assholes and Elbows: Quickly, as fast as you can, in a hurry

BAM: Broad Ass Marine, derogatory term for Woman Marine, Defended by Beautiful American Marine

Bends and Thrusts: four step exercise used for punishment and getting in shape

Boondocks or Boonies: out in the field, or in isolated territory

Boot: recruit or anyone who joined before you, (as in, "he is boot to me")

Brother: black Marine (also Splib)

Bulkhead: wall

Cannon Cockers: artillerymen

Chuck: black Marine's term for white Marine

Chit: paper with written authorization

Chow: food

Chow Hall: mess hall, dining area

C-rations: canned food made during World War II, but still used in 1960's

Corpsman: Navy medic serving with Marines = Medic in Army

Cover: hat

The Crotch: derogatory term for the Marine Corps

Deck: floor

Deuce-and-a-Half: two and a half-ton truck (also 6x6) six wheel drive

Double Time: running twice as fast as normal marching cadence

Duffle Bag: large green bag which held all of your clothing

Every Swinging Dick: all hands, everyman

Field Day: cleanup of barracks usually on Thursday night for Friday Inspection

Fire in the Hole: warning of impending explosion

First Sergeant: company's highest ranking enlisted man (usually E-8) Also called "Top" as in 'top sergeant'

Flak Jacket: heavy vest with armor plating to protect against shrapnel

Force March: walking as fast as you can

Gear: equipment

General Inspection: annual check-up of everything, personal equipment and barracks

Ham and Motherfuckers: horrible tasting c-ration with ham and lima beans

Hatch: door

Head: **toilet (latrine for Army and Air Force)**

Hooch: from Jap. Any shelter with thatched roof (Viet Namese house)

Hump: marching and carrying heavy gear and ammo

Incoming! : fire being received from enemy forces or friendly forces

ITR: Infantry Training Regiment

Jarhead: derogatory nickname for Marines with shaved heads, or stupid (As in head screws on and off)

Junk on the Bunk: inspection of all clothing and equipment laid on the rack, also things on the springs

Klick: kilometer

Ladder: stairs or ladder way

Lifer: anyone who makes a career in the military

Lock and Load: enter a round in the chamber, ready to fire when safety is released

MOS: Military Occupation Status (trained for assigned job specialty)

Office Hours: lowest form of court marshal, or reprimand

Office Pogue: clerk, desk-bound, non-combat

Ontos: track vehicle armed with six 106 recoilless rifles (rockets)

Orders cut: having received a chit for reassignment

Passageway: hallway

Piss Tube: urinal in the field

Pogue: office worker or someone who was lazy, non-combat

Police up: pick up, clean up

Rack: bed, bunk

Rappel: rapid climb down using a rope from a cliff, building or helicopter

Recon: short for reconnaissance, scout

Round: bullet, artillery or mortar shell

Scuttlebutt: (from the olden days when Sailors and Marines drank water from a bucket) now a drinking fountain or rumors and gossip

Seabag: see duffle bag

Shit Bird: to screw up, have a messy uniform, a fuck up

Shit Can: garbage can

Short: (short timer) someone near the end of enlistment or a tour of duty

Short Round: Shell that lands short of target and on friendly troops

Sick Bay: clinic or hospital with doctors or corpsmen

Six-By: 6x6 standard three axle truck

Skivvies: underwear

'Sorry 'Bout That': mock apology

Squared Away: opposite of shit bird, someone who is neat, orderly

Stack Arms: stand three rifles up-right in a triangle

Swabbie: sailor

UA: Unauthorized Absence (former term was AWOL)

Utilities: olive drab work or field uniform

Wing Wiper: anyone in the Air Force or Marine Air Wing

The Word: official information, often confused with scoop or scuttlebutt

Zero-Dark-Thirty: early, pre-dawn

ACKNOWLEDGEMENTS

Putting this book together took a great deal of help from many sources. I want to thank Tom Laemlein for supplying and allowing the use of the photo of the Vietnam era Marine radioman pictured on the cover of this book. Also special thanks to my good friend and fellow teacher Larry Roda, who edited my work. He took what I hope is a well told story and made it a well written story. Also, heartfelt thanks to my son John, the designer who formatted and put this book together. His talents I believe make the book come to life. And to my daughter-in-law Jennifer and my wife, Pat who convinced me that these stories were worth telling and needed to be published. Their patience in reading and re-reading this manuscript, giving many suggestions, really helped take my thoughts and words to a higher level and hopefully made this effort more meaningful to the reader. Heartfelt thanks to all.

Made in the USA
Coppell, TX
25 October 2022

85222475R10177